Romantic and Victorian Long Poems

Romantic and Victorian Long Poems

A Guide

ADAM ROBERTS

Ashgate

Aldershot • Brookfield USA • Singapore • Sydney

Published by
Ashgate Publishing Limited
Gower House
Croft Road
Aldershot
Hants GU11 3HR
England

Ashgate Publishing Company
Old Post Road
Brookfield
Vermont 05036–9704
USA

British Library Cataloguing in Publication Data

Roberts, Adam (Adam Charles)
    Romantic and Victorian Long Poems: A Guide
    1. Epic poetry, English—History and criticism.   2. English
    poetry—19th century—History and criticism.   3. Romanticism—
    England—History and criticism.
    I. Title.
    821.8'09145

Library of Congress Cataloging-in-Publication Data

Roberts, Adam (Adam Charles)
    Romantic and Victorian long poems: a guide/Adam Roberts.
        Includes bibliographical references and indexes.
        ISBN 1-85828-156-7 (alk. paper)
        1. English poetry—19th century—Bibliography.   2. Narrative
    poetry, English—Bibliography.   3. Epic poetry, English—
    Bibliography.   I. Title.
    Z2014.P7R67   1999
    [PR581]
    016.821'030907—dc21   99–18600
                                                                         CIP

ISBN 1 85928 156 7

This book is printed on acid free paper

Typeset in Sabon by Manton Typesetters, 5–7 Eastfield Road, Louth, Lincs, LN11 7AJ and printed in Great Britain by MPG Books Ltd, Bodmin, Cornwall

Contents

Preface

This aim of this guide is to provide easy access to a fairly complete range of the long poetry written in the Romantic and Victorian periods: epics, narrative poems, verse-novels and other work of over a certain length. The format provides title, author, length of work (the number of lines) and prosodic description. Texts are then summarized according to the internal divisions (the markers, for instance *Book 1, Canto 2* or sometimes simply *III* or *4*, correspond to the format used in the original text). In order to avoid proliferating 'q.v.'s, cross referencing within the text takes the form of an asterisk before the title in question (e.g. ' ... Cottle's first epic, *Alfred* (1801) was prefaced with comments on ... '). Titles are keyed to the first significant word (so *The Idylls of the King* is to be found under 'I' rather than 'T').

The limits of inclusion have been determined with a certain degree of flexibility. Mostly only poems self-consciously designed as 'long' are included. Most works over 1000 lines meet this criterion, although narrative poems are included where verse-dramas have been excluded (hence no *Prometheus Bound*). At the lower threshold, though, there has been a certain leeway granted. Tennyson's *Enoch Arden* (941 lines) seemed self-evidently worth a place here, as did Arnold's *Sohrab and Rustum* (845 lines); Keats's *Hyperion: A Fragment* makes it in (at 884 lines) partly because its fragmentary status is suggestively epic, whereas *Lamia*, at 708 lines, comes in just under the line and is excluded.

John Sutherland, in his *Longman Companion to Victorian Fiction* (1988) – one of the points of departure for the present undertaking – comments that 'there are two approved ways of writing a companion to literature of this kind. Team composition, while it divides the workload, can produce a certain deadness of presentation. Single authorship risks a higher degree of error and bias, but sometimes results in a zestier book'. Zest notwithstanding, single authorship in this case has at least provided a certain coherence to the undertaking. Where summaries of the poems aim for disinterested objectivity, the introduction that follows allows itself a trifle more latitude. It is tendentious, deliberately so, and advances a particular, partial argument as to why the nineteenth century was so fascinated with the length that was the ultimate aesthetic rationale for the long poem.

Introduction

This study is a guide to the poetry over a certain length written in the nineteenth century, and this introduction needs to say something intelligent about this particular poetic form. This is easy on one level, and much more difficult on another. The easy level is that of the critical discourse which talks about the fertility of nineteenth-century long-poem production, the number of long poems, epics and romances written during that period. This discourse would stress that many of the poems listed in this guide are neglected today, and would perhaps use the phrase 'unjustly neglected' (although 'justice' is surely a difficult concept to bring into critical history). It would argue that no critic or student of the nineteenth century can properly understand the period without having a sense of the long poems that characterized it, and that because the taste today is for short poetry, where there is a taste at all, a sort of blindness afflicts literary historians. Few today have the time or inclination to read all 900 pages of Bailey's *Festus*, or all the weary bulk of 'Southey's unsaleables'; but nineteenth-century audiences had both time and inclination. Worse (in a way) is the shrinkage that attends syllabus construction. Teachers find it hard enough encouraging their students to read even the most famous of the poems in this book (*The Prelude*, say, or *The Ring and the Book*), and there simply is not enough time in the timetable to fit in any other lengthy works. So it is that 'Romanticism' becomes *Songs of Innocence and Experience* rather than *Vala*, or *Don Juan Canto 1* rather than the whole of Byron's epic, and so it is that the most prominent Romantics of their day, Scott, Southey and Landor, are ignored altogether because they cannot be adequately represented with a few pages in an anthology. This line of critical discourse would conclude by saying what a shame this is: because (it would argue) the nineteenth century was the last time in literary history that long poems and epics 'worked', that long poetic narrative cohered aesthetically and produced masterpieces, before the shredder of Modernism was wheeled in and all long poems became, very deliberately, fragments shored against our ruin. All of this particular critical discourse, this easy level, is true, after a fashion. Researching this volume has meant reading a large number of extremely good long poems, works which previously I had barely even heard of. It is, I am sure, not just academic patch-guarding that leads me to think that no account of nineteenth-century poetry, and perhaps of nineteenth-century literary culture, can be properly understood without taking into account this vigorous, powerful, supple and fascinating mode of writing.

That would be one level. The more difficult level, on the other hand, would try to answer one underlying question: why so *long*? It is one thing to note that, almost without exception, the major writers of this period were drawn irresistibly to epic projects – as indeed they were, in that they all wrote long poems, except for those who only planned to write long poems and were not able to bring it to fruition. But it is quite another to explain what the lure of length was in the first instance. With students of the novel this question has been pretty much shirked, I think, because there are apparently easy answers to this question (chiefly, that in the age of serialization and lending libraries with their penchant for triple-deckers that could be loaned to three borrowers at once, novelists were paid by the page, so a big book earned them more money). But no such argument holds for the long poems, which were never serialized and only rarely published in library-friendly forms. I am not trying to suggest that the writing of long poetry was magically separated from these sorts of materialist or even political contextual questions: quite the reverse, in fact. But I would assert that the answer is not immediately forthcoming.

This introduction, then, sets out to try and sketch answers to the various sorts of questions associated with this form, and by extension to interrogate some of the issues that surround the broader usage of 'epic' as cultural category.

Epic and romance

There is a critical tradition that sees the eighteenth century as the terminus of the epic tradition. We are comfortable describing Homer, Vergil and Milton as epic authors, but the term becomes increasingly contested as we come closer to the nineteenth century. E. M. W. Tillyard's venerable study of *The English Epic and Its Background* closes the book on the eighteenth century, he says, because the Romantics and later epics lacked the 'high quality' and 'high seriousness' that characterize the form as he understands it.[1] Tillyard means something particular and convention-determined by 'epic', of course; but even if we broaden the criteria (as this study does) the eighteenth century is where we find most of the criticism. 'More than any other century,' writes John Barrell, 'the eighteenth century was the age of the long poem: it was by writing at length that poetic reputations were made.'[2] According to this critical paradigm, Romanticism sees a disintegration of epic projects and their replacement by rubbishy verse-romances. So it is we see Coleridge planning a gigantic *Fall of Jerusalem* epic, but in practice only ever able to manage bits and pieces such as the interrupted 'Kubla Khan'; or

Keats breaking off from his Miltonic *Hyperion* project in mid-flow not once but twice; or Wordsworth skirting round the edges of his enormous *Recluse*. And where epic ambitions lack coherence we find in their place a gushing of more-or-less doggerel stanzaic romances, from Scott's *Lay of the Last Minstrel* to *Harold the Dauntless*, from Byron's *Bride of Abydos* to *The Island*, from Landon's *Improvisatrice* to Hemans' *Forest Sanctuary*. It is the snobbery implicit in this setting of 'high' modes of writing against 'low' that renders it suspect today, I suppose. But any caricature of literature such as this involves ignoring material that does not fit with the slur, and in this case the material ignored is probably more significant that the material included. The number of Romantics who were able to integrate their epic projects is far greater than the number that could not: Blake, Shelley, Byron, Southey, Landor, Tighe. And among the Victorians, epic projects were the central expressive endeavour of almost every poet we can name.

In what follows, I use the term 'epic' as a catch-all to describe all long poems, rather than limiting it to a poem that ticks off a list of requisite attributes (twelve books, visit to underworld, etc.). This is partly a gesture towards convenience, but it also registers what strikes me as the crucial thing about long poems – their length – and suggests that it is length in the first instance that informs epic. Or at least it was length that drew nineteenth-century writers to epic in the first instance: not the chance to start a poem in medias res, not the opportunity to write in a catalogue of ships, or weave through allusions to Vergil. It was length that somehow 'mattered' in poetry, just as it was in so many other endeavours of nineteenth-century art and culture. Asking why this was so raises a series of interesting questions about the period.

Before coming to these, though, it is important to recognize that using the one term, 'epic', to describe these productions ignores the wide variety of contra-distinguishing labels used by writers of the time. Actually, these name-tags make an interesting study in their own right. The extraordinary variety of different genres and sub-genres of nineteenth-century long poetry might seem certain to baffle any attempt to make general critical points. Surely (it might be said) by subsuming all this diverse production under the single heading 'epic' I have rendered the term too baggy to be useful? This is not merely a question of conflating 'epic' and 'romance' – two modes which were held to be very different indeed by nineteenth-century writers themselves – but of smoothing away differences between epic and verse-novel, epistolary verse novel, psychological epic, spasmodic epic, monodrama and verse-drama. But, in a sense, this orgy of generic markers exactly demonstrates my point. The eighteenth century knew what an epic was; they knew precisely by what rules it operated. The nineteenth century, on the other hand, enacted a fecundity that breaks these rules apart. The long-poem impulse (if I am interdicted from calling it the epic impulse) pushed into a thousand different directions. It is this fecundity, as much as anything, that determined the height to which these shoots grew, and so the length of the final products.

I need to rehearse the argument in order to dismiss it. Baldly, then, one critical narrative of nineteenth-century long poetics would go like this: there were two forms to which long poems in this period were allied. One was what we might think of as the conventional epic form: poems written as heroic narratives in an elevated style that aim at 'nobility' and 'severity' and that follow some or all traditionally conceived 'epic conventions'. This tradition we might think of (to lapse into Bloomian terminology briefly) as anxious about its Miltonic influence, and therefore either rewriting Milton deliberately (as Blake did well in his *Milton*), or else deliberately tackling the sorts of subjects Milton avoided (Southey's project was to write one epic for every major world religion, relativizing the project of justifying the ways of God to men). In this tradition we find Wordsworth's *Prelude*, Keats's epic pretensions, Bailey's *Festus*, Tennyson's itch to revitalize Milton's Arthurian project with the *Idylls of the King*, even Browning's more high-serious productions. It might seem odd calling a work like Barrett Browning's *Aurora Leigh* 'Miltonic', but there is perhaps a sense (a serious, public-minded sense) in which it is. The second form taken by the long poem in this period was the romance. Where epic was serious and severe, the romance was deliberately racy and entertaining, often garrulous and comical as well. This is the tradition effectively inaugurated by Scott and continued by Byron; the tradition in which Letitia Landon wrote, as well as Felicia Hemans, and that flourished in more satiric form (via *Don Juan*) through Clough's *Amours de Voyage*, Lytton's *Lucile* and beyond. This is a distinction that we might want to press on to international poetics as well, to distinguish (for instance) Hugo's serious, heavy *Les Legendes des Siècles* from Pushkin's light-toned and romantic (if profound) *Eugene Onegin*.

A romance carries with it connotations of improvisation, which has its own cultural value. An epic is slow, weighty, considered. Facility cheapens it. Hence the comic astonishment of the *Edinburgh Review* in 1808:

> A correspondent wrote us lately an account of a tea-drinking in the west of England, at which there assisted no fewer than six epic poets – a host of Parnassian strength, certainly equal to six-and-thirty bards.[3]

Or the tetchiness with which Southey was sometimes received:

An epic poem in 12 books finished in six weeks, and, on its improved plan in 10 books, almost entirely recomposed during the time of printing! Is it possible that a person of classical education can have so slight an opinion of (perhaps) the most arduous effort of human invention as to suffer the fervour and confidence of youth to hurry him in such a manner[?] [*Monthly Review*, 1796; n.s. xix. 361]

The hierarchy of age over youth inflects much epic criticism of the period. Indeed, it is present in much more recent criticism. The epic in the nineteenth century is surely a mode of writing in its dotage – witness its death at the century's end. But the impression gained from reading a mass of these poems is quite other. They display all the gaucheness, the overweaning foundationless ambition and pretension of youth; and at the same time they have youth's energy, inventiveness, vigour and heart-touching *brio*.

The problem with this dichotomous reading of epic versus romance, it seems to me, is not that it fails to find room for the oddities of Victorian poetic production, although it does so fail (how does Dobells' *Balder* fit into the scheme? What about Montgomery's *Pelican Island*?). The problem is that it divides the body of literature before us along a fault-line (serious vs comic) that bears very little relation to the actual dynamics of the poetry. And I do not mean by this that nineteenth-century poetry was always serio-comical; it is not that. Rather I am taking a lead from Colin Burrow's persuasive account of epic development. Burrow tackles the traditional division of categories implicit in 'epic' and 'romance' respectively, the tendency to 'oppose "epic" austerity and purpose to "romance" vagrancy and pity'; and by going back to the classics he manages to demonstrate the ways in which 'pity' represents a complex central to the Homeric project, and by extension to writers working in the Homeric tradition.[4] The importance of Burrow's readings goes, I think, beyond a simple project to resuscitate epic in popular imagination – although that is a worthy project (he is surely right that epic now connotes everything which people are 'not predisposed to like: eulogy, heroism, unity, dull officialdom, maleness'). His insight into the intimacy between epic and romance actually illuminates the whole nineteenth-century poetic tradition, as it must do any tradition based so roundly on Homer.

It is Homer, even more than Milton, who becomes the crucial figure for my account of the nineteenth-century long poem. The centrality of Homer to so much nineteenth-century literary culture has been explored in detail.[5] What is sometimes overlooked is the way this engagement with Homer in particular is less hermeneutic (as W. David Shaw argues) and more *ethical*.[6] Truthful rendering of Homeric epic, getting the translation 'right', elides with truthful living, doing the 'right' thing. This is why commentators could rise to such remarkable heights of passion about the subject.

> Not the slightest deviation from the *ipissima verba* of the original text ought, by rule, to be permitted. We cannot insist too strongly upon this. To us what are called free translations are an abomination. So called 'freedom' of translation we regard as, in most cases, proceeding from nothing else than a defect of conscientiousness, a weakness of moral principle.[7]

Browning's late poem 'Development' expresses the central position Homer had in his own development with less hysterical overstatement, but with the same emphasis on the ethical. What Browning learnt from his passion from Homer was 'to loath ... a lie as Hell's gate' like Achilles, to 'love my wedded wife/Like Hector, and so on' ('Development', 100–102). Browning is adamant in this poem that he could have learnt nowhere near as profound a sense of ethical duty from Aristotle's *Ethics*. Only epic can impart this level of emotional education. The nineteenth century had a word to describe literature that tutored readers in their humanity by means of evoking pity and emotion, a word that now has a wholly negative set of connotations: sentimental. Tastes have shifted, but it does not require too large an adjustment of our critical faculties to appreciate why the nineteenth-century saw 'sentimentality' as a good thing.[8] By making us cry, making us feel for the characters, sentimental texts educate us emotionally, and therefore morally. It was good for us to cry at literature, because doing so taught us to empathize with suffering, and made it less likely that we would cause suffering to others – that, at any rate, was the idea. It seems to misrepresent Homer's *Iliad* to call it 'sentimental'; and yet so it is, in the nineteenth-century understanding of the term, and so it was taken, by the readers and writers of long poems in that period.

We can conflate epic and romance, then, in nineteenth-century practice precisely because of this crucial understanding of their mutual emphasis on 'pity', or 'sentiment' as a contemporary might have put it. It is because of this that poets writing National epics – poets, in other words, who thought they were working in one of the accepted modes of epic – in fact put the emphasis not on the expressly political or ideological, but upon the sentimental. Specifically, national projects uniformly act as backdrops to love stories: the courtship of Arthur and Genevieve in Bulwer's *King Arthur*; King Alfred's loss of and reuniting with his kidnapped wife in Cottle's *Alfred*; Edwin of Deira concludes his epic by marrying his Bertha and converting to Christianity. This is why the less conventional epics of the period are also based around love stories (I am thinking here of *The Ring and the Book* or *The Princess*).

This emphasis on Homeric 'sentiment' might seem to ignore other palpable influences upon long poetry of the period; it is much harder pinning the 'sentimental' label on Milton. And yet Milton's influence on the period was of a curiously fragile kind. Romantic works written in his shadow were either pointlessly derivative (Cumberland's *Calvary*, Pollok's *Course of Time*), fragmented with the impossibility of conclusion (Keats's *Hyperion*) or *sui generis* (Blake). However much the Victorians admired Milton, they did not write Miltonic long poems.[9]

The emphasis on following a conventional series of rules for generating a poem, in other words for sitting down to write with Homer as your model, does rather undermine the Romantic heroism of a Manfred or a Childe Harold. Don Juan settles easily into society life towards the end of *Don Juan*; Festus never really defies God in the way his inspiration, Faust, does. We could invoke the cinematic paradigm here, and compare the case of David Lean's *Lawrence of Arabia* (1962). Here is a text most would agree is epic. We might use the epithet to refer to the length of the film, to its breathtaking cinematography (those 70mm shots of endless desert vistas), and by extension to the portrayal of the birth of a nation from diverse tribes. We might want to link these 'epic' (large) themes to the film's (slightly inchoate but powerful) suggestion of 'epic' passions and conflicts in the heart of the central character. But there is another way of interpreting this text: it would be possible to go through it ticking off the various ways in which it embodies epic conventions that go back to Homer. Homeric tribes battle it out, watched over at a distance by the godlike British officers in their Olympian Cairo mess-hall; the protagonist is a warrior, whose greatest love (the two Arab boys) die, Patroclus-like. He travels widely, like Odysseus, even descending into a metaphorical underworld (the capture and rape by the Turks) and so on. This patterning is not coincidental, of course; in this respect the film follows the archetypal paradigm that Lawrence himself adopted for *The Seven Pillars of Wisdom*. Lawrence, after all, knew his Homer. But if we read the text this way, then doesn't it become a film in some sense about convention and therefore conventionality? Instead of giving us a Byronic hero whose existence is predicated upon an inner freedom, a defiance of convention, the film in fact and at a deep level *reassures* us, panders to the security that can be achieved by deploying familiar patterns.

Almost all the poems included in this guide follow epic convention in this way (although the few that follow epic convention absolutely and to the letter tend to be the deader works epitomized here, and have lasted least well). Wordsworth's *Prelude* gives us a catalogue of books in place of a catalogue of ships; Barrett Browning's *Aurora Leigh* takes us to the seedy streets of Paris, the scene of rape and abandonment, instead of taking us into a more literally conceived underworld. In these cases the adherence to Homeric–Vergillian practice may be deliberate, or it may not. We might want to make the argument that epic constitutes, as Northrup Frye thought it did, a fundamental archetype, one of the ways human beings structure their reality. But it is difficult to ignore the particularities of literary production. Ordering reality according to certain pre-existent categories is another way of thinking about the particular conservative, traditional mores of the Victorian period itself.

Epic proportions: great length in literature

Victorian writers, then, working in what they considered to be an epic tradition, found in Homer (more than other influences, howsoever important) the matrix of length, of heroic pity, and of aesthetic unity that chiefly motivated them. For the sake of discussion, it is worth dilating upon these two formal features of epic: unity and length. The first is, in a manner of speaking, the point of epic, and that is the vision of aesthetic and ethic coherence embodied in all classical epics. Homer, Vergil, Milton: all these poets wrote of, or out of, a unity difficult for the post-Romantic mind to comprehend. Homer's unity was heroic, in the sense that a certain conception of character under the pressures of war (in the *Iliad*) or exile (in *Odyssey*) informs a vision of the universe in which everything fits together. The gods in heaven, the dead in the underworld, mankind struggling between, everything in Homer has a place. This, at any rate, was what appealed to the Victorians about him. Death might be painful, Priam might weep for Hector; but death *had its place* in the epic scheme of things, and in a sense precisely because it was death that defined heroism. In Vergil the unity was more narrowly conceived of as national, patriotic; but similarly every virtue that pious Aeneas demonstrates is a civic virtue, and helps towards a definition of the ideal Roman. To suggest that Milton's poem articulates a religious coherence sounds limiting today, but only because we have lost Milton's certainty that religion could be the central fact of a person's existence, rather than a peripheral or lifestyle choice.

But it is in the Romantic and Victorian periods that these ethico-aesthetic certainties began their long process of erosion, that wearing-away that has culminated today in a postmodern unweaving of all master narratives (and, in case I sound too reactionary here, I should add: what a necessary release from straightjacketing that process has been). Victorian poets no longer had A Theme to write poetry about, and could no longer count on agreement as to what poetry was. Bakhtin has written of epic as one of the few monologic modes of literary art, and I take it he means something similar to my own observations here.[10] But the epics dealt with by this guide are far from monologic; it is their dialogism, often unintentional, that makes them interesting.

The second criterion of epic is the more recognizable. Epics need to be long; indeed, today, anything long enough is liable to be called epic. To achieve even a whiff of 'epic' the short poem needs, like Coleridge's 'Kubla Khan', to suggest a poetics of aposiopesis. In this regard, the nineteenth century was famously suited to epic production. Victorian literature is some of the most prolix in the canon. It is a shame, indeed, that 'prolix' carries such negative connotations, because it is part of the glory of the Victorian literary project that it was able to dilate upon its subject.

Today, the pre-eminent long literary form is the novel, and since long novels will still find readers where long poems will not, it might seem that the novel has best claim today to being the repository of epic form. There is even a certain sense of appropriateness in thinking that the inheritor of Romance (and the verse-tales and verse-novels of the nineteenth century) should also be the representative of the epic today. Of course, we might wish to broaden our parameters and argue that in fact it is cinema that has furnished the most striking 'epic' productions of our age. But in either case, the pedigree is poetic. As far as this goes, there is some point to the contemporary vernacular usage of 'epic' to mean 'of large proportions'. A film such as *Titanic* (1997) is predicated upon an aesthetics of *size* in the first instance: a very big boat, a very long film, a very great deal of money put into the making of it. The point of this aesthetic, of course, is in transference: with so much grandness of scale about we are encouraged to read the film's love affair as imbued with a similar enormity. It is not ordinary, or small-scale; theirs is a monumental love, a cosmic passion. And so on. A postmodern deconstruction of this followed, of course: *Godzilla* (1998) is a film enamoured of size simply for the sake of size. Form here casts no sublime light upon subject in this text; the surface vastness of the central monster (and of the film's budget, and of the marketing exercise brought to bear on it) is a simulacrum only of the vastness of the profits that can be accrued by the successful author of these sorts of texts. We are a long way from the hugeness of Milton's Satan, sprawled on his lake of fire. Or, indeed, from the lines in Darwin's *Botanic Garden* describing the creation of the universe:

– 'LET THERE BE LIGHT!' Proclaimed the ALMIGHTY LORD,
Astonished Chaos heard the potent word;
Through all his realms the kindling Ether runs,
And the mass starts into a million suns;
Earth round each sun with quick explosions burst,

And second planets issue from the first;
Bend, as they journey with projectile force,
In bright ellipses their reluctant course;
Orbs wheel in orbs, round centres centres roll,
And form, self-balanced, one revolving Whole.
– Onward they move amid their bright abode,
Space without bound, THE BOSOM OF THEIR GOD!
[*Botanic Garden: Economy of Vegetation*, 1: 103–14]

Horace Walpole thought these lines 'the most sublime passage in any author, or in any of the few languages with which I am acquainted'. The Romantic fascination with the Sublime informs his judgement of course, just as it was to spur many writers into battles with epic projects. And the point of the Sublime is one of scale, the intimation of the infinite, the way the enormity of Wordsworth's Alps, or Shelley's Mont Blanc, strike the authors not as very large but paradoxically as very small compared to the infinitude of God, or the Absolute, or Power, or whatever one's name for the mystic totality. This was behind Coleridge's enthusiastic championing of 'the Vast', not the least in his unwritten vast epic *The Fall of Jerusalem*: 'From my very early reading of Faery Tales & genii &c &c', he wrote in his notebook, 'my mind had been habituated *to the Vast* – '. Romantic Sublimity surely carries less force for us today, perhaps (it has sometimes struck me) because our scientific perception of the universe has expanded it appallingly in our imaginations. When Shelley thought of the 'everlasting universe of things' he thought of something very large, of course, but something still measured implicitly by human scales. Nowadays the distances between the stars beggar human measurements. A human being is measured in feet, but we could not count the distance between galaxies on that register.

Darwin's scientific-poetic epic of everything, his *Botanic Garden*, stirred Walpole with its hugenesses because Walpole could connect the size of form and subject to a correlative enormity of concept (in his case, God). Without such a correlative, enormity becomes a hollow and echoey thing, a vast cavern instead of a mighty mountain. The blossoming of uncertainties that characterizes the nineteenth century eroded this aspect of epic: its correlation with any system of belief that might be thought to possess epic cogency. Darwin's pious-sounding description of the Creation, from *Genesis* out of Alexander Pope, belie his own atheistical beliefs. The nineteenth century was the epoch of what J. Hillis Miller has called 'the Disappearance of God', and all the time it was happening poets returned again and again to grandiose religiose themes, as if in desperate denial. The fattest epic of them all is Bailey's *Festus*, and it demonstrates better than any the futility of this sumo-esque bulking up. Although the 900 pages of Bailey's version of Faust work their ponderous way towards a conventionally religious affirmation of the majesty and sublimity (that is to say, the Size) of God, the effect of reading his poem is quite otherwise. The line-to-line pressures of the piece, its spasmodic intensity, the vividness of its minutiae as compared to the vague windiness of its larger themes – all this frays *Festus* into a million pieces. It becomes a kind of anti-epic in a way more profound than the mock-epics of Pope or Byron could ever achieve: because it becomes a poem precisely about the impossibility of coherence. It is here that the distinctiveness we tend to think of as Modernist originates. The parent-text for this whole tradition arguably is Landor's *Gebir*. The weird garblings of epic expectation in this wonderful poem showed its apostles (particularly Shelley and Browning) how to break the epic into lucid monads, the juxtaposition of which modelled the world not as a smooth contiguity (the version of epic Auerbach so powerfully argued for in his *Mimesis*) but instead a muscular awkwardness that worked towards a new beauty.

This also brings in the way epic functioned historiographically for the nineteenth century, and the Victorians in particular. History can be big or small depending on how you wish to take it; but if you perceive the present state of your nation to be very large – imperial, indeed – then the history that leads up to that state of affairs is liable to be seen as very large as well. Carol Christ has argued that it is precisely this habit of historical comparison that characterizes the Victorian age in general, and that therefore underlies the resurgence of interest in long poetry.[11] She quotes John Stuart Mill's *The Spirit of the Age* to the effect that 'never before was [historical comparison] itself the dominant idea of any age'. Christ's own Victorian long-poem examples (*The Ring and the Book* and *Idylls of the King*) do indeed seem embedded in a historiographic imaginative act. Moreover, Carlyle repeatedly insisted that history was the only proper subject for the epic. In his own (prose) history of *The French Revolution* (1837) he deliberately modelled himself on *The Iliad*. Allusions to and quotations from Homer were paralleled with Homeric tricks, such as awarding all the main players epic epithets: 'Mirabeau, King of Men', 'Sea-green Robespierre' and so on. His characters die Homerically, too, like Marat, whose 'life with a groan rushes out, indignant, to the shades below'.

But history is not the end-point of this aesthetic value. Carlyle himself valorized history over fiction for one reason only. He was less interested in the uses of the historiographic imagination in establishing the ideological vagaries of the present (for instance), and more interested in a single, monolithic, idealist notion of 'truth'. And so we find ourselves back at the ethical imperative that underlay Homer's own influence. The reason why history was the proper subject for epic, said Carlyle, was that history was true, and that truth was the highest ethical value. Epic, as the highest art form, ought to mirror this.

> Epic Poems of old time, so long as they continued *epic*, and had
> any impressiveness, were Histories, and understood to be narra-
> tives of *facts* .... Fiction, whilst the feigner of it knows that he is
> feigning, partakes, more than we suspect, of the nature of *lying*.[12]

It was this ethical commitment to veracity, rather than an abstract
interest in representing history, that was behind nineteenth-century historical projects. Browning, for instance, justified his historical epic *The
Ring and the Book* (based on an actual court-case in Rome in 1698) on
exactly these grounds: a Carlylean concern for 'fact'.

> The business has been, as I specify, to explain *fact* – and the fact is
> what you see ... here my pride was concerned to invent nothing:
> the minutest circumstance that denotes character is *true*.[13]

Writers working in the nineteenth century were in general happy to
accede to this vision of the historico-epic. In other words, works such
as Scott's poems, or Cottle's *Alfred*, or *The Ring and the Book* were
historical, both in the sense of recreating (or 'being set in') a particular
historical period, and in the sense of establishing a retro aesthetic, a
looking-backwards. The most significant corollary of this is to configure
our understanding of history as epical. It sets in train a long tradition
where the past – be it the French Revolution, or (say) the events of
War and Peace or *Lawrence of Arabia* – are perceived as epic because
they are history, rather than the other way around. This is not what
Carlyle intended. For him the first thing about history was its truth,
and the epic form was simply the way of embodying that. For
subsequent thinkers, perhaps even for us, the first thing about history is
that it is *very big* and that it follows certain (culturally conditioned)
narrative conventions. As Barthes was the first to point out, it is now
not only impossible to access the past (it was always impossible to do
that); it is even impossible to *conceptualize* the past as anything but a
series of stock images from mythic and therefore fictional discourses.
Even the scholar who buries herself with parchment sources and ar-
chaeological evidence is never going to be able to banish the romance
version of (say) Scott's Highland from her mind. Just as size supersedes
meaning, so the romance externalization of experience as history *becomes* history. It is symptomatic, then, that one of the most popular
'historical' subjects for nineteenth-century epic was Arthurian. Poets
turned to King Arthur in exactly the ways we turn to history – to tell us
where we come from, to open up the determinants on today, to define
(in this case) 'Englishness'. At the same time, though, there is not a
single Arthurian work in the whole century but that scrabbles a whole
range of epochs into one (primitive, Dark Ages, medieval, Renaissance,
contemporary) – indeed, not only do they do this, but they self-

consciously do it. Arthur is history as cultural melange: a simulacrum, then, but not the less fiercely believed in for that. Critics who attacked Tennyson's *Idylls of the King* for anachronism egregiously missed the point. History as epic and anachronism are the same thing.

The historical pedigree of epic writing in the nineteenth century went hand in hand with psychological epic: epic attempts to anatomize the working mind, the machine of consciousness. We think of this sort of interior monologue as distinctively Victorian, as the most 'modern' feature of the literature; but in terms of long poetry these epic-dramatic monologues almost always had a historical component: medieval Italy in *Sordello*, seventeenth-century Italy in *The Ring and the Book*. Even a contemporary monodrama like Tennyson's *Maud* worked to create a sense of scale by tying in the maunderings of the insane protagonist with the ongoing history of the Crimean War. The parent-text for these, as it were, is Wordsworth's epic autobiography: but since it was not until 1850 that the 'egotistical sublime' of *The Prelude* was presented to the reading public the actual effect of the work is to link Wordsworth's interiorization with a big-scale historical event (French Revolution) that Carlyle has already shown to be Homeric in form as well as mood.

The question of size, then, finally brings these poems back to the age in which they were written. A poem like *Festus*, to come back to that example, is predicated upon an encyclopaedic aesthetic. Its theme is (to quote Bailey's own preface) 'world-life' based on a 'theory of spiritual things'; and its overall structure can seem banal in precis – Festus and Lucifer tour the universe, have various adventures, Festus puts his soul at risk but is eventually saved. But to look to the overall *pattern* is surely to miss the point, and the point in this case is not architectonic so much as scalar. The effectiveness of *Festus* is local, in its legion moments and striking images ('ye hate the truth as a slug salt: it dissolves ye'), and in particularly in the tension between this atomism and the poem's enormous scale. Viewed at in this way, the poem becomes a textual dramatization of diversity being gathered together in one huge metanarrative, with the emphasis as much on the wide range of diverse constituent elements as on the Christian unifying power. This, I think, acts as a description of most of the works in this volume. Tennyson's national epic, his *Idylls of the King*, become a series of separate poems – poems whose separateness is almost multicultural (so different are the tenors of each separate idyll) – gathered together and held only by the imperial name of the King of the title.[14] Bailey in *Festus* was actually imitating Goethe's *Faust*, after his own inimitable nineteenth-century fashion, and Goethe is a relevant figure to invoke here. Homi Bhaba's *Location of Culture* quotes from Goethe's 1830 'Note on a world literature' to the effect that the Napoleonic wars changed the conditions of cultural production by opening writers to a material existence (as opposed to the sort of idealized, literary existence that had prevailed before). After Napoleon, wrote Goethe:

> Nations could not return to their settled and independent life again without noticing that they had learned many foreign ideas and ways, which they had unconsciously adopted, and come to feel here and there previously unrecognized spiritual and intellectual needs.[15]

Bhaba, of course, reads Goethe's observations in a positive light as prefiguring a 'cultural dissensus and alterity', with Goethe's imagined 'world literature' as the place where cultures recognize themselves through their projections of 'otherness'. But there are less upbeat interpretations of the sentiment.

Put it this way: there is no doubt that nineteenth-century long poetry is profoundly committed to this vision of 'world literature'. Southey conceived his entire epic project as an exploration of many varied, differing cultures, religions and races. Byron's verse tales range over the East, travelling as widely as his horse in *Mazeppa*. Browning wrote epics set in Italy and France, not England. Morris's *Earthly Paradise* is a bringing together of many cultural alterities. But if this list starts to sound like a cheerful celebration of cultural difference, then we need to remember the ways in which a nineteenth-century poet was likely to conceive of cultural difference, or even of a 'world literature'. The chief context, it seems to me, is necessarily going to be *imperial*.

Which, in turn, brings us back to epic antecedents. If it strains Homer to see him as an imperial poet (although that did not stop Gladstone, whose certainty in the universality of the *Iliad* lead him to believe its political universality, and to use it as a textbook for dealing with the Eastern question) – if, then, it strains Homer to see him as imperial, there was never any doubt that Vergil was exactly that. The place where all these diverse cultures and peoples came together was precisely the British Empire; and imperial Britons distinguished themselves from their Roman forebears not in terms of an ideology of 'civilizing the uncivilized', but rather in terms of size. The British Empire was, as the British were fond of reminding themselves, the biggest the world had ever seen. The ideological underpinnings of size exist outwith all the other rationales for empire-building: putting together an empire upon which the sun never sets can so easily become entangled in a belief in size as a value in and of itself: a political correlative to the *Godzilla* or the *Titanic* aesthetic. Valorizing bigness, then, justifies itself on its imperial foundation.

As with any such explanation that depends upon ideological underpinnings, this is an answer to the question 'why so big?' that needs to be applied carefully. I am not suggesting that Bailey sat down to write an enormous poem because he saw that the British Empire was, or was becoming, enormous. Nothing is so straightforward. But I do declare a belief that ideology operates in culture in exactly the sorts of submerged ways that might prompt a writer to believe that size is a virtue, and that the only way to bring together diverse narratives is within some overarching boss-structure (in Bailey's case, an overarching boss-structure from Christian teleology, which was used widely enough as an imperial justification itself). The urge to build big poems, and the urge to build big empires, are various manifestations of the same ideological root patterns. But, the advantage for us is that although the architectonic shell (the 'epic' with its bad, official, boring connotations) may remain as unappealing to contemporary tastes as 'empire', there is so marvellous, so brilliant and so diverse a world of discourses contained within as to make the study of them the most rewarding activity there is.

Notes

1. E. M. W. Tillyard, *The English Epic and Its Background* (London: Chatto and Windus, 1954), p. 5.
2. John Barrell, *Poetry, Language and Politics* (Manchester: Manchester University Press, 1988), p. 79.
3. Quoted in Stuart Curran, *Poetic Form and British Romanticism* (Oxford: OUP, 1986), p. 158.
4. Colin Burrow, *Epic Romance: Homer to Milton* (Oxford: Clarendon Press, 1993), p. 3.
5. See Frank Turner, *The Greek Heritage in Victorian Britain* (New Haven: Yale University Press, 1981); Richard Jenkyns, *The Victorians and Ancient Greece* (Oxford: Blackwell, 1980); Warren Anderson, *Matthew Arnold and the Classical Tradition* (Ann Arbor: University of Michigan Press, 1965); Geoffrey Highet, *The Classical Tradition: Greek and Romance Influence on Western Literature* (2nd edn, Oxford: OUP, 1951).
6. W. David Shaw argues that it was the interpretive, hermeneutic aspects of translation that motivated Victorian fascination with Homer; Shaw, *The Lucid Veil: Poetic Truth in the Victorian Age* (London: Athlone, 1987).
7. [David Masson], 'Translations from the Classics', *North British Review*, 16 (1851), 261.
8. See, for instance, Fred Kaplan's *Sacred Tears: Sentimentality in Victorian Literature* (Princeton: Princeton University Press, 1987).
9. Milton was more of an influence on Romantic writers than Victorian. See Curran's work in this field: Stuart Curran, *Shelley's Annus Mirabilis: The Maturing of an Epic Vision* (San Marino: Huntingdon Library Press, 1975); Stuart Curran, ' "The Mental Pinnacle": *Paradise Regained* and the Romantic four book epic', in Joseph Wittreich (ed.), *Calm of Mind* (Cleveland: Case Western Reserve University Press, 1971).
10. Bakhtin sees the epic as retrogressively monologic, as compared to the fertile dialogism of the novel. He describes the form as 'congealed and half-moribund': Mikhail Bakhtin, *The Dialogic Imagination: Four Essays*,

trans. C. Emerson and M. Holquist (Austin Texas and London, 1981), p. 14.

11. Carol Christ, 'Myth, history, and the structure of the long poem', *Victorian and Modern Poetics* (Chicago: University of Chicago Press, 1984), pp. 101–41.

12. Carlyle, *Miscellanies*, III, 49–50.

13. Letter, Browning to Julia Wedgwood, 19 November 1868; in Roberts (ed.), *Robert Browning* ('The Oxford Authors', Oxford: Oxford University Press, 1997), pp. 709–10.

14. Cecil Lang has argued already that 'the real subject of this great poem is the British Empire', *Tennyson's Psycho-drama* (Harvard: Harvard University Press, 1983).

15. Quoted in Homi Bhaba, *The Location of Culture* (London: Routledge, 1994), pp. 11–12.

: *A* :

Abencerrage, The (1819), by Felicia Hemans. 1555 lines, heroic couplets. Hemans came across the story for this work in tedious book entitled *Historia de las Guerras Civiles de Granada*.

Canto One. The poem opens to the noise of battle, an assault on Granada, and the flight of the Moorish ruler of the city, Abdallah. The story then flashes back, and we follow the story of Hamet the Moor, young chief of the tribe of Aben-Zurrah (the 'Abencerrage' of the title). For unspoken reasons, Abdallah has executed Hamet's father and brother, and banished Hamet himself from Grenada. Hamet has one last meeting with his love, the beautiful Zayda, who comes from the rival tribe of Zegri. He announces to her that he must leave, and swears himself to vengeance. *Canto Two.* Christian soldiers lay siege to Grenada, part of the crusade to drive the Moors from Spain: Hamet and his Aben-Zurrah warriors have joined with the Christian Knights. Disguised as a 'wandering Fakir', Hamet steals into the besieged city to meet with Zayda; but he discovers that his support for the Christians has turned her against him – 'not the chief who leads a lawless band/To crush the altars of his native land;/The apostate son of heroes ... not *him* I loved'. Hamet leaves with anguish in his heart. *Canto Three.* The Christians storm and overrun the citadel, and Abdallah flees. A band of Moors retreat to the rocky fastnesses of the Alpuxarras. Hamet leads a troop in pursuit; but he is no longer seeking military glory, rather 'his hope is but from ceaseless pangs to fly,/ To rush upon the Moslem spears, and die'. His reckless courage in battle scatters the remaining Moslems, and he single-handedly pursues the stragglers up a cliff-face. At the top he encounters Zayda, nursing in her arms the corpse of her father, killed in the skirmish. She accuses Hamet ('Did he not perish, haply by thy hand,/In the last combat with thy ruthless band?'), but when a band of Moors comes upon them and rushes at Hamet in a fury of revenge for the death of Zayda's father, she interposes herself between the two parties and receives a fatal wound. Her dying prayer saves Hamet's life ('spare him, my kindred tribe! forgive and spare!'); Hamet sings a funeral dirge, and in 'a few short years' he too is buried in the 'lonely cave/Where sleeps the Zegri maid'.

Alastor; or, the Spirit of Solitude (1815), by Percy Bysshe Shelley. 720 lines, blank verse.

The story concerns the fate of an unnamed Poet; we learn of his unhappy childhood (his 'cold fireside and alienated home') and his wanderings around Europe and Asia visiting the sites of antiquity (Athens, Tyre, Jerusalem). In Arabia a native woman brings him food, apparently in love with him, but the Poet hardly seems to notice. Instead he has a dream of erotic consummation with a dream maiden ('with frantic gesture and short breathless cry/Folded his frame in her dissolving arms'). The Poet goes off into the wilderness in search of this ideal partner, travelling far from humanity. Eventually, hopeless in his quest, he dies unmourned.

Alfred; an Heroic Poem, in Twenty-Four Books (1801), by Joseph Cottle. 13,031 lines, blank verse. Cottle's first major epic betrays the heavy influence of Wordsworth, both in style and subject.

Book 1. The Pagan Ivar the Dane is preparing to leave Denmark with an army and attack England: 'death to our foes! My spirit thirsts to see/ The blood of Saxons flowing, ocean like'. Before going he wants to seek out a certain Sorceress, but when a mariner refuses to take him to 'her secret dwelling', Ivar kills him. He finds another mariner to take him to the witch, but is spooked to find this new sailor is actually the revivified corpse of the man he killed. Shaken, he vows never to slay an unarmed man again. When he finally meets the Sorceress (there are actually three Macbeth-like witches), they give him a magic banner marked with a crow which he believes will give him victory. *Book 2.* King Alfred is in Somersetshire, having been once again defeated by the Danes ('never till that day/Had Alfred known so great an overthrow'). He retreats to Selwood Forest and regroups, before dismissing his men and walking away with his wife, Alswitha, and his child. *Book 3.* Alfred crosses the moonlit heath ('"thou lovely moon!" cried Alfred, as he roam'd/Across the trackless moor, all wide and waste,/Bearing his infant child'). He meets a beggar and, despite his wife's remonstrances, shares his last loaf with him ('this is our all, old man! one half is thine!'). At Glastonbury Abbey he deposits his spouse and baby, and goes off mysteriously. *Book 4.* Alfred, more and more Wordsworthian in cast, contemplates kingship as he wanders.

> He had learned to weigh
> What, of the mass of miseries we mourn,
> To this our state was needful, what the effect
> Of hostile innovation, and he thought,
> With fervent joy of all a king might do.
> Long had he fed on intellectual food:
> The love of Nature and of nature's God
> Had harmonized his spirit, he had felt
> His heart attuned to love.

He finds shelter in the neatherd's hut, and stays for many weeks. He burns the cakes. He hears that Glastonbury has been sacked by the Danes, and his wife killed. *Book 5*. A knight brings Alfred's son to the neatherd's hut. Acca, the neatherd himself, recognizes Alfred ('art *thou* our king? and this forsaken child/Our noble prince, prince Edward? ... View in me thy friend!'). Alfred decides to leave his son with Acca. *Book 6*. Sigbert, Abbot of Wilton and Alfred's loyal deputy, is captured by the Danes. *Book 7*. Alfred, leaving the hut and wandering some more, meets the remnants of a Saxon army fleeing Ivar and the Danes. Inspiring them with patriotic speech ('The glorious day of triumph hastens fast./There is a point in human wretchedness/Beyond whose bound, the wretched cannot feel ... Look on to happier times, Cheer up, brave men!'). *Book 8*. Sigbert returns to Alfred and reports that Alswitha is still alive. *Book 9*. At Selwood Forest, Alfred musters his men. He decides to burn the Danish ships. Sigbert becomes animated with war-lust, but Alfred rebukes him as a churchman ('Discard the priesthood! or, renounce the sword!') and Sigbert agrees to give up his 'sacerdotal robe'. *Book 10*. Alfred burns the Danish fleet. *Book 11*. The Saxons return safely to their fort in Selwood. *Book 12*. Ivar is far from happy to hear of the destruction of his fleet. He decides on the human sacrifice of 'a saxon slave' ('a female captive, fair as Gimer's child!') to 'appease the Gods'. *Book 13*. Alfred, distressed at the predicament of his wife 'unfriended, far away' resolves on infiltrating the Danish camp disguised as a Harper: 'for my fingers well can sweep/Its bold, or gentlest strings ... for music has a charm/Melting all hearts'. *Book 14*. Alfred, as the Harper, gets into the Danish camp, where he is a big hit: 'like famished birds around their prey, the Danes/Again encircle Alfred, crying loud,/"A song, O harper"'. *Book 15*. Alfred, as the Harper, gets close to the leaders of the Danish invasion. *Book 16*. Ivar and his chiefs, with disguised Alfred in attendance, bring in captive Alswitha. She is commanded to take the Harp from her disguised husband (whom she recognizes), and sings a coded song warning him away. But Alfred stays to hear a spy report the Saxon strength to Ivar. *Book 17*. Alfred ('gloom pervades his brow') returns to the Saxon camp. He rallies his men, and marches out to give battle to the bloodthirsty Danes. *Book 18*. The Battle of Eddington begins. The Danes attack with 'demon shouts' and 'savage yells'. Confident in his magic banner (from Book 1), Ivar cries out to his comrades to leave Alfred to him ('Touch not one hair of Alfred! ... My might shall lay him low'). The Book ends with the two in one-to-one combat. *Book 19*. The Danes are defeated ('spare the vanquish'd', Alfred cries as they fly). Alfred has killed Ivar, and the remaining Danes retreat to a castle. *Book 20*. The Danes, now under the command of Guthrum, refuse to yield to Alfred, although they do relinquish the captive Alswitha, who is joyfully received by Alfred ('My soul still pure!' she tells him). *Book 21.* Alswitha tells the story of her captivity. She is worried about their son, but Alfred reassures her that he is being brought from the lowly cottage. *Book 22.* Guthrum is now persuaded to surrender to Alfred. He pleads to become a Christian. *Book 23.* That night, the sleeping Alfred has a vision of his guardian angel: 'He saw, or thought he saw, a Spirit, tall,/And of majestic port. His eye was mild,/Yet one fixed look he had, as though he stood,/Immoveable, from ages infinite'. This Angel stresses the importance of the Bible, and foretells an age when 'men will arise' from 'grov'ling superstition'. He goes into a lengthy sectarian diatribe against Catholicism (at nearly 2000 lines long this is by far the longest section of the poem). *Book 24.* Guthrum is baptised, and Alfred addresses his victorious troops for the last time.

Amours de Voyage (first published in the *Atlantic Monthly* 1858; in volume form 1862), by Arthur Hugh Clough. 1243 lines, unrhymed hexameters. The poem is in the form of various letters, mostly from Claude to Eustace, but other correspondents are also quoted.

Canto 1. Claude, the world-weary traveller, writes to his friend Eustace from Rome ('Rome disappoints me much; I hardly as yet understand, but/*Rubbishy* seems the word that most exactly would suit it'). It is the time of the French invasion of the short-lived Roman Republic (1849), and the city is under seige. He spends some time with another English family abroad, the Trevellyans, and particularly with one of their daughters, Mary; but Claude is more in love with the idea of being in love ('But for Adam, – alas, poor critical coxcomb Adam!/But for Adam there is not found an help-meet for him') than he is actually in love. *Canto 2.* Claude contemplates the ongoing war with insouciance ('*Dulce* it is, and *decorum* no doubt, for the country to fall ... but/On the whole we conclude that the Romans won't do it, and I shan't'). He is growing closer to Mary: 'I am in love, you say: I do not think so, exactly'. *Canto 3.* The Trevellyans leave for Florence. Claude is supposed to follow, but he encounters practical difficulties and is anyway spooked by talk of his 'intentions'. *Canto 4.* Claude finally arrives in Florence to find the Trevellyans already departed for Milan; he follows them around Italy hoping to run into them, but keeps just missing them. *Canto 5.* Claude, now in Florence, has realized that he does love Mary, but is oppressed by the sense that their moment has passed: 'So plumb I the deeps of depression,/Daily in deeper, and find no support, no will, no purpose'. He returns to Rome, but cannot bear it now that the French have conquered ('Rome will not suit me, Eustace; the priests and the soldiers possess it'). He resolves to return to England.

Emerson wrote to Clough that he could not forgive him for 'the baulking end or no end of the *Amours de Voyage*'; but more recent critics have seen its downbeat anticlimax a powerful mode of expressing the ambivalence of Clough's vision.

Angel in the House, The (1854–56), by Coventry Patmore. 3812 lines, octosyllabic quatrains. The two parts of this work were *The Betrothal* (published 1854) and *The Espousals* (1856); two related poems, *Faithful for Ever* (written 1860) and **The Victories of Love* (written 1861) were published together under the latter title in 1863.

More a collection of various interconnected lyrics than a coherent long poem, *The Angel in the House* traces the courtship and marriage of Felix Vaughan, a poet, providing us with numerous examples of his poetic productions, which tend to be brief lyrics on aspects of love, and which preface each of the twenty-four cantos. Rather than summarize each of these (usually extremely brief) cantos one by one, I give the broader drift of the poem as a whole; but the cantos all have titles, which are given below:

Book 1.
Canto 1.   The Cathedral Close
Canto 2.   Mary and Mildred
Canto 3.   Honoria
Canto 4.   The Morning Call
Canto 5.   The Violets
Canto 6.   The Dean
Canto 7.   Ætna and the Moon
Canto 8.   Sarum Plain
Canto 9.   Sahara
Canto 10. Going to Church
Canto 11. The Dance
Canto 12. The Abdication

Book 2
Canto 1.   Accepted
Canto 2.   The Course of True Love
Canto 3.   The County Ball
Canto 4.   Love in Idleness
Canto 5.   The Queen's Room
Canto 6.   The Love-Letters
Canto 7.   The Revulsion
Canto 8.   The Koh-i-noor

The work deals with two idealized courtships and marriages, but the title refers not to the figure of the ideal wife herself, but to the 'spirit of love' that dwells in the house of the happy marriage.

Book 1. Felix, a poet, returns to Salisbury ('Sarum') after being away. He finds his old friend, the Dean of Salisbury Cathedral, in good health, and bearing up during his widowhood by fixing his thoughts on Heaven ('Well might his thoughts be fixed on heaven's content,/Now she was there!'). He renews his acquaintanceship with the Dean's three daughters, Honor, Mildred and Mary, and quickly falls in love with the first. Spurred to action by the rival attention of Frederick Garaham, he visits often, makes morning calls, and eventually summons the courage to ask the Dean for permission to woo his daughter, which he receives. He approaches her, and she smiles upon him (a scene his poetic imagination sees as the Moon smiling tranquilly on the volcanic Mount Etna), but events conspire to delay his proposal. Honor goes to London for some weeks (which time without her company becomes 'Sahara' to Felix). After a Dance, Felix finally summons up the courage ('twice rose, twice died my trembling word'), but finally he proposes and is accepted. *Book 2.* The wedding is fixed for July; Felix makes a rule, 'in Sarum Close/To make two visits every week'. He prepares a house in which they can live together, sends love-letters, and flatters his fiancée egregiously (on the grounds that 'a woman, like the Koh-i-noor,/Mounts to the price that's put on her'). Eventually they marry, and honeymoon by the sea: 'And she assumed the maiden coy,/And I adored remorseless charms,/And then we clapped our hands for joy,/And ran into each other's arms.'

Aristophanes' Apology; including a Transcript from Euripides: being the Last Adventure of Balaustion (1875), by Robert Browning. 5711 lines, blank verse. As with its prequel, **Balaustion's Adventure*, *Aristophanes' Apology* uses the fictional figure of the Rhodian girl Balaustion to explore issues of art and life, centred on the reputation of the Attic tragedian Euripides. Here, however, the narrative element is very thin, the language is ferociously complex and esoteric, the argument immensely long and involved. The translation of Euripides it contains (the *Herakles*, or *Hercules Furens*) is rendered in a much spikier, less accessible verse than was the *Alkestis*, and contemporary reviewers were almost all baffled and negative.

Since we last met Balaustion, she has grown older; she has met her beloved Euripides, kissed his hand and received from him a copy of the *Herakles*. Euripides is now dead, Athens has finally lost the long-running Peloponnesian war, and has had its walls pulled down in its defeat. Balaustion herself has got married, and with her husband Euthykles, she is sailing back to Rhodes. The bulk of the poem consists of Balaustion's recollection of the events of the day on which news reached Athens that Euripides was dead.

To celebrate the life of the great tragedian, Balaustion and Euthykles have gathered to give a private reading of the *Herakles*; but before they can begin there is a knocking at the door and in bursts Aristophanes, the great comic poet, ruddy and drunk.

> On the bulge
> Of the clear baldness – all his head one brow, –
> True, the veins swelled, blue network, and there surged
> A red from cheek to temple ...
> Huge the eyeballs rolled ... nostrils wide.

What follows, at great length, is essentially a head-to-head debate between Balaustion and Aristophanes on the relative merits of Tragedy (represented by Euripides) and Comedy (Aristophanes). Aristophanes argues that comedy, including all the material that Balaustion thinks of as obscene, scatological and pornographic, is the broad expression of natural life. He argues the case of the body, of action rather than thought. Balaustion replies as the representative of 'soul', of art that questions, that explores the life of the mind rather than the body, of becoming rather than being. For Balaustion, Aristophanes' satire is mere destructiveness, not creation; his celebration of the body is mere sensual indulgence. The argument continues with Balaustion reading the *Herakles*, Euripides' last play, as a testament to his powers. Aristophanes responds by singing a fragment of a lyric, 'Thamuris Marching'; it breaks off 'in laughter'. It is dawn; Aristophanes leaves, saying 'Farewell, brave couple! Next year, welcome me!'

Balaustion concludes her narration with a narrative of the fate of Athens, defeated by Sparta; the city's defensive walls were pulled down to the sound of flutes, but the city itself was not destroyed and the inhabitants either killed or sold to slavery (as was the Greek way) solely because of the Spartan respect for the genius of Euripides.

ARNOLD, Sir Edwin (1832–1904). Not related to the more famous Matthew, Arnold was born in Gravesend to a well-to-do family, and studied at Kings and University Colleges, London. His final degree was only a third, but his passion for Greek poetry (which he read avidly) spurred him on to his own writing. *Belshazzar's Feast* won him the Newdigate Prize for poetry, and was published (1852). It was also included in *Poems, Narrative and Lyrical* (1853), the year of Matthew Arnold's *Poems* with its famous preface (*Blackwood's Magazine* published a review entitled 'The Two Arnolds').

Arnold worked as a schoolteacher, and then in 1856 took up the post of Principal of Deccan College, in Poona, India. He was also elected a fellow of Bombay University. It was here that his fascination with India, and the East in general, took him over. He translated Sanskrit poetry and published pamphlets on various subjects. He returned to England in 1862, and began working as a leader writer for the *Daily Telegraph* (George Sala remembered an 'eastern aroma' settling on the *Telegraph* after Arnold's appointment). By 1873 Arnold had worked his way up to editor of the newspaper. His great work, *The Light of Asia, or the Great Renunciation* was published in 1879; it set out to 'depict the life and character and indicate the philosophy of that noble hero and reformer, Prince Gautama of India, founder of Buddhism'.

ARNOLD, Matthew (1822–88). Arnold's literary life divides roughly into two consecutive periods, a poetic and a prosaic. Disillusionment with the first, insofar as Arnold found himself unable to write the sort of poetry he felt ought to be written, lead him on to the prolific production of critical writings from 1853 onwards. Although he continued writing verse until 1866, for our purposes it is the poetry written before 1853 that is most interesting.

Arnold was born in Laleham-on-Thames, the eldest son of Thomas Arnold, the famous Headmaster of Rugby school (from 1828) and eminent Victorian. The pressures of growing up under the shadow of so overwhelming a pater took their toll on the young Arnold, and emerge in various ways in his verse (for instance, in *Sohrab and Rustum*). He went to Oxford, where he met and befriended Arthur Hugh *Clough, with whom he discussed poetic and aesthetic ideas. He graduated with a second-class degree in 1844, and worked for a time as the private secretary to Lord Landsdowne. He also travelled abroad, most significantly to Switzerland in 1848. It was here, in Thun, that he met the woman referred to in his poetry by the pseudonym 'Marguerite'. It is hard to determine precisely what happened with Marguerite, but it seems likely that Arnold and she fell in love, but that something (maybe Arnold's own social fastidiousness) prevented marriage. He returned to Thun the following year, and again met Marguerite, but her presence in his poetry is an entirely valedictory one, as in 'Parting' and 'Farewell', and the famous 'To Marguerite

– Continued', where Arnold asks why the lovers should be separated, and replies:

A God, a God their severance ruled!
And bade betwixt their shores to be
The unplumb'd, salt, estranging sea.

1849 saw the publication of Arnold's first collection of poetry, *The Strayed Reveller, and Other Poems*, which was favourably received. In 1851, still (to judge from his verse) melancholy over the unsucessful affair with Marguerite, Arnold married Lucy Wightman, daughter of Sir William Wightman, Justice of the Queen's Bench. The same year, Arnold (who believed that a man must work, whether financially compelled or not) took a job. He was appointed Inspector of Schools – work which was rendered extremely physically demanding by the long distances Arnold had to travel. The strain of this job almost certainly contributed to the heart attack that eventually killed him.

Empedocles on Etna, and Other Poems was published in 1852; the lengthy title poem was particularly well received, and Arnold's reading public were all the more puzzled when he excluded it from his collected *Poems* of 1853. In fact, Arnold had decided (as his preface to the 1853 volume explained) to suppress *Empedocles on Etna*; not because it was a badly written work, or because it had in some artistic sense 'failed', but simply because Arnold judged the *effect* of the work to be too negative. In the story of a philospher wracked with misery and finally committing suicide, Arnold had delineated a subject in which the suffering found no vent in action; for Arnold, the prime directive for any poetry was not 'is this poem well written?' but 'will this poem *do good?*' He insisted that all art must 'animate' and 'ennoble' its readership, and art which failed to do this was, no matter how beautiful it might be, deplorable.

Arnold's problem was that he was not particularly skilled at producing animating and ennobling works of poetry; his genius lay in the evocation and dissection of melancholy, as with the bleak but lovely Marguerite poems. His *Tristram and Iseult*, from the 1852 volume, was another work influenced by his unhappy love affair. In correspondence with Clough, Arnold himself declared *Sohrab and Rustum* (1853) to be the only one of his works that 'animated' like the great heroic poetry of past ages. Otherwise, his attempts to create a proper poetry tended, like his dry and tedious recreation of Sophoclean tragedy, *Merope* (1857), to fail.

Arnold found increasing pleasure in writing prose, a medium which he always preferred as more immediately communicative than verse. From 1857–67 he was the elected Oxford Professor of Poetry, a post that enabled him to express his poetics. In his later life he published a great deal of critical prose, including *On Translating Homer* (1861), *Essays in Criticism* (1865), *On the Study of Celtic Literature* (1866), and his most famous book, *Culture and Anarchy* (1869). During his later years he expended a great deal of energy examining religious and dogmatic questions, with works such as *St Paul and Protestantism* (1870) and *God and the Bible* (1875). His personal life was not entirely happy, with three of his children predeceasing him, although he did eventually (1884) become Chief Inspector of Schools, and he was widely acclaimed as the nation's most influential spokesman on issues of culture. He died of a heart attack at the age of 66, at Liverpool docks, awaiting the boat on which his daughter was returning from America.

Aurora Leigh (1856), by Elizabeth Barrett Browning. 10,938 lines, blank verse. Barrett Browning's aim was to write 'a true poetical novel – modern, and on the level of the manners of the day', and this work can claim to be the first female *Kunstlerroman*. *Book 1*. Aurora Leigh is born in Italy to a Tuscan mother and English father. Her mother dies first, and Aurora has an Italian childhood until her father also dies. The thirteen-year-old Aurora then moves to England to stay with her aunt, where she meets her cousin Romney Leigh, an idealistic young would-be social reformer. She spends most of her time in books ('I read much ... The world of books is still the world ... And both worlds have God's providence, thank God.') and starts writing poetry. *Book 2*. Aurora is twenty, and Romney (in line to inherit the family fortune) proposes marriage: 'I ask for life in fellowship/Through bitter duties' – the chief 'duty' in question being to 'help' the 'social strait' of the time. Aurora cannot accept ('What you love/Is not a woman, Romney, but a cause:/You want a helpmeet, not a mistress, sir,/A wife to help your ends, – in her no end.'). *Book 3*. Aurora's aunt has died (partly of shock that Aurora could turn down Romney's proposal) and she moves to London, where 'in a certain house in Kensington/Three years I lived and worked' as a writer. A gentlewoman, Lady Waldemar, calls one day with news that Romney (whom she claims to love) is about to marry beneath him, one 'Marian Erle ... Upon whose finger, exquisitely pricked/By a hundred needles, we're to hang the tie/'Twixt class and class in England'. Aurora meets Marian (telling us 'Nowise beautiful/Was Marian Erle ... Too much hair perhaps') who relates how Romney proposed to her out of a sense of social duty. *Book 4*. On the day of the wedding Marian fails to turn up at the church. Romney goes in search of her. *Book 5*. Aurora discusses her various poetic experiments: 'What form is best for poems? Let me think/Of forms less, and the external. Trust the spirit.'

She goes to a party thrown by Lord Howe to cheer herself up, but to no effect ('now I'm sadder that I went tonight/Among the lights and talkers at Lord Howe's'). There she discovers that Romney is 'soon to marry' Lady Waldemar. After bickering politely with the Lady herself, Aurora is forced to confront her feelings: 'Why should I be pained/That Romney Leigh, my cousin, should espouse/This Lady Waldemar?' She decides to return to 'My Italy,/My own hills!' *Book 6*. On her way to Italy, Aurora encounters Marian in Paris, and goes with her to her home ('a room/ Scarce larger than a grave, and near as bare') where Marian tells her story. Lured onto a ship by Lady Waldemar with the promise of a better life in Australia, Marian was kidnapped, taken off the ship at the first French port-of-call, drugged and raped. Turned loose, she had to fend for herself. *Book 7*. Marian describes how she worked as a maid to a Parisian woman, but lost this job when her pregnancy became obvious. She contemplated suicide, but thought instead of 'the sinless babe that should be' and found work. Aurora writes to England to tell Marian's story to Lord Howe and Lady Waldemar (to this latter writing 'I'm very glad/I never liked you ... since you're proved so vile') and the two women go on to Italy. *Book 8*. Romney visits the women in Italy and asks their forgiveness for his mistakes. He reports that Leigh Hall, in which he had established a Utopian socialist community, has been burnt to the ground by one of the inmates. It transpires that Romney has not married Lady Waldemar after all. *Book 9*. Romney declares that he has come to marry Marian, but Marian demurs ('I do not love you, Romney Leigh'). We then discover that Romney is blind, having lost his sight in the fire at Leigh Hall, and Aurora is moved to confess 'weeping bitterly ... I love –/I love you, Romney'.

AUSTIN, Alfred (1835–1913). The greatly mocked Austin was not a particularly good poet; but he is interesting for our purposes here because of his lifelong commitment to the long poem. His father was a wool-stapler in Leeds and a Catholic. Austin took his BA from London University (1853) and was called to the bar in 1857. His first publica-tion, a lumpish satire called *The Season*, appeared in 1861. It was poorly received, but Austin responded to negative critical notices with tremendous energy and vitriol – a habit he was to continue all his life, and which was to win him a great many enemies. The first version of his great epic and self-declared life's work, *The Human Tragedy*, ap-peared in 1863 but failed to make an impression. Discouraged, he wrote no more poetry until 1871, and instead pursued his political career with the Conservative Party (he was a fanatical Disraelian). He stood unsuccessfully as a Tory candidate at various seats, and made his living mostly from his political journalism (in 1883 he was a co-founder of the *National Review*, which he then edited to 1895).

In 1870 he published an article attacking just about all the major poets of the age: Tennyson ('third-rate'), Browning ('not specifically a poet at all'), Morris, Arnold, Clough and Swinburne were all lambasted. The problem, in Austin's view, was that their poetry was either 'feminine' (a pejorative term in his critical vocabulary) or else lyrical, and lyric poetry is essentially 'childish'. What was wanting, he argued, was a masculine poetics. No poem, he declared, could be called great unless it was an epic or dramatic romance on a theme combining 'love, patriotism and religion'. His own *Human Tragedy* was designed to be just this; he reworked it and published a new version in 1876 (other reworkings appeared in 1889 and 1891). He appointment as poet laureate in 1896 was more as a result of his political work (and his devotion to Lord Salisbury's Conservative administration); appropriately one of his first actions as laureate was to write an ode celebrating the Jameson Raid (the trumped-up South African military expedition in which the British attempted to annex Boer land). But in literary circles Austin was a figure of ridicule; Browning responded to Austin's attack by writing him into his satire *Pachiarotto* as 'Quilp Hop O' My Thumb' (Austin was of diminutive height).

AYTOUN, William Edmondstoune (1813–65). Born into a well-to-do Edinburgh family, Aytoun grew up with a passion for Scott (he later claimed that from the age at which he learned to read, not a year went by when he did not reread the entire works of Scott) and absorbing the Jacobite sympathies of his mother. He studied at Edinburgh University, and published his first collection of poems at the age of 19 (*Poland, Homer and Other Poems*, 1832); an unremarkable collection of pieces. After university, he was articled to his father's legal firm, and much of his adult life was divided between law and literature. He began writing pieces (articles and poems) for *Blackwood's Magazine* in 1836, and swiftly became their 'No 1' contributor, particularly for humorous or parodic pieces. Many of the ballads he published in the magazine were patriotic Scottish pieces (collected in 1849 as *Lays of the Scottish Cavaliers*), but he was better known (and was altogether a better poet in) the various parodies of contemporary poetry he wrote with Theodore Martin. These appeared under the pseudonym 'Bon Gaultier' (meaning *'bon viveur'*) between 1845 and 1857. His genius for parody lighted on the 1850s craze for the febrile, psychological poetry of disjointed imagery and moral dislocation associated with *Bailey, *Dobell and *Smith, and for which Aytoun coined the name *'Spasmodic'. He wrote a mock-review of an imaginary new poem called *Firmillian ('A Spas-modic Tragedy') for *Blackwood's Magazine*, May 1854. The piece was such a hit that friends suggested he actually write this tragedy, which he did. *Firmillian appeared in 1854, and banged the last nail into the Spasmodic coffin. Although he possessed a genius for parody, Aytoun yearned for serious poetic success. He stopped contributing to *Blackwood's* in order to concentrate on writing a lengthy Scottish poem, *Bothwell, which (despite respectful contemporary reviews) is quite bad. Aytoun in later life became an elder statesman of Scottish litera-ture. He was Professor of Rhetoric at Edinburgh University in 1845, and Sheriff of Orkney in 1852. He published little else of note after *Bothwell*, and died at the age of fifty-two.

: B :

BAILEY, Philip James (1816–1902). Born in Nottingham, the young Bailey was encouraged in his enthusiasm for poetry by his father, who, for instance, insisted that he learn the whole of Byron's *Childe Harold* by heart. After matriculating at Glasgow, Bailey entered Lincoln's Inn in 1834, and was called to the bar in 1840. Although he never actually practised law, Bailey was always proud of this achievement, and his title-pages style him 'Barrister-at-Law'. It was while studying for the bar that Bailey first read, and was captivated by, Goethe's *Faust*; and throughout the 1830s he worked at an English version of the same legend, which was eventually to emerge in 1839 as Bailey's first, and most famous, publication: *Festus.*

Initial reviews of the work were mixed (the *Athenaeum* called it 'a mere plagiary from the *Faust* of Goethe, with all its impiety and scarcely anything of its poetry'); but the popular success of what was, in fact, a fairly desiccated, blank-verse fantasia on philosophical and religious themes, only occasionally leavened by striking or beautiful images, was remarkable. Bailey was never to move beyond the impact of *Festus*; and the fact that he repeatedly revised and augmented the work for later editions meant that it constitutes in effect, and despite its early initial publication, his life's work. Some sense of the quantity of additional material Bailey incorporated into successive editions of the poem can be garnered by the swelling size of the volumes as they appeared. The first edition (1839) ran to 360 pages; the second to 396; the fifth to 562; the seventh to 602 and the tenth to 688 pages. By the time of the eleventh 'jubilee' edition, *Festus* had inflated to nearly 40,000 lines of verse, making it one of the longest single works by any Victorian poet – or any poet. Although Bailey was castigated by *Aytoun as the father of the *Spasmodic movement, and although *Festus* remains the classic or paradigmatic Spasmodic text, contemporary opinion was often not so dismissive. Robert Chambers's *Cyclopedia of English Literature* (1860) bracketed Bailey with Robert *Browning as 'philosophical poets – men of undoubted talent, learning and poetical imagination, but too often obscure, mystical and extravagant.' Chambers, aptly, describes Bailey's typical poetic production as possessing 'one tendency and object – to describe the history of a divinely instructed mind or soul soaring upwards to communion with the universal life'.

Festus was popular with a wide variety of people, many of whom (as his contemporaries noted) did not otherwise read poetry; and publications such as *The Festus Birthday Book* (1882), the selection (by 'a student') of *The Beauties of Festus* ('with descriptive index', 1884) and H. Henry Brown's *Selections from Festus* (1893) kept his work in the public eye to the end of the century. Bailey's other works did not succeed on the same scale. The windy, philosophical blank verse of *The Angel World, and Other Poems* (1850) and *The Mystic, and Other Poems* (1855) is fairly unremarkable; although the title poem of the latter collection, in which the narrator passes 'the flaming bounds of space and time' to encounter the 'fontal deity', won comparisons with Milton. His Pope-influenced satire, *The Age: a Colloquial Satire* (1858), however, was roundly condemned as banal and doggerel, as for instance in this attack on the concept of the Christian Solider:

> Of all conceits mis-grafted on God's Word,
> A Christian soldier seems the most absurd.
> That Word commands us so to act in all things
> As not to hurt another e'en in small things.

Apart from his continual tinkerings with *Festus*, Bailey published little from 1860 onwards. A dry *Universal Hymn* was issued as a separate volume in 1867, although it amounts to little more than a pamphlet. In 1872 Bailey toured Europe, and saw Vesuvius erupt, although proximity to the volcano injured his health. He retired to England, where he died (of 'flu) in 1902.

Balaustion's Adventure, Including a Transcript from Euripides (1871), by Robert Browning. 2705 lines, blank verse. The 'transcript' or translation of Euripides' *Alkestis* that makes up the bulk of this work marks Browning's first attempt at translating Greek tragedy; further efforts included Euripides' *Herakles* and Aeschylus' *Agamemnon*. All these display Browning's idiosyncratic literalism, in which Greek names are rendered in English letter-for-letter rather than being simply anglicized.

Balaustion is a beautiful Rhodian girl, brought up in Athens. It is the time of the Peloponnesian war (5th century BC), and the Athenian fleet has been defeated at Syracuse. Balaustion and others take flight on a ship at Kaunus, a sea-port that belongs to Rhodes. They run into trouble, and are pursued by a pirate ship, but Balaustion gives heart to the rowers by singing an Aeschylean song that had been sung at the battle of Salamis. The ship arrives at Syracuse and asks for shelter, but the Syracuseans refuse the request on the grounds that they are at war with Athens. When the people on the ship insist that they are Karians, subjects to Rhodes, and not Athenian at all, they receive the reply that 'all Athens echoed in that song from Aeschylus which was ringing over the sea'. All seems hopeless, it looks as though the ship will be turned away to face doom at the hands of the pirates, when somebody on shore cries out: 'Wait. Do they know any verses from Euripides?'

Balaustion (her name means 'wild pomegranate flower') not only loves and knows Euripides, but has particular lyric and narrative gifts herself. The Rhodians are brought ashore to the temple of Herakles, and on the temple steps Balaustion recites the story of Euripides' play *Alkestis*, half repeating Euripides' words, half describing a performance she has seen 'at Kameiros this very year'. The bulk of *Balaustion's Adventure* is taken up with this retelling of the *Alkestis* –how Admetus is doomed to die young unless somebody is prepared to take his place, how nobody is prepared to make the sacrifice except his loving wife Alkestis; how she then dies, and is finally rescued from the underworld by Herakles himself as a return for Admetus's selfless hospitality. The recital delights the Syracusians, who accept the Rhodians to their hearts, for:

> Greeks are Greeks, and hearts are hearts,
> And poetry is power ...
> What's poetry except a power that makes?
> And, speaking to one sense, inspires the rest,
> Pressing them all into its service?

For Browning, whose wife had recently died, the story of *Alkestis* had particular resonance, and Elizabeth Barrett is quoted and eulogized towards the end of the text.

We are given another portion of Balaustion's adventures in the sequel Browning wrote four years later, **Aristophanes' Apology*.

Balder. Part the First (1854), by Sydney Dobell. 7813 lines, blank verse with lyric interludes. Dobell originally planned three parts of *Balder*, but the negative criticism with which this **'Spasmodic'* work was received discouraged him. The work is mostly monodrama, with an occasional second actor introduced.

Scenes I–XV. Balder is in the study of his tower home, working on an epic poem (he spends quite a lot of time reading sections from this work in progress) which appears to be about a battlefield populated with allegorical figures. In between reading from his epic, he meditates on life, the universe and almost everything. Meanwhile, heard but unseen in an adjacent room, his wife Amy sings a variety of lyrics, many of which are addressed to her baby: 'Awake, awake, my babe, my only babe, ... thou art my heart/And only by its pulse I know I live.'

Scenes XVI–XXVII. Amy's songs from the next room makes us aware that the baby has died (Balder 'sinking his head into his hands' wails 'So soon, so soon! My lamb, my lily-bud,/My little babe!'). Amy goes slowly mad, her songs becoming increasingly disjointed, and a repeated refrain emerges: 'That I might only die and be at rest,/That I might die and sleep the sleep of peace'. Balder calls in a doctor to help, but little can be done. *Scenes XXVIII–XXXVIII.* Amy grows worse. The doctor returns. Balder takes him out on the balcony and threatens to throw him off unless he promises to 'cure her!' (terrified, he says 'I will!', and Balder replies 'Thou wilt NOT!/Liar! Begone!'). Amy's repeated 'That I might die and be at rest, O God!' prompts Balder to consider murdering her to put her out of her misery, although at first the prospect fills him with guilty terror, expressed in the famous (or notorious) lines:

> No, no, it cannot be, it must not be,
> It shall not be! – Amy!
> > *[Looking up, his eye catches the clouds.]*
> > You white full heavens!
> You crowded heavens that mine eyes left but now
> Shining and void and azure! –
> > Ah! ah! ah!
> Ah! ah! ah! ah! ah! ah! ah! ah! ah! ah!

Scenes XXXIX–XLII. Balder resolves to murder Amy, but cannot steel himself to commit the act (despite her best efforts to help him along, as in the stage direction '*striking her head against the stone wall*'). The poem ends with Balder finally holding Amy in his arms, unable to murder her. Dobell declared that, had he been able to finish the second and third parts, Amy would have played a large part in the subsequent growth of Balder out of the state of obsessive self-contemplation that characterizes him in the first part.

Battle of Marathon, The (1820), by Elizabeth Barrett. 1462 lines, heroic couplets. Barrett's first published work (she was thirteen when she wrote it) does not represent her finest hour. As she says in her preface of her chief influence, 'perhaps I have chosen the rimes of Pope ... injudiciously'.

Book I. Greece, 490 BC, the Persians are massing for invasion. The Athenians are debating the situation when a Persian herald arrives, and demands their immediate capitulation to the Persian king Darius. The Athenians are unimpressed ('We scorn Darius and his threats defy') and offer to kill the messenger. He pleads for his life, but 'the Sire of Gods' booms forth a command from the clouds, and the poor fellow is slain. The book ends with Jove and Athena in conversation. *Book II.* The

Athenian Senate is divided as to the wisdom of war ('Before superior force will Athens fall' say some); a herald from Sparta relates that the Lacedaimonians had agreed to help Athens, and had even marched an army out to join them, when direct divine intervention had sent them home again. The herald is apologetic ('If Athens fall – it is by wrath divine'). *Book III.* The Athenian preparations for war are lengthily described. *Book IV.* Battle is joined, the few thousand Greeks matched, we are told, against 'warlike millions' of Persians. The fighting is bloody, but the Greeks are eventually triumphant.

Beppo: a Venetian Story (1818), by Lord Byron. 752 lines, ottava rima. Byron's first experiment in ottava rima (*Don Juan* and *The Vision of Judgement* were to follow) was prompted by his reading of Frere's *Whistlecraft.*

The scene is set at a luxurious Venetian carnival ('a time liked less by husbands than by lovers', as the poet tells us). Beppo, a Venetian merchant, has been absent on a trading mission to Aleppo for many years and is generally assumed dead; his wife, the beautiful Laura, has taken a lover (or 'Cavalier Servente') known as the Count, and together they are attending the Carnival. They come across a Turk 'the colour of mahogany', who cannot keep his eyes from Laura. He follows them home and reveals himself to be Beppo; the Count invites him in to discuss matters in a civilized fashion over a coffee. Beppo reveals he has been shipwrecked, taken in slavery, escaped to become a pirate and that he now returns with great riches. Rebaptised, he takes possession again of his wife and house and everything ends agreeably, with the Count and he 'always friends'.

BLAKE, William (1757–1827). The first great genius of the long poem in the nineteenth century, and the only Romantic poet to be able to fully integrate his poetic vision at great length, Blake remains nonetheless *sui generis.* Not only are his epics unlike anything that had gone before, or anything that was to come after; but they also existed only in the complex patternings of words, designs and pictures that Blake published himself out of his own print shop (no other publisher issued them during his lifetime). To summarize their narrative lines, as this study does, is to represent them in a extremely feeble manner. They remain among the most beautiful composite poetic/visual arts productions in English.

Of all the poets dealt with in this guide, Blake has the least by way of personal biography. He was born in London, the son of a hosier; and apart from three years living on the Sussex coast, he lived his whole life in London. He was apprenticed to James Basire, an engraver; and from 1779 was employed in this capacity by a bookseller. In 1782 he married Catherine Boucher, who became his lifetime companion. There were no children. With financial help from a friend, Blake set up his own print shop at 27 Broad Street in 1784; out of which emerged the self-illustrated and self-engraved lyrics and ballads of the famous *Songs of Innocence* in 1789. It was here also that Blake began formulating his idiosyncratic personal mythology; early short works in the epic mode of his later masterpieces begin to express it (*The Book of Thel* and *Tiriel* in 1789). In 1790 the Blakes moved to Lambeth, where he continued his creative work: *The Marriage of Heaven and Hell* (1790–93), *The French Revolution* (1791), *America: a Prophecy* and *Visions of the Daughters of Albion* (both in 1793). *The First Book of Urizen* and *Europe: a Prophecy* both appeared in 1794; *The Song of Los* and *The Book of Ahania* in 1795. All these are relatively short works, particularly when compared with the later epics.

In 1794 he added *Experience* to his earlier collection of *Innocence*; *The Songs of Innocence and Experience* was the only volume of Blake's works to establish any sort of reputation during his own life. Since these poems remain the best known of Blake's life, it is worth pointing out how very different they are from the later, long poems that are the concern of this study. These latter began emerging in the first decade of the nineteenth century, with Blake working on the monumental (but unpublished) *Vala* (also called *The Four Zoas*) throughout the decade, and also condensing down this myth into *Milton* (1804–08) and *Jerusalem* (1804–20). These works embody the distinctive Blakean myth.

Scholarship spends a great deal of time tracing this personal schema of symbolic quasi-gods through eighteenth-century traditions of mysticism, particularly the work of the Swedish visionary Emanuel Swedenborg. Blake was certainly well versed in Swedenborgism, and other obscure Gnostic cults, just as his work has evident affinities with strands of political radicalism and revolutionary theory. But to trace these influences on Blake is profoundly to miss the point of Blake's whole life, which was to be free of influence, to remake oneself and one's art on one's own terms. The consistent evils of the Blakean universe are restriction, imprisonment, repression, oppression and all ideology (including organized religion); the consistent virtues are freedom, energy, imagination and non-inhibition. To inhabit another system of belief, poetic or spiritual, was for Blake a form of slavery ('I must Create a System,' says Los in *Jerusalem*, 'or be enslaved by another Man's'). Thus Blake's unusual subject matter, his unique mode of book production, even his unrhymed long lines (freed from the fetters of rhyme and metre) are a form of poetic self-manumission. Blake took what inspired him out of a wide range of texts, most especially the Bible and Milton, as well as the Swedenborgian mystic tradition, and then made them wholly his own. Accordingly, he offers us his own personal mythology absolutely not in a proselytizing spirit: it would be a grotesque error to form our own beliefs out of Blake's personal mythic universe – we must make the imaginative, fiery effort to create our own. What this means in practice is that Blake had no need (because he was printing his own work) and no desire (because of his own beliefs) to make his work accessible, or even especially attractive to other people. This can give his longer poems a rather awkward, difficult feel to them; and even with modern annotation his myths come over as the arcane and complex code they undoubtedly are. But these works are very much worth persevering with for their powerful sweep and many muscular beauties.

From 1800 to 1803 Blake lived in a little cottage on the Sussex coast, at Felpham, provided for him by his friend and patron Hayley. During his time here Blake was charged in the Courts that he had 'uttered seditious and treasonable expressions such as "Damn the King, damn all his subjects"'. Blake was acquitted of this charge, but he took the accusation (and the man who had originally made it, a soldier called Scholfield) deeply personally, as examples of eternal evil and enmity. Scholfield re-emerges in *Jerusalem* as a demon. In 1803 he moved back to Lambeth in London, where he spent the remainder of his life. He worked at engraving *Milton* and *Jerusalem*, and undertook various other commissions, but he remained an unknown, regarded by those few who encountered his work as an eccentric. At his death (in relative poverty), Wordsworth remarked that 'there was no doubt that this poor man was mad, but there is something in his madness that interests me more than the sanity of Lord Byron and Walter Scott'. He remained an obscure figure, existing outside the currents of poetical tradition until Gilchrist's 1863 biography and Swinburne's 1867 study. Even then, it was not until Modernism and later twentieth-century poetry (particularly Beat poets like Ginsberg) that his influence was felt most profoundly.

Blake detested Wordsworth. Reading the 'Prospectus' to the *Excursion* infuriated him so much that he fell into a sort of fit, out of which developed a fever that came close to killing him. He saw in his eminent contemporary an oppressive desire to fit the imagination into the shapes and forms of the natural world, and to subordinate the individual mind to a grand theistic pattern. From Blake's point of view this could not be more wrong, or more dangerous. He regarded the manifestations of the external world as delusive, as a sort of prison in which the eternal spirit was trapped. The aim of his poetic was (to invoke his much-quoted proverb from *The Marriage of Heaven and Hell*) to cleanse the 'doors

of perception', and reveal Infinity. Accordingly his poetry is little concerned with describing the external world, and more interested in
elaborating Blake's personal myth. This myth (dangerously truncated in
precis) is as follows: the reality we all inhabit is the result of a fall, or
disintegration of an Eternal Man or Being (variously Albion, Jesus, the
Lamb of God). This fall broke the Eternal Man out of timeless paradise,
and trapped him in pieces in the world of time. These pieces, or Zoas,
are fourfold, and each of the four (male) pieces has his female partner,
or emanation. The Zoas exist either in their eternal shape, or else in
fallen versions: Urizen is the Rational, controlling intellect; his emanation (female partner) is Ahania. Luvah (whose fallen form is called Orc)
is passionate and desiring, particularly in a sexual sense; his emanation
is Vala, who exists in various forms as a beautiful woman (sometimes
called Jerusalem) and a temptress/harlot. Tharmas represents compassion, and his emanation is Enion. Urthona (whose fallen form is Los)
represents the fiery energy of the imagination, and is the Zoa that most
approximates Blake himself; his emanation (who has similarities to
Blake's wife Catherine) is Enitharmon. When harmoniously combined,
these four Zoas produce the perfect eternal balance; but if any one
achieves a primacy over the others disaster follows. It is usually Urizen,
the Jove-like Law-god, who upsets this balance by attempting to seize
power; but each of the Zoas, in various poems, try to assert themselves
at the expense of the others. Blake's great poetic subject is the fall of the
divine man and his breaking into components, the troubles that ensue,
and the eventual reintegration of the whole.

BLOOMFIELD, Robert (1766–1823). Born at Honington, Suffolk,
3 December 1766, Bloomfield was one of six children of a poor tailor,
who died when he was a year old. His mother kept a village school,
where he learnt to read, and after she married again (in 1774) Bloomfield
was taken to her brother-in-law's farm. However, Bloomfield was so
small of stature that he was not of much use on the farm, and eventually he was sent up to London to learn shoemaking from another
relative. For several years he lived in a garret in which five separate
cobblers worked, and his main occupation was reading aloud from the
newspapers to these illiterate artisans as they laboured. Via this reading,
and particularly from scanning the 'poet's corner' of the *London Magazine*, Bloomfield enlarged his literary vocabulary to the point where he
decided to write poetry. He composed in his head in the cobbler's
garret, being accustomed to memorize anything from fifty to a hundred
lines of verse before he could write it down. He married in 1790, and
continued living in the most abject poverty.

By 1798 the manuscript of *The Farmer's Boy* was finished, and it came to the attention of one Capel Lofft, by whose efforts it was published in March 1800. It was an immediate and huge hit, and had sold 26,000 copies within three years. Despite this popular success, however, the pastoral visions of *The Farmer's Boy* did not please the literary establishment. Lamb wrote to Manning, in 1800, that the author (whom he had not met) had 'a poor mind ... I have just opened him and he makes me sick'. Bloomfield went on to write and publish *Rural Tales* (1802), *Good Tidings, or News from the Farm* (1804) and *Wild Flowers* (1806). He also travelled through Wales, and recorded his impressions in *The Banks of the Wye* (1811). But his fame did not greatly increase his happiness, and a few years later, half-blind and hypochondriacal, he retired from London to Shefford in Bedfordshire, where he died in 1823.

Botanic Garden, The (1789, 1792), by Erasmus Darwin. 4484 lines, heroic couplets. The two parts of this work were published separately, *The Loves of the Plants* (actually Part II) coming out in 1789, and *The Economy of Vegetation* (Part I) in 1792 (although dated 1791). Darwin declared his aim (in the Advertisement to the whole) 'to inlist Imagination under the banner of Science'. To this end he included in his epic a fantastical supernatural apparatus ('The Rosicrusian doctrine of Gnomes, Sylphs, Nymphs and Salamanders,' he announces, constituting 'the proper machinery for a Botanic poem') while also rooting the whole in a body of up-to-the-moment scientific knowledge (there are many hundreds of pages of notes, as well as beautifully etched plates of plants and flowers).

The Economy of Vegetation (1791; 2448 lines). Despite its title, this poem has very little to do with vegetation, being more concerned with rocky, fiery and watery natural phenomena.

Canto 1. The theme of this canto is 'Fire'. The 'Genius' of the poem invites the Goddess of Botany to speak to various Rosicrucian beings ('GNOMES, ascending from their earthy beds, ... Gay SYLPHS ... Blue NYMPHS'). The Goddess relates the whole history of the universe, beginning with the creation, 'when LOVE DIVINE, with brooding wings unfurl'd,/ Call'd from the rude abyss the living world'

> the mass starts into a million suns;
> Earths round each sun with quick explosions burst,
> And second planets issue from the first;
> Bend, as they journey with projectile force,
> In bright ellipses their reluctant course;
> Orbs wheel in orbs, round centres centres roll,
> And form, self balanced, one revolving Whole.

The Goddess describes the molten core of the Earth, various geological and atmospheric features (lava, 'phosphoric lights in the evening') and zoological oddities ('Luminous Sea-insects', 'electric eels'). The canto closes with great men of science who had harnessed fire (and therefore steam) and electricity – Bacon, Savery, Franklin – with each example mirroring scientific advance with mythological parallel (so Franklin discovers electricity with his kite and his key, 'and seize[s] the tiptoe lightnings, ere they fly'; the scene is compared to when Cupid 'snatch'd the raised lightning from the arm of JOVE'). *Canto II.* The second canto is concerned with the element of Earth, and its tutelary spirits the Gnomes ('And now the Goddess with attention sweet/Turns to the Gnomes that circle round her feet'). The Goddess explains the creation of the earth, out of a volcano of the Sun ('From the deep craters of his realms of fire,/The whirling Sun this ponderous planet hurl'd'), and the creation of the moon, out of a cataclysmic split of the Earth early in its history:

> GNOMES! how you shrieked! when through the troubled air
> Roar'd the fierce din of elemental war; ...
> And Earth's huge sphere exploding burst in twain –
> GNOMES! how you gazed! when from her side
> Where now the South-Sea heaves its waste of tide,
> Rose on swift wheels the MOON's refulgent car,
> Circling the solar orb, a sister-star.

The Goddess goes on to detail the formation of various stones (limestone, marble, granite), salt, and various metals: iron, 'refulgent tin', copper, zinc, which leads into a condemnation of slavery ('Hear, oh BRITANNIA ... Now AFRIC's coasts thy craftier sons invade,/And Theft and Murder take the garb of Trade!'). The Goddess concludes with the circulation of all matter ('mass obeys its changeful doom'), and the Gnomes depart. *Canto III.* The Goddess now addresses the Sylphs, the spirits of the Water. She explains how sea-water circulates into the atmosphere, and falls as rain; how oil stills water ('oil effusive lull[s] the waves to sleep'); the importance of the great rivers of the Earth (the Tiber, the Nile); of medicinal springs and various other watery things. Finally, the nymphs depart 'like water-spiders': 'to each bright stream on silver sandals glide'. *Canto IV.* Now the Goddess addresses the Sylphs, the spirits of the air. The canto moves from 'the production of vital air from oxygene and light' (mythologized as the marriage of Cupid and Psyche), to hot-air ballooning ('bold MONTGOLFIER ... Outstretch'd his buoyant ball with airy spring,/And bore the Sage on levity of wing') and submarine sea-balloons ('Huge SEA-BALLOONS beneath the tossing tide'). Via a passage on airborne distribution of seeds, the Goddess finally comes to the subject of vegetation, and the canto closes with a variety of observations on plant-life, where technical terms are blended with mythological fancy and Biblical allusion ('Form the green *Calyx*, fold including fold;/Each widening *Bracte* expand its foliage hard ... Thus when in holy triumph Aaron trod,/And offer'd on the shrine his mystic rod'). The poem closes with a peroration to Kew Gardens ('Imperial KEW by Thames's glittering side'). The Goddess, finally, binds the Zephyrs to her car, and 'climbs into air' to 'pierce the low-sailing clouds'.

The Loves of the Plants (1936 lines). Where *The Economy of Vegetation* encompassed a wide range of topics, its companion piece is more focused on its topic, the reproductive mechanisms of the vegetable world.

Canto I. After invoking the 'BOTANIC MUSE', Darwin details how various plants court and mate, how the Indian reed *Canna* 'plights his nuptial vow'; how *Collinsonia* is more profligate (for the female plant, '*three* unjealous husbands wed the dame'), and so on through a list of, in all, ninety-six plants. All the plants in this poem are personified, and their cross-pollination related in human-sexual terms. *Canto II*. Among the plants discussed here are Papyrus (which leads to a discourse on paper, and thence learning: 'to astonish'd realms PAPYRA taught/To paint in mystic colours Sounds and Thought'); and Digitalis ('bright DIGITALIS' dress and air/Her ruby cheek, white neck, and raven hair'). *Canto III*. The canto is concerned with plants that have a more baleful influence on humanity. It begins with the hallucinogen Circaea, or Enchanter's Nightshade, and a description of the nightmares that follow ingesting it: 'So on his NIGHTMARE through the evening fog/Flits the squab Fiend o'er fen, and lake, and bog;/Seeks some love wilder'd Maid with sleep oppress'd,/Alights, and grinning sits upon her breast'). It goes on to attack, with the vine, the evils of alcohol ('Fell Gout peeps grinning though the flimsy scene,/And bloated Dropsy pants behind unseen'). The Canto closes with an attack on slavery. *Canto IV*. The Canto goes from the cactus ('to the skies she lifts her pencill'd brows') to the Oat, Avena, and thence to Cannabis:

> Slow treads fair CANNABIS the breezy strand,
> The distaff streams dishevell'd in her hand;
> Now to the left her ivory neck inclines,
> And leads in Paphian curves its azure lines.

After detailing various other herbs and flaxes, the poem concludes with the departure of the Goddess.

Bothie of Toper-na-Fuosich, The: A Long-Vacation Pastoral (1848), by Arthur Hugh Clough. 1732 lines, English hexameters. The poem is named after a real Bothie (a single-roomed hut in the countryside, at which hunting parties and the like would stay) that Clough had come across on a map; but after publication he discovered that the Gaelic translated as an obscenity – it means 'the well under the woman's beard' (which is to say, the vagina). He changed the title for subsequent editions to *The Bothie of Tober-na-Vuolich*, which does not mean anything in Gaelic.

The poem concerns a party of young Oxford undergraduates who travel to Scotland during the university summer vacation, to read books together and generally amuse themselves: 'they bathed, read, and roamed, all in the joy of their life and glory of shooting jackets'. One of the party, a young poet and political radical called Philip Hewson, 'Hewson, the radical hot, hating lords and despising ladies', decides to put into practice his philosophy of classlessness and the dignity of work. Hewson argues with his Tutor, Adam, over politics: Adam thinks society is the result of Divine Providence, and that people should do their duty 'in the state of life it has pleased God to call you'. Hewson, on the other hand, sees society as a mess: 'infinite jumble and mess and dislocation'. He flirts with a peasant girl called Jane ('smit by the charm of a lovely potato-uprooter'). With a certain abruptness, he then swings to the opposite extreme, and goes off to woo the high-class beauty Lady Maria. He sends a letter to his friends outlining his volte-face in political opinions: 'What of the poor and needy? their labour and pain is needed./Perish the poor and the needy! what can they better than perish?/Perish in labour for her who is worth the destruction of empires'. The final twist comes with Hewson's third inamorata, the highland girl Elspie Mackaye, the self-reliant, self-educated daughter of an ex-blacksmith, ex-soldier and ex-schoolmaster (now a potato farmer). At the poem's end 'Elspie, the quiet, the brave' is married to Hewson:

> So won Philip his bride. They are married and gone to New Zealand.
> Five hundred pounds in pocket, with books and two or three pictures,
> Tool-box, plough, and the rest they rounded the sphere to New Zealand.
> There he hewed and dug; subdued the earth with his spirit.

Bothwell: a Poem in Six Parts (1856), by W. E. Aytoun. 4192 lines, rhymed octosyllabics and ballad metres. Aytoun, a Scot of mild Jacobite sympathies, wrote this work to vindicate Mary Queen of Scots and present Bothwell as the unwitting dupe of Scottish nobles. He himself thought highly of the Scott-influenced *Marmion*esque work that resulted, although it is dull and serious, and particularly disappointing after the comic fireworks of *Firmillian*.

Part First. Bothwell narrates the whole poem from the castle of Malmoe where he is imprisoned. He recalls how, upon first seeing Mary Queen of Scots, he fell in love with her according to the old chivalric code of *amour cortois*: 'I worshipped; and as pure a heart/To her, I swear, was mine'. He despises Darnley, Mary's husband ('His pride provoked the nobles' hate,/His folly stirred their spleen'). Darnley ordered the murder of Mary's private secretary Riccio; although Bothwell does not object to this death (Riccio was 'sharp and sly') he does despise the men who carried it out on chivalric grounds: 'base it was for belted knights/So poor a wretch to kill'. *Part Second*. Bothwell reveals how he was manipulated by the Scottish nobles, who used his love for Mary as leverage, to plot against Darnley's life. *Part Third*. Bothwell blows up Darnley's Edinburgh house, killing him ('flashed the glare,/And with a hoarse infernal roar/A blaze went up and filled the air!'). *Part Fourth*. Bothwell is legally absolved of complicity in Darnley's murder (because the nobles, who control the courts, want first to implicate Mary). In a moment of hubris he decides he should marry Mary ('the strength of Scotland backs my claim'). *Part Fifth*. Bothwell forces Mary to marry him; as narrator, he is full of remorse for this action ('It might be foul, it might be wrong/To slay the man I hated long;/But O what mercy from above/Can he entreat who strikes at love?'). *Part Sixth*. Still enamoured of the chivalric ideal, Bothwell leads an army against the Scottish nobles: 'I stood upon Carberry's height,/Eager, intent, resolved to fight'. But instead of battle, he issues chivalric challenges for personal combat. His captains (and their troops) slope away in disgust at his 'chivalrous display'. Bothwell is forced to flee, and is ultimately captured.

Bride of Abydos, The: A Turkish Tale (1813), by Lord Byron. 1214 lines, octosyllabic couplets and various other metres. Byron claimed to have written this tale in under a week.

Canto the First. Old Giaffir is the Turkish Pasha, or ruler. He has decided to marry his beautiful young daughter, Zuleika ('The might, the majesty of Loveliness ... Such was Zuleika') to the ageing and wealthy Bey of Carasman. Zuleika confides her misery to her brother, Selim. *Canto the Second*. It is late at night, and 'the winds are high on Helle's wave'. Wrapped in a black cloak, Selim comes to Zuleika's tower and takes her away. They travel to a grotto, where he uncloaks to reveal himself dressed as a pirate. He then reveals that he is not her brother at all but her cousin; not a mild-mannered prince but the leader of a band of desperadoes. He begs her to marry him. She seems keen (saying 'bid me be thy slave!'), but then Giaffir's soldiers arrive. Battle is joined, but

Selim cannot help looking over his shoulder to catch a glimpse of Zuleika in the midst of it ('Ah! wherefore did he turn to look/For her his eye but sought in vain?/That pause, that fatal gaze he took/Hath doom'd his death'). Selim being killed, Zuleika dies of grief.

BROWNING, Elizabeth Barrett (1806–61). Born into a wealthy upper-middle-class family (Edward Moulton Barrett, the father, had made a small fortune via Jamaican plantations), Elizabeth Barrett wrote poetry from an early age. Her first publication, a mini-epic in heroic couplets called *The Battle of Marathon appeared when she was fourteen; *An Essay on Mind came out in 1826, and a translation of Aeschylus, Prometheus Bound and Other Poems in 1833. She spent her childhood in a country house in Herefordshire, reading widely and educating herself in a variety of disciplines. In 1832 the family moved to Sidmouth, and in 1835 on to London. 1838 saw the publication of her first popular and critical success, *The Seraphim, and Other Poems; but this was also the year in which her health, never strong, gave way. She was diagnosed as suffering from a burst blood-vessel in her chest, and was sent to Torquay to convalesce. But here tragedy struck: Edward, her eldest brother, drowned while swimming in the sea in 1840. The grief of this event overshadowed her life. She returned to London in 1841, and was now confined (or confined herself) almost wholly to bed, her health extremely delicate. Her next publication, a collected *Poems* (1844), dedicated to her father, won great plaudits.

In 1845 she began corresponding with Robert Browning; the two met, and (eventually) fell in love. The snag was Elizabeth Barrett's father. Perhaps slightly unhinged by the death of his son, this overprotective man had become a domestic tyrant, refusing to let any of his children marry. In the face of this, Robert and Elizabeth married secretly in 1846 and eloped together to the Continent. Her health apparently not so delicate after all, she and her new husband travelled by coach over the Alps to Italy where they set up house together. After several miscarriages, Elizabeth Barrett's only child, Robert Wiedemann, was born in 1849.

By now her poetic reputation was so high (much higher than her husband's) that she was, on Wordsworth's death, openly canvassed for the laureateship. *Sonnets from the Portuguese*, love poems addressed to Robert, appeared in 1850; in 1851 a poem given over to themes of Italian Liberty, *Casa Guidi Windows. She worked on her masterpiece *Aurora Leigh for several years, before it finally appeared in 1857. Despite its often risqué themes (class injustice, rape, female emancipation) the poem was a tremendous success. The unashamedly political collection *Poems Before Congress* came out in 1860; but Barrett's health, never good, was failing, and she died in 1861.

BROWNING, Robert (1812–89). Browning's life divides into three main periods: the years of his youth, before he met Elizabeth Barrett (in 1845), the courtship and marriage years (1845–61) and Browning's life as a widower (1861–89). Criticism has tended to concentrate on the first two periods, but the bulk of Browning's poetic output actually occurred in the last.

Browning was born and brought up in Camberwell, south-east London. His father was a widely-read employee of the Bank of England (his personal library contained over 6000 volumes) who conveyed his love of literature and his eclectic tastes to his only son. Browning's interest in writing poetry began young, under the contrary influences of his mother's strong nonconformist faith, and the often radical impulses of much of his early reading (especially Shelley). His first published work, *Pauline* (1833) dramatizes his struggle between these opposing forces, although it received little notice. *Paracelsus* (1835) was more successful with reviewers, and a meeting with the actor-manager William Macready convinced Browning that he ought to write for the stage. *Strafford* (1837) resulted, but closed after only a short run, and none of the other six stage plays Browning wrote were successful. His attempt at epic, *Sordello*, was published in 1840 to an astonished, outraged and noncomprehending reception. With *Sordello*, Browning established a reputation for obscurity and literary affectation that dogged him for much of his writing life. The collections of shorter poems published in a series of pamphlets called *Bells and Pomegranates* (there were eight of these, 1841–46) were much more accessible. On 10 January 1845 the celebrated romance with the bedridden Elizabeth *Barrett began, and over the next two years the two poets exchanged hundreds of letters, meeting frequently. Elizabeth Barrett's father was hostile, and the couple resorted to covert action. On 12 September 1846 they secretly married, and on 19 September they left England together for Italy. The following year they settled in Florence, where their house (Casa Guidi) became their home for the remainder of their time together. The marriage produced a single child (Robert Wiedemann Barrett Browning, known as 'Pen', 1849–1913). Under Elizabeth's influence, Robert published the religious poem *Christmas-Eve and Easter Day*, and then his famous collection *Men and Women* (1855). An 1856 legacy of £11,000 from John Kenyon, an old friend of the couple, solved their financial problems, although Elizabeth, never hale, sickened, and died 29 June 1861. Browning left

Florence in August that year, never to return. After a few months travelling in France, he settled in London.

A collected *Poetical Works* (3 vols, 1863) went some way to restoring Browning's currency as a great poet, and his reputation was further enhanced by the publication of a new collection of dramatic monologues, *Dramatis Personae*, in 1864. He was awarded an honorary fellowship by Balliol College in 1867. But it was *The Ring and the Book* (1868–69) that really cemented Browning's reputation with Victorian readers. Although never matching the sales of Tennyson, Browning was virtually lionized during this second residency in London, and a Browning Society was established in London (1881) for the promulgation and explication of his works. In September 1869 Browning seems to have proposed marriage to the beautiful and eligible Lady Ashburton; her rejection stung him deeply, and he reacted with hostility. After a short break, he launched into his most productive decade, the 1870s. His next work, *Balaustion's Adventure* (1871) is a sunny and positive poem set in ancient Greece; and *Prince Hohenstiel-Schwangau* (1871) examined the political situation of France under Louis Napoleon. *Fifine at the Fair* (1872) is a more complex work, exploring the dynamics of married life, and *Red Cotton Night Cap Country* (1873) is also set in France, this time based on a contemporary *cause celebre*. If reviewers found *Fifine* hard going, and were nonplussed by the brutality of the story in *Red Cotton Night Cap Country*, Browning's next poem was his longest work (after *Sordello* and *The Ring and the Book*), and baffled reviewers completely. *Aristophanes' Apology* (1875) is a sequel to *Balaustion's Adventure*, but where the former poem is light and accessible, the latter is a vastly detailed and complex web of classical allusion, quotation and argument. In November of the same year, Browning published another long poem, *The Inn Album*, and the following July saw a collection of shorter poems, *Pacchiarotto and How He Worked in Distemper* (1876). The title work was a satirical attack on Browning's critics. Translation from Attic tragedy had formed part of both *Balaustion* and *Aristophanes' Apology*, and in 1877 Browning published his famous 'literal' version of *The Agamemnon of Aeschylus*. Other works, mostly collections of shorter poems included *La Saisiaz: The Two Poets of Croisic* (1878), *Dramatic Idylls: First Series* (1879) and *Dramatic Idylls: Second Series* (1880). *Jocoseria* (1883), as its title suggests, was a collection combining jocular and serious works; and *Ferishtah's Fancies* (1884) consisted of twelve poems illustrating the sayings of the fictitious Persian Sage of the title, although the collection is often considered Browning's poorest. The remarkable and difficult *Parleyings with Certain People of Importance in their Day* appeared in 1887, and Browning (still hale at 76) supervised his sixteen-volume

Poetical Works in 1888–99. His final collection of short lyrics and dramatic monologues, *Asolando* was published on 12 December 1889. Browning died later in the same day, in Venice. His body was returned to England for burial in Westminster Abbey.

Browning's impact and influence on poetry was immense, particularly in terms of his development of the dramatic monologue, and his vigorous, muscular experiments with style. The standard biography is Irvine and Honan, *The Book, the Ring and the Poet: A Biography of Robert Browning* (1974).

BULWER-LYTTON, Edward (1803–73). Bulwer (as he was known before inheriting his family estate in 1843, when he changed his name to Bulwer-Lytton) is remembered today chiefly as a novelist whose novels are now little regarded (they are overlong, artificial and overwritten, although one of them, 1830's *Paul Clifford*, begins with the memorable sentence: 'It was a dark and stormy night'). Bulwer's career as a novelist produced an enormous amount of books, many of which were highly regarded in his own day; and he was friendly with Charles Dickens, with whom he founded the Guild of Literature and Art in 1850.

Bulwer also wrote plays (*Money*, which was first performed in 1840, is still highly thought of) and poetry. He had won the Chancellor's medal for poetry at Cambridge in 1825, and his first publication had been a *Byron-influenced verse-tale called *Ismael: An Oriental Tale* (1820). In among his prolific output of novels in the 1830s and 1840s he also wrote a series of satires on the literary scene (*The New Timon*, 1846), and hoped to crown his career with his epic production, *King Arthur* (1848–49). The public were less interested in his poetry, however, and after this he devoted himself to his novels.

BYRON, George Gordon, Sixth Baron Byron (1788–1824). Byron was one of the two great names (the other being *Scott) who helped cement the popularity of verse-tales and long poems with the public in the early years of the century. Indeed, it was Byron's success that encouraged Scott to concede the field to his rival and turn to writing novels. Although among his lesser studied works today (*Don Juan* excepted, of course), his longer tales contain a great deal of extremely interesting work.

Byron was born in London, the son of the strikingly nicknamed 'Mad Jack' Byron, and the grandson of the equally strikingly nicknamed Admiral 'Foulweather Jack' Byron. He inherited the baronetage at the age of ten on the death of his great uncle (known as the 'wicked Lord', the fifth baron Byron, had killed a man while duelling, and had subsequently adopted a reclusive life attended only by his mistress and a single servant). Byron's Scottish mother was similarly unconventional, a descendant of James V (of Scotland) and given to violent temper. When we take this heritage into account, and add the fact that Byron was born with a club-foot ('No action of Lord Byron's life –' wrote Mary Shelley later, 'scarce a line he has written – but was influenced by his personal defect') and that he was initiated into the sexual life at a very early age by an overzealous nurse, then we have the important ingredients in the famous 'Byronic' persona.

He was educated at Aberdeen Grammar School and Harrow, and from 1805 at Trinity, Cambridge (where, true to his family character, he debauched wildly and kept a pet bear). A collection of poems, the less-than-impressive *Hours of Idleness*, appeared in 1807. The individual poems were derivative and feeble, but Byron took extreme exception to the poor reviews the volume garnered, particularly a swingeing piece in the *Edinburgh Review*. By way of revenge, Byron published *English Bards and Scotch Reviewers* (1809), an energetic and still entertaining satire on pretty much the whole literary scene of the day. 1809 saw Byron taking up his seat in the House of Lords, and over the next three years he travelled widely over Europe. The poem which emerged from this peripatetic experience was the extraordinarily popular *Childe Harold's Pilgrimage*. The first two cantos of this work appeared in 1812, Canto 3 emerging in 1816 and the final Canto in 1818. It was the sudden success of this work that prompted Byron's famous 1812 statement: 'I awoke one morning and found myself famous'. His social life continued energetically: a hectic affair with Lady Caroline Lamb (who famously called the poet 'mad, bad, and dangerous to know'), an intimacy that was perhaps sexual with his half-sister Augusta, and a poorly-judged marriage with Annabella Milbanke (in 1815).

Meanwhile, capitalizing on his success, Byron starting producing verse-tales at a remarkable rate. *The Bride of Abydos* was written in a week and *The Corsair* in ten days: both were published, along with *The Giaour*, in 1813. The following year saw *Lara. Hebrew Melodies*, a collection of shorter pieces, came out in 1815, the same year that saw his separation from his wife. Rumours concerning his unconventional sexual life were growing, and in 1816 Byron, ostracized by polite society and profoundly bitter, left England for the Continent. He never returned. 1816 also saw the last two of his pot-boiler verse-tales, *The Seige of Corinth* and *The Prisoner of Chillon*.

He lived for a time in Geneva, sharing a villa with his friend Shelley. Here he wrote the first two acts of a play, *Manfred*, and conceived a daughter (Allegra) with Clare Clairmont. But by the time she was born

(January 1817) Byron had moved to Italy, where he was enjoying a particularly riotous life. In Rome he wrote the comic and rather charming *Beppo (1818), in the *ottava rima* stanza that he was later to utilize so famously in *Don Juan*. *Mazeppa (1819) is another poem that marks the transition from the slushy, romantic style of the earlier verse-tales to the dry, witty style of *Don Juan*. The first two cantos of *Don Juan appeared in 1819, to be greeted by the British press with outrage, and branded as pornographic and heretical. Byron continued working intermittently on this unfinished masterpiece for the rest of his short life, producing eventually sixteen full cantos and the fragment of a seventeenth. In addition to continuing this work, Byron wrote a variety of plays (in particular *Sardanapalus* and *Cain*). His satire on Southey's laureate sycophancy, *The Vision of Judgement, was written in 1821 and was published in 1822 by the daring journal *The Liberal*. Libel problems associated with this poem in particular hastened the death of the magazine.

His daughter Allegra died in 1822 aged five; Byron's habit of absentee fatherhood added guilt to his grief. The satirical *Age of Bronze* and *The Island appeared in 1823, but Byron was becoming increasingly dissatisfied with the life of a writer. Despite the fact that he was now corpulent and far from healthy (although still apparently attractive to women) he yearned for a soldier's life. To this end he sailed to Greece to help the Greeks in their war of independence. He landed at Missolonghi in January 1824, founded a brigade that he named after himself, and spent a great deal of money on the cause. But before he could see any military action he caught fever, and was bled to death by his rather over-enthusiastic doctors on 19 April 1824.

Byron's significance for the development of poetry is difficult to overstate. His influence has been vast, to an even greater degree on the continent than in his native land. Both his early, romantic verse-tales and his later witty *Don Juan* style had tremendous influence on subsequent poets; but arguably of even more importance is his personal myth, the attributes we today invoke with the adjective 'Byronic'.

: C :

Calvary, or the Death of Christ (1792), by Richard Cumberland. 6624 lines, blank verse.

Book 1, The Assembling of the Devils. On an earthly mountain top, Satan assembles his Devils from 'the farthest bounds/Of Pagan isle or continent'. This hellish crew debate the best way to confound Christ, and decide that the task should be given to Mammon. Satan sends him on his way. *Book 2, The Last Supper.* Mammon assumes the form and character of a Levite, seeks out Judas, and pretends to offer him a commission from the priests and elders to deliver up Christ to them. A variety of cunning arguments win Judas over ('If he be very CHRIST, death shall not dare/To aim his dart at immortality' and so on), and he promises to give his answer that evening. At the last Supper, Christ foretells Judas's treachery. *Book 3, The Treason of Judas.* After a soul-searching soliloquy, Judas goes to a meeting of the High Priests and betrays Christ. The priests head off to the Mount of Olives, and no sooner are they gone than Satan and his cohorts occupy their seats. Satan congratulates Mammon. A demon named Chemos enters, wounded by Gabriel as he spied on Christ at the Mount of Olives ('I felt his spear's sharp point with forceful thrust/Deep plung'd into my side' he tells the assembly) and reports on Jesus's sorrows. Satan swears vengeance on Gabriel for injuring Chemos, and leads his Devils out. *Book 4, The Agony in the Garden.* Christ prays in the Garden while the disciples sleep. Satan arrives and 'takes post near the spot' where Christ is praying. Christ discovers and reproves Satan, and the demon is unable to rise from the ground when the guards seize and carry Jesus away. Discovered by Mammon, Satan announces he has had a presentiment of his own defeat, and the terrified minor devil flies away. *Book 5, The Condemnation of Christ.* Christ is brought before the priests of the Council, and then before Pilate. Peter denies him three times. Pilate washes his hands, and Christ is taken away. *Book 6, The Crucifixion.* Mammon, in the disguise of the Levite, meets Judas and convinces him to kill himself. Judas does so, and is reproved by the narrator ('A losing game, friend Judas, thou hast play'd'). Mammon then departs and greets a convocation of devils with the news that Satan is soon to be banished from the world; 'sudden panic seiz'd/The Stygian host'. Meanwhile Christ is crucified, and 'the sun is darkened, the earth quakes, the rocks are rent, and the bodies of the saints and prophets are raised from the dead and appear upon the earth.' *Book 7, The Descent into Hell.* Christ's spirit descends to Hell, 'the dark confines of Death's engulph'd domain … that immeasurable blank'.

> A pillary cloud arose
> Of sulph'rous smoke, that from hell's crater steam'd;
> Whence here and there by intermittent gleams
> Blue flashing fires burst forth, that sparkling blaz'd
> Up to the iron roof.

Satan, expelled from Earth, falls at the feet of Death and implores mercy; but none is forthcoming and the fiend is bound in the bottomless pit. Death humbles himself before Christ, aware that his power has been superseded. Christ gives the key to Gabriel to release the Saints. *Book 8, The Resurrection from the Dead.* Christ addresses the souls of those Saints just released, and reveals what awaits them in the New Jerusalem. He then reascends to Earth, 'high-soaring to this orb terraqueous bound'. The angel Gabriel, left behind, explains the purposes of Christ's resurrection to the assembled Saints, and the poem ends with the spirit of God descending on the hearts of the righteous.

CAMPBELL, Thomas (1777–1844). Campbell was born in Glasgow, the youngest of the eleven children of a wealthy Virginia merchant. The American wars seriously damaged the family fortune, and by the time he came of age Campbell was forced to consider a career. Too poor to approach the bar, he contemplated medicine but found himself revolted by surgery. After working as a clerk in a Glasgow mercantile house he went to the outer Hebrides to work as a tutor. His trunk having been mislaid, he was reduced to scribbling verses on the whitewashed walls of his room for want of paper. His tutoring continued on his return to the mainland half a year later. *The Pleasures of Hope* was published in Edinburgh in 1799, and brought him a degree of fame. He toured Europe, a dangerous undertaking at that time, and had to flee with the (re)declaration of war in 1801. In 1803 Campbell married his cousin, Matilda Sinclair; of this union only one child survived to adult life, and this son was confined in an asylum for the insane in later life. The poet settled in Sydenham, London, and in 1805 a Crown pension of £200 a year helped ease his financial difficulties. He was writing a great deal of (Whig) journalism, something he continued all his life. *Gertrude of Wyoming* appeared in 1809, and had gone through nine editions by 1825. Campbell's reputation began to grow, with his lectures on poetry to the Royal Institution being accounted a great success (1812), and his election as Lord Rector of Glasgow University in 1826. He was also connected with the founding of the University of London (the present

University College). He continued publishing, with *Theodric and Miscellaneous Poems* appearing in 1824, and *Poland* in 1831. In his later years he spent a great deal of time and money helping Polish refugees; and at his funeral his coffin was carried by a guard of Polish noblemen. But by the time of his last collection, *The Pilgrim of Glencoe* (1842) he was a lonely and embittered old man, his wife dead, his only son in an asylum; and at this time he viewed the world with what his biographer describes as 'exaggerated gloom and despondency'. In his final year he sold his house and furniture and moved to lodgings in Boulogne with his niece, where he died on 15 June 1844. Campbell's reputation was high at his death, and he was buried in poet's corner in Westminster Abbey amid much public grief. He is rather less regarded, or indeed remembered, today.

Casa Guidi Windows: A Poem, in Two Parts (1851), by Elizabeth Barrett Browning. 2002 lines, continuous pentameters rhyming ababab. Barrett Browning claimed that 'no continuous narrative or exposition of political philosophy' was attempted in this meditation upon the contemporary Italian political scene.

Part I. Written in 1848, this part of the poem is filled with revolutionary optimism. The poet is sitting at the window of her house when she overhears a child pass underneath singing '*O bella liberta, O bella!*'; this propels her into a reverie, where she contemplates the glories of Italy's past (Michelangelo, Savonarola, Cimabue, Giotto, Fra Angelico, Dante, and the spontaneous love of liberty of the Florentine populace); this, she suggests, should prompt contemporary Italy to resist Austrian occupation and declare a free Italy: 'Will, therefore, to be strong, thou Italy!/Will to be noble! Austrian Metternich/Can fix no yoke unless the neck agree'. *Part 2.* Written in 1851, after the revolutionary hopes of 1848 had come to nothing, this is a more sombre reflection on the themes of Italian liberty. Once again at the window of her Florentine house, Casa Guidi, the poet recalls watching the invading Austrian troops occupy the city: 'the armament of Austria flow/Into the drowning heart of Tuscany'. She calls on the other European nations, and England in particular, to come to Italy's aid. The poet ends with a peroration to her two-year-old son, 'Penini'.

Childe Harold's Pilgrimage: a Romaunt (1812, 1816, 1818), by Lord Byron. 4700 lines, Spenserian stanzas with interspersed songs. The extraordinary success of the first two cantos of this travel-poem in 1812 was so sudden that it occasioned Bryron's memorable statement: 'I woke one morning to find myself famous'. The poem was written at various times over six years.

Canto the First (1812). Harold is a young Englishman who has spent his life 'in riot most uncouth ... sore given to revel and ungodly glee'. One day, feeling the 'fulness of Satiety' ('for he through Sin's long labyrinth had run'), he bids farewell to his native shore and travels to Portugal. As a classic 'Byronic' hero, Harold can admire the beauties of the land through which he travels, but he is forever alienated from it ('To horse! to horse! he quits, for ever quits/A scene of peace, though soothing to his soul'). He goes from Portugal (where he mediates upon the treachery of the Convention of Cintra), into Spain ('Oh, lovely Spain! renowned, romantic Land!'), a country then resisting Napoleon. He observes a bullfight, which is vividly described. *Canto the Second* (1812). Harold travels by boat to Greece, where he sails among the Ionian islands. Disembarking, he travels through Greece and into Albania. There are various passages lamenting the passing of Greece's glory, and its modern degradation under the rule of the Turks. *Canto the Third* (1816). This canto reads much less like a guide book to Europe, although it does relate Harold's travels through northern Europe (Belgium, the Rhine, the Alps) and his thoughts on Waterloo, Rousseau and others. Instead we get what Byron himself called 'a fine indistinct piece of poetical desolation'. Harold muses on the contrasts between Society and Solitude, and as 'the wandering outlaw of his own dark mind' is drawn particularly to the latter. Standing atop an alp he observes 'is it not better, then, to be alone?':

> I live not in myself, but I become
>> Portion of that around me; and to me
>> High mountains are a feeling, but the hum
>> Of human cities torture.

Canto the Fourth (1818). Readers had always identified Childe Harold directly with Byron himself, and in the fourth canto the author abandoned the fiction of the 'pilgrim' and instead spoke in his own voice. The mood is less dark than the previous canto, and instead we have meditations on various Italian cities and the famous poets associated with them: Venice and Tasso, Arqua and Petrarch, Florence and Boccaccio. The poem concludes at Rome, overlooking the Mediterranean ('Dark-heaving – boundless, endless, and sublime—/The image of Eternity').

Christmas-Eve and Easter-Day (1850), by Robert Browning. 2399 lines, various rhymed metres.

Christmas-Eve is a fantasy narrative, much of it written in a gro-tesque-comic tone, although the poem has a serious moral. The narrator takes refuge in the porch of a little dissenting chapel on a particularly inclement Christmas Eve evening, and mockingly observes the various ugly-mugs and idiots going inside to hear the 'preaching man's immense stupidity'. Afterwards the narrator encounters a vision of Christ (as we assume, although he is never named):

> All at once I looked up with terror.
> He was there.
> He himself with his human air.
> On the narrow pathway, just before
> I saw the back of him, no more –

Christ carries him to Rome where he sees the swarms of worshippers at St Peters, and thence to the lecture hall of a rationalist German profes-sor, who is discoursing on the 'myth of Christ'. Returning him to London Christ leaves, and the narrator enters the dissenting Chapel to hear the sermon. He is still aware of its deficiencies, but is open to the spiritual 'cup of water' it nonetheless implies. *Easter-Day* is a dialogue that has to do with the questions of religious doubt and faith. One speaker declares 'How very hard it is to be/A Christian'; the other announces that without direct proof he will not believe anything. The first speaker describes a vision he had in which he imagined it was the day of the Last Judgement, and the consequent moral to be drawn from the experience, that all the treasures of the world are nothing without Love.

CLOUGH, Arthur Hugh (1819–61). The son of a well-to-do Liverpool cotton merchant, Clough was sent to Thomas Arnold's Rugby, where he became lifetime friends with the headmaster's son, Matthew *Arnold. He won a scholarship to Balliol, and high things were expected: but he only managed a second-class degree (he wrote to his old headmaster to tell him 'I have failed'). Friends in the university thought better of him, and he was offered a fellowship at Oriel, which he took only to resign when he decided that he could not sign his agreement to the XXXIX Articles as university dons were legally required to do (the Articles are the tenets of faith of the Church of England, and in a country without official separation of church and state they embodied the establish-ment). In 1848, the year of this resignation, he travelled widely around Europe, witnessing at first hand the French siege of Rome. A intelligent, quick-witted and likeable man, Clough spent a great deal of his time in anxious pondering of questions of religious faith and doubt, and also attempting to reconcile the conflict of urges that resulted from his highly sexed nature and his equally deeply felt belief in a more Victorian moderation. He married Blanche Smith (Florence Nightingale's cousin) in 1854. His working career was varied: he became principal of University Hall, London, and afterwards an Examiner in the Education Office. His correspondence with Arnold contains some of the most trenchant analyses of poetry in general and nineteenth-century writing in particular. Arnold also encouraged him in his poetic career. Clough published the witty and yet carefully considered *Bothie of Tober-na-Vuolich in 1848, and soon after put out a collection of his earlier shorter pieces (Ambarvalia, 1849). Clough's attempts to resurrect the hexameter as a plausible mode of modern English poetry attracted a great deal of critical attention; but in many ways more significant than his form was his modernity of tone. This is even more evident in the other long poem he published during his life, the epistolary *Amours de Voyage (1858), in which the rootless, sardonic, troubled hero Claude and the oblique, psychologically plausible narrative seem to belong in the twentieth century rather than the Carlylean nineteenth. Most readers of Clough are struck by this up-to-datedness, and the sophistication and polish of his surface intelligence can disguise his more hollow substance.

Advised to travel for his health, Clough left England in 1861. He went to Greece, Turkey and Italy; where, in Florence, he had a stroke and died.

Corsair, The (1814), by Lord Byron. 1864 lines, heroic couplets with interspersed songs.

Canto the First. The Corsair is Conrad, a pirate chief ('his name on every shore/Is famed and feared') who lives on a Greek island with his band of desperadoes and his lover, the beautiful Medora. We are given Conrad's character – 'he knew himself a villain', yet 'quickening round his heart/One softer feeling would not yet depart ... Love!'. A ship arrives, bearing the news that the Turkish Pasha is about to attack the island. Rather than wait for the assault, Conrad decides to infiltrate the Pasha's camp. He bids a lengthy farewell to Medora. *Canto the Second*. Conrad arrives at the bay of Coron, where the Pasha Seyd has assembled his attack fleet. He presents himself to the Pasha, pretending to be a 'dervise' (or dervish) escaped from the Pirate's island. The Pasha accepts him, and questions him through the night, until realization dawns upon him:

> 'Ha! it cannot sure be day?
> What star – what sun is bursting on the bay?
> It shines a lake of fire! – away – away!

Ho! treachery! my guards! my scimitar!
The galleys feed the flames – and I afar!
Accursed Dervise! – these thy tidings – thou
Some villain spy – seize – cleave him – slay him now!'

Conrad fights off the Pasha's guards, rescues a beautiful young Haram slave (Gulnare) from out of the thick of the fighting, is wounded and finally captured. Loaded with heaviest chains, Conrad is locked in a high tower to await impalement at dawn. Gulnare meanwhile, who has fallen in love with the stranger, creeps to this cell at midnight and promises to try and dissuade the Pasha from his grisly revenge. *Canto the Third*. Back on the Pirate island, Medora hears the news that Conrad has been killed; she swoons. In fact the Pasha has not yet executed Conrad, if only because (as he puts it) 'thirsting for revenge, I ponder still/On pangs that longest rack and latest kill'. On the fourth night Gulnare returns to Conrad's cell, offers him a knife and tells him to go and cut the sleeping Pasha's throat. Conrad, however, has too strong a sense of honour to do any such thing ('the scimitar/Such is my weapon – not the secret knife'). On hearing this news, Gulnare goes off and slits the Pasha's throat herself. The two escape together, and return to the Pirate island; but there Conrad discovers that Medora has died of grief at the reports of his death. The following morning Conrad has vanished, 'and Conrad comes not, came not since that day:/Nor trace, nor tidings of his doom declare/Where lives his grief, or perish'd his despair.' In fact, Conrad returns under a different name in Byron's next verse romance, *Lara*.

COTTLE, Joseph (1770–1853). Cottle became a bookseller in Bristol, and despite his lack of a classical education claimed an unusual interest in literature and literary developments of his day (he claimed to have read 'more than a thousand volumes of the best English literature' by the time he was twenty-one). He made enough money from selling and publishing books to be extremely generous with the sums he paid authors – particularly Coleridge and Southey. Inded, it was his connection with the Lake poets that was deep rooted. He published Wordsworth and Coleridge's *Lyrical Ballads* in 1798, and helped Coleridge out with sums of money when at his lowest opium-induced ebbs. His own literary production bore the stamp of these influences. A collection entitled *Malvern Hills* appeared in 1798, filled with nature poetry of a distinctly Wordsworthian kind. His first epic, *Alfred, an Heroic Poem in Twenty-Four Books* (1801) was prefaced with an essay that stressed the importance of a (quasi-Wordsworthian) plain style in epic poetry. The work was well received in a small way, and he published a similarly national epic, *The Fall of Cambria* in 1809. His third major production, a 24–book *Messiah* (1815) was an old-testament epic, the latter books of which were concerned with the doings of David, but which nonetheless fitted into a broader contemporary vogue for religious epic writing (see, for instance, Cumberland's).

Cottle's *Early Recollections, Chiefly Relating to Samuel Taylor Coleridge* (1837) was deemed rather ungentlemanly in its day, with its minute descriptions of Coleridge's opium abasements, but it remains a lively and entertaining account of the Lake School by somebody who was close to it.

Course of Time, The: A Poem in Ten Books (1825), by Robert *Pollok. 7890 lines, blank verse. Derivatively Miltonic, this pious epic relates the entire history of the universe, from the Scots Presbyterian perspective that shaped Pollok's life. It was, however, extraordinarily popular. It went through 25 editions by 1867, and had sold a remarkable 78,000 copies by 1868.

Book One. The poem begins in a timeless future Paradise, after the Day of Judgement. Two angels see the approach of a stranger, flying 'on wing of holy ardour strong' from a far distant world. The stranger relates that his journey had taken him past a place containing myriad souls in suffering. Seeking explanation for these sights, he is referred to

> an ancient bard of Earth,
> Who, by the stream of life, sitting in bliss,
> Has oft beheld the eternal years complete
> The mighty circle round the throne of God.

The angels and the stranger repair to the bard's bower, where he reveals that 'the place thou sawst was hell'. *Book Two.* The bard begins 'in brief the history of man', beginning with the story of Genesis, and the Fall. The stranger is surprised (the people on his world 'never fell' but 'in virtue stood/Upright'), and the bard identifies the root of the problem as 'self-adoring pride'. *Book Three.* The bard describes how 'the Son of God descended' as Saviour, but laments 'how few returned from folly's giddy chase'. *Book Four.* The varieties of human life are touched on, and the many ways in which people fell into sin enumerated, with secular literature in particular chastised ('A Novel was a book/Three-volumed, and once read, and oft crammed full/Of poisonous error, blackening every page'). The bard explains how inequalities in God's distribution of worldly wealth, and individual intellect, demonstrated the indifference with which He regarded these things. *Book Five.* The holy and righteous inhabitants of earth are described, and the bard praises his native Scotland. Babylon falls, and a utopia is established for the occupation of the devout: 'Messiah reigned,/And Earth kept Jubilee a thousand years'. *Book Six*. The millenium ends, and the bard resumes his 'song of woe'. Wickedness rises again, men haunt dens of iniquity (such as the theatre – 'The theatre was, from the very first,/The favourite haunt of Sin'). The end is nigh. *Book Seven*. The world ends, and the dead rise from their graves. *Book Eight*. A huge congregation gathers to see God give judgement, and the variety of the accused is elaborated. *Book Nine*. The bard hymns the Virtues, and praises a poet (unnamed, but clearly Milton), 'the bard, by God's own hand anointed'. Pollok is keen that we do not confuse this figure with another poet, one who 'sold/The incommunicable heavenly gift,/To Folly' and made 'himself the hero of his tale' (presumably *Wordsworth). *Book Ten*. God appears, ushers his saints into Paradise and condemns the wicked to eternal Hell.

The poem was praised in its own day for its religious seriousness. The *Quarterly Review* described it as 'never feeble', adding that although 'some sections are prolix' there are passages 'of the highest and sublimest poetry'. It is, nonetheless, hard going.

CUMBERLAND, Richard (1732–1811). Remembered today principally as a second-rate dramatist (allegedly the original for the character of Sir Fretful Plagiary in Sheridan's *The Critic*), Cumberland in later life wrote pious poetry.

His early life seems peculiarly connected with Trinity College, Cambridge. He was born there, in the Master's lodge, 19 February 1732 (his father was a fellow-commoner at the College). He lived there, and eventually was educated there, graduating in 1751. He then worked as Ulster secretary for Lord Halifax, and afterwards as clerk of reports in the Board of Trade. It was in this latter, lowly-paid post that Cumberland turned to writing plays; and he was later to boast in his memoirs that he eventually wrote more plays than any other English dramatist. He enjoyed a certain success with *The Brothers* (1769) and *The West Indian* (1771), and with other such sentimental comedies. He moved on to tragedy (with *The Battle of Hastings*, 1778) to less success. He also wrote two novels (*Arundel*, 1789, and *Henry*, 1795, about Henry Fielding), and translated Aristophanes. His interest in writing poetry came late in his life, and his religious epic *Calvary* (1792) sold well, going through seven editions between 1800 and 1811. Another religious epic, based on the book of Exodus, *The Exodiad* (1808), was less successful. He died at Tunbridge Wells, 7 May 1811.

Curse of Kehama, The (1810), by Robert Southey. 5131 lines, varied metres, rhymed. A conscientious attempt to write epic poetry based on Hindu mythological apparatus, part of Southey's scheme (conceived while still a schoolboy) to write one epic for every major world religion.

1. *The Funeral*. Arvalan, son of the cruel Raja of the World, Kehama, is dead; he is burned on a funeral pyre with his wives. 2. *The Curse*. After the funeral Kehama summons the spirit of his son, who demands vengeance on his killer. Kehama summons the man responsible, the peasant Ladurlad, from the crowd. He comes forward with his daughter Kailyal (guards try to seize her and she tries to escape, falls into the river and apparently drowns). Ladurlad begs for mercy, explaining that the Prince had attempted to rape his daughter Kailyal, and that he had killed him to defend her. But Kehama issues his curse: Ladurlad will never die or be injured, never be able to eat or drink to satisfy his hunger or thirst:

> Thou shalt live with thy pain
> While Kehama shall reign
> With a fire in thy heart,
> And a fire in thy brain;
> And Sleep shall obey me
> And visit thee never
> And the Curse shall be on thee
> For ever and ever.

3. *The Recovery*. Ladurlad 'staggers from the dreadful spot', and leaps into the river; in accordance with Kehama's curse, the water shrinks before him, and he is able to save his daughter's life. 4. *The Departure*. 5. *The Separation*. Ladurlad wanders aimlessly through the countryside in the company of his daughter Kailyal. She sleeps, but the curse prevents Ladurlad from doing so; he decides that he alone should bear the burden of his curse and creeps off by himself. The spectre of Arvalan attempts to seize the now solitary Kailyal, but she escapes into a nearby temple. 6. *Casyapa*. 7. *The Swerga*. The Immortals, impressed with Kailyal's beauty and innocence, take pity on her. Casyapa, the Father of the Immortals, sends down his son Ereenia with a Ship of Heaven into which Kailyal is placed and whisked across the sky. They arrive at the Swerga, Ereenia's 'bower of bliss'. Anxious about her father, Kailyal goes to the Paradisical Garden of Indra, God of the Elements, to plead on his behalf. But this God confesses that even he is not powerful enough to 'pierce the sphere of power' with which Kehama is circled. Kailyal begs to be, and is, returned to the Earth. 8. *The Sacrifice*. Kehama sacrifices 99 pure-bred horses on 99 consecutive days; one more will grant him the power to unseat the God of the Elements and take his place. At this final sacrifice, Ladurlad leaps forward and

profanes the ceremony, rendering it useless. Kehema's rage can do nothing to hurt him, and he retires. *9. The Home Scene. 10. Mount Meru.* Ladurlad and Kailyal are reunited by the gods on Mt Meru, the source of the holy Ganges, whose magical waters allow Ladurlad respite from his sufferings. *11. The Enchantress.* The shade of Arvalan recruits the help of an evil enchantress, Lorrinite. *12. The Sacrifice Completed. 13. The Retreat.* Kehema repeats the sacrifice of horses, this time with success: he rises 'through the conquered sky' to seize Indra's kingdom 'for his proud abode'. *13. The Retreat.* Ladurlad and Kailyal flee through the wilderness. *14. Jaga-naut.* Kailyal falls into the hands of a 'band of Yoguees', seeking a bride for their seven-headed Idol, Jaga-naut. The enchantress Lorrinte manages to spirit the ghost of Arvalan into the fleshly form of this evil God. Indra's son, Ereenia, attempts to rescue her, but is carried away by a band of demons. Rather than face defilement Kailyal sets fire to her marriage bed. She is rescued at the last minute by Ladurlad. *15. The City of Baly. 16. The Ancient Sepulchres.* Ereenia has been carried away to the ruined city built by the Giant Baly in ancient times, long since swallowed by the sea. Ladurlad travels there, passing easily through the water ('the broad ocean ... closed and arch'd him o'er') and locates the eerie submerged streets of this ruined city. He battles a sea-monster, and frees Ereenia. *17. Baly. 18. The Descent of Kehama.* Ladurlad and Ereenia return to the shore where Kailyal is waiting. The evil Kehama himself comes down and proposes marriage to Kailyal ('To be the Queen of Heaven and Earth,/And whatever Worlds beside/Infinity may hide ... '). She rejects him and he angrily withdraws. *19. Mount Calasay.* Furious at her refusal of him, Kehama strikes Kailyal with leprosy. Ereenia flies off through heaven to seek justice at the Court of the mighty God Seeva (the Destroyer). The brilliant light of the presence of the God is too much for him to bear, and he falls from Heaven, hearing as he does so a voice telling him to seek justice with Yamen, Lord of the Underworld. *20. The Embarkation. 21. The World's End.* The three of them cross the outermost World Ocean in a magic ship and reach the End of the World. Passing beyond Kehama's dominions, the Curse is lifted from Ladurlad. *22. The Gate of Padalon.* At the World's End they plunge into the gulf, and so enter the world of Night, the land of Padalon on which this world is built. *23. Padalon. 24. The Amreeta.* They travel on a magic Car through a vividly described Underworld. Coming before Yamen, God of the Underworld, they make their case. But before Yamen can respond, Kehama makes a sudden appearance to seize the throne of the Underworld for himself. Kehama easily defeats Yamen: 'a smile/ Gleam'd on his dreadful lips'. He commands the liquor of immortality to be brought to him, and so it is, but as he drinks it Seeva transforms it into a poison that combines 'torture at once and immortality'. Kehama's body 'glows/ Like molten ore ... doomed thus to live and burn eternally'. Ladurlad, Kailyal and Ereenia are received into Heaven.

: D :

Disciples, The (1873), by Harriet E. Hamilton King. 7568 lines, blank verse. The title refers not to the disciples of Christ (although the poem does have an overtly Christian theme), but to the disciples of Italian revolutionary Giuseppe Mazzini, whom the author idolized as a hero of freedom. A framework to the poem reveals that Mazzini 'he, the Seer, the Master, and the Saint' had named Hamilton King 'his poet, crowned me laureate/Of his Republic – therefore are these words'. What follow are dramatic monologues put into the mouths of four Mazzinists: Jacopo Ruffini (who speaks, dying of poison and imprisoned by the enemy in a Genoese tower, 1833), Ugo Bassi (the great bulk of the poem is taken up with this monologue, narrated by a follower of the anti-establishment and saint-like priest Bassi, up to his death in the cause of Italian freedom in 1849), Agesilao Milano (who speaks a stanzaic hymn of praise to Mazzini ('Master, singer of the sunrise') after the fall of Naples, 1856) and Baron Giovanni Nicotera (who awaits his execution in Selerno, 1858, with equanimity). A long section from the 'Ugo Bassi' monologue, consisting of one of Bassi's sermons, was published separately as *The Sermon in the Hospital*.

DOBELL, Sydney (1824–74). On the strength of *Balder*, Dobell was tarred with the *Spasmodic brush; although (in that work and elsewhere) much of his poetry is quietly conventional and expressive of standard pieties. Born the son of a wine merchant in Cranbrook, Kent, he grew up in middle-class prosperity in Cheltenham. He never went to school, or university, but studied zealously at home. Aged twenty he went to work in his father's business. In 1844 he married Emily Fordham, an engagement contracted five years previously when he was fifteen; it is said by his biographer that in the subsequent thirty years of married life, they were not separated more than thirty hours. *The Roman*, a verse-drama, was published in 1850, inspired by the question of Italian liberty; it met with small but significant success, and Dobell began publishing regularly. Four years later he published his most famous work, *Balder*. This ambitious work, an attempt to explore the disintegration and (in a never-completed second section) the re-integration through love, of an extreme and morbid consciousness, became something of a laughing stock, and was taken as a representative text of the school of strained, involuted and peculiar verse known as *Spasmodic. Critical hostility and, indeed, hilarity was such that Dobell's slim reputation never really recovered, despite more conventional (in theme and treatment) patriotic publications such as the Crimean-war *Sonnets on the War* (1855), co-written with Alexander *Smith, and *England in Time of War* (1856).

Dobell was advised to rest from 'strenuous mental work' and travel abroad, a plan that backfired somewhat in 1865. Visiting the ruins of Pozzuoli, near Naples, Dobell stepped on a place where only a thin crust of earth covered an opening into one of the ancient tombs. He fell ten feet, banged his head and (in the words of his biographer Dr John Nichol LL.D) 'was never quite the same after'. He consolidated his position as a respected citizen of Cheltenham, and wrote pamphlets on the dangers of one-man one-vote democracy, but he wrote no more poetry. He died in 1874, aged 51.

Don Juan (1819–1824), by Lord Byron. 16,064 lines, ottava rima. Byron's unfinished comic-epic was his masterpiece, the pinnacle of his poetic achievement, and one of the few undisputed works of comic genius in English literature. Byron had discovered the possibilities of the English ottava rima stanza on reading Frere's *Whistlecraft*, and had already produced the witty *Beppo* in that form. He launched into the project of modernizing the story of the famous philanderer Don Juan with (as he told John Murray, his publisher) 'no plan ... the Soul of such writing is its licence'. The first sixteen cantos of the poem were published in irregular instalments between 1819 and 1824. Only a brief part of the last extant canto (XVII) had been written when the poet died in Missolonghi on 19 April 1824.

Byron's digressive and satirical style is unique. It is possible, as I do here, to summarize the peripatetic narrative line of the poem, but to do so gives no flavour of the lengthy, witty, sidetracking digressions that give the poem its peculiar impact, and which (in many cantos) are far more important than the actual plot. The poem opens with a dedication to Robert Southey, who epitomized for Byron the hypocrisy and pettiness of the age (he is repeatedly referred to in *Don Juan* in much the same way that Pope invokes Cibber in the *Dunciad*).

The first two cantos were published in 1819. *Canto the First.* The poet begins in mock-epic fashion ('I want a hero –'), and discusses the inadequacy of contemporary heroism before settling on 'our ancient friend Don Juan'. ('Juan' is pronounced throughout the poem as two syllables, the emphasis on the first: '*Dju*–enn'.) Juan comes from Seville: his aristocratic father 'traced his source/Through the most Gothic gentlemen of Spain', while his mother 'was a learned lady famed/For every branch of science named'. Indeed, the narrator ascribes the marital disharmony between these two to Donna Inez's learning (leading to the famous couplet: 'But Oh! ye lords of ladies intellectual,/ Inform us truly, have they not hen-pecked you all?'). Juan (at thirteen) starts an affair with Julia, the young and beautiful wife of the fifty-year-old Alfonso. Eventually growing suspicious, Alfonso bursts into Julia's bedroom one night hoping to find her young lover; and he and his servants search everywhere ('Closet and clothes press, chest and window seat ... Under the bed they searched, and there they found/No matter what – it was not what they sought'). Julia protests her innocence tearfully, but Juan is in fact hiding between her legs under the sheets. Eventually he is discovered and forced to flee. To prevent further scandal, Juan's mother has him shipped off by sea to travel round Europe. The canto ends with lengthy, and witty, observations upon the current state of English letters. *Canto the Second.* Juan's ship is caught in a fierce storm and sinks; the survivors drift in an open boat, and resort to eating Juan's pet dog. A sailor called Pedrillo is bled to death and eaten, although Juan and some others do not partake – luckily, as it turns out, when the cannibal-sailors run 'raging mad' and die with 'hyena-laughter'. Sighting land, the survivors overset the boat in their rush to reach it, and only Juan (a strong swimmer) survives. He is cast ashore on a Mediterranean island, which happens to be home to a vicious pirate named Lambro. Juan's senseless body is discovered on the beach by Lambro's beautiful daughter, Haidee; falling in love with the handsome youth, Haidee and her maid carry Juan to a cave where they can nurse him back to health without Lambro finding out. As he slowly recuperates, Juan finds himself falling in love with Haidee. They consummate their love.

Cantos III–V were published in 1821.

Canto the Third. A report avouches the death of Haidee's father, the pirate Lambro. Haidee accordingly keeps house on her own account, openly entertaining Juan, although in fact Lambro is not dead. He arrives home in the middle of a particularly spectacular banquet, with Juan and Haidee seated in state; but then the narrator veers off into a lengthy digression on poetic styles, which includes the lyric 'The Isles of Greece', and in which the classics are praised ('Milton's the prince of poets') and the Romantics wittily put-down ('We learn from Horace, "Homer sometimes sleeps";/We feel without him, Wordsworth sometimes wakes'). *Canto the Fourth.* Haidee recognizes her father and 'shrieking she arose, and shrieking fell/With joy and sorrow, hope and fear'. Lambro insists Juan gives himself up. Juan resists, and is wounded, captured and bound. Haidee falls into a swoon and eventually dies. Juan is taken on board one of Lambro's ships to be sold as a slave on the Turkish market. *Canto the Fifth*. At the slave market ('a crowd of shivering slaves of every nation,/And age, and sex') Juan falls in with an insouciant Englishman, called Johnson. Both are sold to the same bidder. They are taken to a beautiful palace, dressed in fine clothes, although a black slave insists that Juan dress in woman's garb: 'being femininely all arrayed ... he looked in almost all respects a maid'. Juan is lead into a huge hall, and presented to the beautiful young sultana Gulbeyaz. It turns out that 'Juan, the latest of her whims, had caught/Her eye in passing on his way to sale'. The female disguise is necessary to avoid the wrath of the Sultan, whose fourth spouse Gulbeyaz is. To begin with Juan, still thinking of Haidee, resists Gulbeyaz's blandishments, incurring her wrath ('Her first thought was to cut off Juan's head;/Her second, to cut only his – acquaintance'). But Juan soon gives way.

Cantos VI–XIV were published in 1823, under the imprint of a more radical publisher (John Hunt) who was more willing to run the gamut of libel and blasphemy laws. Byron wrote a preface to this part of the poem, in which he gloated over the suicide of Castlereigh and defended his work against charges of immorality.

Canto the Sixth. Juan becomes friendly with his fellow women of the harem, and in particular a certain Dudu. Gulbeyaz spends the night with the Sultan her husband (whom she 'abhors'); but in the morning he gets up, drinks 'six cups of coffee at the least' and goes off to consult about the war raging between Turkey and Catherine the Great's Russia. Gulbeyaz hurries back to Juan in the harem, but flies into a rage upon discovering that he has been intimate with Dudu in the night. She orders the pair to be killed. *Canto the Seventh*. The narrator shifts the scene to the Turkish city of Ismail, on the coast and under attack by the Russians (this assault actually took place in 1790). He struggles to fit the names of the Russian commanders into ottava rima:

> there was Strongenoff, and Strokonoff,
> Meknop, Serge Lwow, Arseniew of modern Greece,
>   And Tschitsshakoff, and Roguenoff, and Chokenoff,
> And others of twelve-consonants a-piece;
>   And more might be found out, if I could poke enough
> Into gazettes.

Into the Russian camp come Juan, the Englishman (Johnson), two harem girls and an eunuch, escaped from the Sultan's palace. Juan and Johnson enlist with the Russians, and prepare for the assault on Ismail. *Canto the Eighth*. Juan distinguishes himself by his heroism in battle ('out of inexperience more than anything – his virgin valour never dreamt of flying'); in the course of the fighting he saves an orphaned ten-year-old Turkish girl (Leila) from certain death. After the city is taken, Juan is given the honour of conveying the news of Victory to

Catherine the Great herself in St Petersburg; and 'the Moslem orphan went with her protector' since Juan 'made a vow to shield her, which he kept'. *Canto the Ninth*. The canto begins with an ironic panegyric to Wellington ('the best of cut-throats'); Juan travels to St Petersburg, where the Empress Catherine takes a fancy to him: 'the Sovereign was smitten,/Juan much flattered by her love, or lust'. *Canto the Tenth*. Juan lives it up at the Russian court: 'he lived ... in a hurry/Of waste, and haste, and glare, and gloss, and glitter'. He writes to tell his family of his good fortune. Then he grows sick – perhaps poisoned by a jealous former favourite of the Empress. Physicians agree that the Russian climate is too cold for him ('Meridian born' as he is) to bloom in; Catherine consequently sends him on a diplomatic mission to England. Juan and Leila travel through Poland, Germany, Holland and on to Dover, through Canterbury and finally they arrive at London: 'a mighty mass of brick, and smoke'. *Canto the Eleventh*. Some cockney thugs attempt to rob Juan's carriage, but he coolly shoots one (who falls over yelling 'Oh Jack! I'm floored by this 'ere bloody Frenchman!'). They arrive at their hotel. Juan is presented in Society, where his good looks excite interest from various women ('He was a bachelor – of arts/And parts, and hearts'). *Canto the Twelfth*. 'But first,' says the narrator, 'of little Leila we'll dispose.' Juan, discovering he is 'no tutor', leaves her 'with a lady, whose last grown-up daughter' had left home. Unencumbered he enters the 'game' of Society ('for good society is but a game,/ "The royal game of Goose" as I may say'). At first he does not find English women pretty, but gradually he decides they are 'fairer far' than Eastern beauties. *Canto the Thirteenth*. The Lady Adeline Amundeville, an arrogant but beautiful noblewoman and the wife to Lord Henry, becomes infatuated with Juan. At the end of the winter ('The English winter – ending in July,/To recommence in August – now was done') Lord Henry, Lady Adeline and their guests decamp to their country estate, Norman Abbey. Juan makes up one of the party. The various, mostly ennobled, guests are described. *Canto the Fourteenth*. Juan hunts and dances, to general admiration, and the particular attentions of the 'fine and somewhat full-blown blonde' Duchess of Fitz-Fulke, whose flirting provokes Lady Adeline's jealousy. Adeline resolves to put a stop to it. *Canto the Fifteenth*. Adeline decides it is time for Juan to get married, and suggests various eligible but unappealing bluestocking women. Juan, though, is drawn to Aurora Raby, 'rich, noble, but an orphan ... a Catholic too, sincere, austere', despite Adeline's objections ('such a baby ... prim, silent, cold'). Aurora, though, does not seem impressed by Juan's good looks. *Canto the Sixteenth*. Juan retires for the night, but feels 'restless, and perplexed'. He goes for a night-time wander, and thinks he hears 'a supernatural agent – or a mouse'. In fact 'it was no mouse – but lo! a monk arrayed/In cowl and beads'. Juan is terrified, and the apparition passes before him three times and disappears. Juan goes back to bed. At breakfast he learns from Lord Henry that the house is reputedly haunted by the 'Black Friar'. Henry is engaged upon electioneering, and he invites various local people in the evening. Lady Adeline entertains sparklingly, but after these people have finally taken their leave, everybody exclaims against 'their hideous wives, and horrid selves and dresses'; everybody except Aurora and Juan, the latter still silenced by his encounter with the ghost. That night he sees the ghost of the Black Friar once more. Initially terrified he overcomes his fear to reach out and touch the spectre, and finds 'a hard but glowing bust,/Which beat as if there was a warm heart under'. Juan pulls back the cowl to reveal 'in full, voluptuous, but *not o'ergrown* bulk,/The phantom of her frolic Grace – Fitz Fulke!' *Canto the Seventeenth*. Only fourteen stanzas of this canto were written; we get the briefest glimpse of Juan and Fitz-Fulke both worn out at breakfast the next day.

: E :

Earthly Paradise, The: a Poem (published in four volumes 1868–70), by William Morris. Twenty-five individual long poems (some in heroic or octosyllabic couplets, some in Chaucerian seven-line stanzas; this mixture follows the metrical model of the *Canterbury Tales*), 42,681 lines in all. This titanic poem, the longest published in the modern era (although Bailey's *Festus* is almost as long, and does constitute a single poem, instead of the variegated narratives of Morris) was extremely popular in Morris's own day, although many more recent critics have tended to see it as static and rather monotonous. Morris himself played up the escapist element in the work; its opening lines encourage us to:

> Forget six counties overhung with smoke,
> Forget the snorting steam and piston stroke,
> Forget the spreading of the hideous town;
> Think rather of the pack-horse on the down,
> And dream of London, small, and white, and clean,
> The clear Thames bordered by its gardens green.

But in fact this poem is not the work of an 'idle singer of an empty day' (Morris's self-characterization), but a complex, elegiac and melancholic poem about the impossibility of the utopia suggested by its title.

Prologue: the Wanderers. A company of thirteenth-century Norsemen arrive at a 'nameless city ... white as the changing walls of faerie', a haven of ancient Greek culture somewhere in the Mediterranean, where the Olympian gods are still worshipped. The Elder of the City asks for their story, and the wanderers tell of how they left Scandinavia fleeing an outbreak of Plague, and hoping to reach the fabled Earthly Paradise 'across the western sea where none grow old'. They search fruitlessly for most of their lives, and have many adventures, before returning east 'old and grey/Before our time'. The Elder of the City invites them to spend the rest of their days on the island. Twice a month the Norsemen and the Greeks meet at a great banquet, and a representative from each people tells a tale; the tales of the former being based on Norse mythology and the latter on Greek. Morris divides the rest of the poem into months, from March to February, introduces each section with a brief lyric section, and relates each tale. These tales are integrated to the time of year, from the cheerfulness of Spring to the tragic cast of Winter and back to Spring. Detailed summary of each of these twenty-four tales would prove unwieldy, so the accounts below follow only the basic shapes of the poems.

March. Atalanta's Race (636 lines, stanzaic). The virgin and athletic Atalanta, daughter of the Greek king, Schoenus, wishes to avoid wedlock, and so she challenges any suitors to a race, promising to marry them only if they can beat her. Her speed ensures no man is able to claim her hand. But Prince Milanion, taking advice from the goddess Venus, wins the race by strewing the field with golden balls: Atalanta cannot resist pausing in the middle of the race to pick these up and so loses. *The Man Born to be King* (2223 lines, octosyllabic couplets). A wealthy and powerful king hears a prophesy that his successor will be low-born and poor. The king tries various strategies to avoid this: he sends the man in question to his daughter the princess with orders that she kill him, but she falls in love with him instead and marries him, thus fulfilling the prophesy.

April. The Doom of King Acrisus (2523 lines, heroic couplets). Acrisus, the King of Argos, learns that his daughter Danae will give birth to a man destined to kill him. To avoid this fate, Acrisus has Danae imprisoned in a tower 'fashioned of mere molten brass'. Although sequestered from mortals, Jove visits Danae as a shower of gold ('the chamber, scattered o'er with shining gold/That grew, till ankle-deep she stood in it') and she gives birth to a son, Perseus. She and the child are cast adrift, but arrive at the island of Seriphos where Perseus grows to manhood. After many adventures (cutting off the Gorgon's head, winning the hand of a princess) Perseus and his mother return to Argos, where he unwittingly fulfils the prophesy by killing Acrisus. *The Proud King* (849 lines, stanzaic). A king grew proud in his greatness and declared himself God ('What need have I for temple or for priest?/Am I not God, whiles that I live at least?'). But he subsequently discovers that nobody recognizes him as king any more. He suffers a variety of humiliations before learning humility and encountering an angel who tells him the moral ('That God that made the world can unmake thee').

May. The Story of Cupid and Psyche (2541 lines, heroic couplets). Venus is jealous of the beauty of Princess Psyche, but her son Cupid (or 'Love') marries her. Cupid visits his bride only in the night, and insists that she never see him; but her curiosity eventually gets the better of her, and she is banished. She wanders through the world, suffering much at the hands of Venus, until she is eventually reconciled to her husband, and made immortal by Jove. *The Writing on the Image* (366 lines, octosyllabic couplets). In Rome there is 'an image cut of cornel wood' upon which is written 'PERCUTE HIC' ('strike here'), although nobody knows what this means. One day a scholar decodes the message: digging at the spot marked by the image's shadow at noon he uncovers a 'winding staircase wrought of stone'. Going down in search of treasure he winds up trapped there 'until the judgement day'.

June. The Love of Alcestis (1352 lines, heroic couplets). Admetus, a Thessalian King, can avoid death if he can find somebody to die in his place; but nobody will do so except his wife Alcestis. *The Lady of the Land* (546 lines, stanzaic). An Italian sailor lands on a Greek island and falls in love with a beautiful woman in a splendid mansion:

> Naked she was, the kisses of her feet
> Upon the floor a dying path had made
> From the full bath unto her ivory seat.

This woman lives under a spell cast by Artemis, and although a beautiful woman on one day of the year she is 'a fork-tongued dragon' the rest of the time ('And through the island nightly do I range/Or in the green sea mate with monsters strange'). The mariner promises to break the spell by kissing the woman in her dragon manifestation; but encountering her the next day he runs away in fear, and afterwards dies.

July. The Son of Croesus (539 lines, stanzaic). Croesus has a vision of his son Atys being slain by an iron weapon. Understandably eager to avoid this fate, he sets up Adrastus as the captain of a band of guards specifically remitted to protect the boy but Adrastus accidentally kills Atys when the two are hunting. *The Watching of the Falcon* (912 lines, octosyllabic couplets). Any person who watches a certain falcon for seven days and nights is granted a wish by a fairy maiden who appears to them. Many people do this and wish for various things, but a King watches the falcon and when the fairy appears he declares his wish that they be man and wife. He goes with her to the Fairy kingdom, but his bliss is also his ruin and he dies.

August. Pygmalion and the Image (700 lines, stanzaic). Pygmalion is a sculptor from Cyprus, and he creates a beautiful sculpture of a woman; so beautiful in fact that he falls in love with it. He prays to Venus, and the goddess transforms the statue into a real woman, whom Pygmalion marries. *Ogier the Dane.* (1609 lines, heroic couplets). Ogier is visited when still in his cradle by six fairies: five give him conventional gifts (that he be brave, happy and so on), but the sixth gives herself, to be his love after he has lived in the world a long time. He grows to manhood and, after adventures, marries the fairy and lives with her in Avallon even to the present day.

September. The Death of Paris (739 lines, stanzaic). Paris has been wounded with a poisoned arrow at the siege of Troy. He is carried up Mount Ida to converse with the nymph Oenone, whom he once had loved, hoping that she can cure him: but such knowledge is beyond her and Paris dies. *The Land East of the Sun and West of the Moon* (3375 lines, octosyllabic couplets). John, the idle son of a churl, sees seven swans shed their swan-skins and appear as beautiful women. He falls in love with one of them, and she offers him the choice to 'be great among the sons of men ... and forget/That here amid the hay we met/Or else be loved, and love, the while/Life's vision doth thine eyes beguile'. John chooses the latter, and the swan-maiden carries him away to Faeryland. After three years of bliss, something begins to bear down on John's soul, and he returns to our world. Here he lives in hope of returning to his love, but becomes bitter as the years pass. He curses Love, but the faery maiden turns up one Christmas and tells him 'my feet, lost Love, shall wander soon/East of the Sun, West of the Moon.' Next morning she is gone, and John sets out on a quest to find the impossible land she named. After many adventures he does so and is reunited with his love; although they are both changed, worn and weary.

October. The Story of Acontius and Cydippe (1192 lines, octosyllabic couplets). Acontius visits Delos, and falls in love with the beautiful Cydippe, vowing to have her at all costs. He writes '*Acontius will I wed today*' on an apple with a thorn, and casts it into the folds of her gown during a festival of Venus; they are afterwards wed. *The Man Who Never Laughed Again.* (1624 lines, stanzaic). Bharam has lost all his wealth and is despondent; an old friend, Firuz, comes across him, and invites him back to a spectacular hidden palace, where six other miserable men live. Bharam is offered the chance to oversee this mansion while the despondent men pine away and die, the deal being that when they are all dead he can take the house's treasure and return to the real world wealthy. Firuz also gives him a key, the secret (it seems) behind the depression of the seven. After they have all died Bharam returns to the city with his money, but he cannot quell his curiosity as to the root of the men's misery. Returning to the mansion he unlocks an iron door in the garden and passes into an underworld kingdom; there by a sea shore a black barge approaches and two beautiful women invite him to come with them. They sail over the sea to a green, paradisaical land:

> Upon the green slopes Bharam could behold
> The white tents and the spears of many men,
> And on the o'erhanging height a castle old,
> And up the bay a ship o'erlaid with gold,
> With golden sails and fluttering banners bright,
> And silken awnings 'gainst the hot sun dight.

Bharam's eyes are wet 'with happy tears' as he approaches the Queen of this fair land and declares his love. He lives two years in that place, after which the Queen departs for a hundred days, telling him not to look in a certain room; but in his loneliness he does so, and the punishment for his curiosity robs him of his paradise. He returns to our world as 'THE MAN WHO NE'ER SHALL LAUGH AGAIN'.

November. The Story of Rhodope (2093 lines, stanzaic). Rhodope is a beautiful but poor Greek maid; she dresses in splendid clothes her father had long ago chanced upon and journeys to the town, where the splendour of her clothes and her beauty win for her a princely husband. *The Lovers of Gudrun* (4945 lines, heroic couplets). The longest of the tales in *The Earthly Paradise* concerns (briefly) the love that two friends, Kiartan and Bodli, both have for one woman, Gudrun; Gudrun marries Bodli, although her heart is with Kiartan. After various adventures Bodli kills Kiartan, and afterwards is destroyed by his remorse ('And such a storm of grief on him did fall ... That men for shame must turn away their eyes,/Nor seem to see a great man fallen so low').

December. The Golden Apples (598 lines, stanzaic). A Tyrian ship carries Hercules to the Hesperides, where he steals the golden apples of the Sun. *The Fostering of Aslaug* (1505 lines, octosyllabic couplets). Aslaud is the daughter of Sigurd and Brynhild (of *Ring of the Neibulung* fame); she is fostered when still a baby to Heimar the old bard. He seeks shelter in the forest one night, carrying the baby, but is killed by the peasants for his golden jewellery and his fine harp. They raise the girl as a drudge under the name 'Crow'; but after various adventures her true royalty shines through and she is restored to her rightful place, and marries Ragnar.

January. Bellerophon at Argos (2436 lines, heroic couplets). Hipponous is the son of the King of Corinth; one day he accidentally kills his brother, Beller. He flees his country and eventually ends up at the court of Proetus, King of Argos. Proetus purifies Hipponous of the blood-guilt and renames him Bellerophon (telling him 'with this new hapless name that thou hast won/Go forth, go free'). Bellerophon lives contentedly for a while, until the jealousy of Proetus' queen Sthenoboea brings about his downfall: she conceives a passion for him, and when he does not respond she tells her husband that he had attempted to rape her. Proetus is agonized ('And must I slay him then,/Him whom I loved above all earthly men?'). He then sends Bellerophon to his father-in-law, King Jobates of Lycia, with a message that contains the instructions for his execution. Sthenoboea hurls herself from a cliff in remorse. The story is continued in February (below). *The Ring Given To Venus* (1352 lines, octosyllabic couplets). It is Laurence's wedding day; he puts his wedding ring on the finger of a brazen statue of Venus as a testament to the fact that 'I, even I, must sigh for thee!' But then he cannot get the ring off again, and without it he cannot consummate his marriage. The goddess plays various games with him, but in the end he gets his ring back.

February. Bellerophon in Lycia (3585 lines, heroic couplets). Completing the story begun in January, we follow Bellerophon to Lycia, where the king Jobates reads the secret message and tries several times to have him killed: sending assassins against him (but 'small avail/Man's weapons are against him') and so on. His daughter Philonoe falls in love with him. After various vicissitudes the two marry and all ends happily. *The Hill of Venus* (1700 lines, stanzaic). Walter, a medieval knight, riding through Germany, encounters the goddess Venus and goes with her to her underhill home. This seems at first a bliss ('No rest but rest of utter love to find/Amidst the marvel of new-born delight') but the knight eventually wearies of his bliss: 'twixt lessening joy and gathering fear, grew thin/That lovely dream' and the knight eventually leaves that place, but he can find no acceptance in our world. An abbot advises him to seek absolution for his sin with the Pope, and so he travels to Rome: but he cannot fully repent of his love for Venus, and the Pope refuses to cleanse him of sin, telling him that 'just so much hope I have of thee/As on this dry staff fruit and flowers to see!' Walter returns to the Hill of Venus, and the next day the Pope is amazed to find his dry staff 'grew wondrous flowers/That earth knew not'. *Epilogue* (92 lines, heroic couplets). We are told that the wanderers lived peacefully until their death, and the narrator concludes by saying that 'all these images of love and pain/Wrought as the year did wax, perfect, and wane' are now 'cold':

> And thou, O tale of what these sleepers were,
> Wish one good-night to them thou holdest dear,
> Then die thyself, and let us go our ways,
> And live awhile amid these latter days!

Morris concludes with an *Envoi* in which he acknowledges the influence of 'My Master, GEOFFREY CHAUCER'.

Economy of Vegetation, The (1792), by Erasmus Darwin. See *Botanic Garden*.

Edwin of Deira (1861), by Alexander Smith. 3275 lines, blank verse. Based on the Venerable Bede's history of the Northumbrian King who came to the throne in AD 617 and held power until 633, and whose name is commemorated in the city he founded (Edwin's Burgh or Edinburgh). Four years in the writing, Smith was disappointed by the lukewarm reception his historical epic received; coming soon after *Idylls of the King* many reviewers accused Smith of simply plagiarizing *Tennyson.

Book I. Edwin, defeated in battle by the wicked King Ethelbert, flees alone to the court of his father's friend King Redwald. He renews his friendship with the King and his seven sons – and his beautiful young daughter, Bertha, with whom Edwin falls in love. *Book II.* Returning to Redwald's castle after a hunting trip Edwin is warned that Ethelbert has found out his location, and is threatening Redwald with dire consequences unless he gives him up. Unable to enter the castle, Edwin waits uncertainly outside that night, where he meets a mysterious and apparently supernatural 'dark-robed man'. This figure promises to help Edwin back to power and 'send teachers that will teach thee more/Of the dark world that lies beyond the grave'. In the morning Edwin discovers that Redwald has sent Ethelbert's messengers away and is ready to assist Edwin recapture his kingdom, and even marry Princess Bertha. Ethelbert is subsequently defeated in battle, but at the cost of the life of Redwald's favourite son, Regner. *Book III.* Edwin begins to rebuild his realm. He woos and marries Bertha (or as Smith puts it, 'at last, the Prince/Drew [her] green bud to a sweet rosy tip,/Thence to an open flower'). They have a son. Edwin purges the land of various robbers and bandits. An assassin stabs him ('"It was not I/'Twas Ethelbert stabbed thee from beyond the grave"') and Edwin swoons. *Book IV.* Bertha nurses Edwin slowly back to health. He wonders about 'the apparitional man,/When will he reappear?' Christian missionaries appear in Edwin's land, and explain the new religion. After a battle with his conscience, and the reappearance of the mysterious apparitional man, Edwin is converted: 'I here ... Unclothe myself of the religion dark/Which I and all my forefathers have worn,/And put on Christ like raiment white and clean'.

ELIOT, George (1819–80), pen-name of Mary Ann, or Marian, Evans. Eliot's genius, of course, was prose; her novels remain among the most admired and studied of the Victorian period. Her poetry occasionally comes under critical scrutiny, but usually as a means of fleshing out our sense of the complete artist, or in an attempt to throw light on the concerns of the fiction.

Eliot wrote verses, mostly pious and derivative short poems, from an early age. Her busy literary career of translation (Strauss's *Life of Christ* in 1848, Feuerbach's *Essence of Christianity* in 1854) and, later, fiction (*Adam Bede* in 1859, *The Mill on the Floss* in 1860, *Silas Marner* in 1861, *Romola* in 1863 and *Felix Holt* in 1866) did not entirely distract her from poetic endeavour. During a trip to Spain in 1867 she conceived the idea for *The Spanish Gypsy, a project which was to occupy her for the next two years. She wrote it first as a play, then rewrote it as closet-drama, a form of *verse-novel. It appeared in 1868. Despite being fairly well received, Eliot returned to fiction for her next project, *Middlemarch* (1872). Critics see in *The Spanish Gypsy*, and particularly the heroine's struggle between individual romance and racial destiny, a foreshadowing of the main subject of Eliot's last novel, *Daniel Deronda* (1876). Eliot published shorter poetry in magazines from 1865 onwards, and these were eventually collected in *The Legend of Jubal and Other Poems* (1874).

Empedocles on Etna (1852), by Matthew Arnold. 1121 lines, blank verse and various lyric metres. Regarded by many as Arnold's masterpiece, Arnold himself suppressed this lyric-drama for much of his life on the grounds that it was 'painful, not tragic' – that however well written and beautiful the text its effect on readers would be to depress them, and that this was unacceptable.

Act I, scene I. The scene is laid on the lower slopes of Mount Etna, in the forest region; the time is 'between two and three thousand years ago'. Callicles, a young harp player and optimistic lyric poet, is talking with Pausanias, a physician and friend of the philosopher Empedocles. Callicles declares of Empedocles that 'as most men say, he is half mad/ With exile, and with brooding on his wrongs'; Pausanius agrees that 'one of his moods is on him', and goes off after his friend. *Act I, scene II*. The scene is higher up Etna; Pausanius urges Empedocles to rest. The sound of Callicles' harp playing drifts up from lower down the mountain, and Empedocles is greatly struck by it. After an optimistic little poem by Callicles, Empedocles embarks on a lengthy, stoic but ultimately rather gloomy philosophical poem.

> Scratch'd by a fall, with moans
> As children on weak age
> Lend life to the dumb stones
> Whereon to vent their rage,
> And bend their little fists, and rate the senseless ground;

Act II. Empedocles has now climbed, alone, to the very summit of Etna ('Etna's great mouth/Round which the sullen vapour rolls'). He speaks a long blank verse monologue, the pessimism and misery of which ('I alone/Am dead to life and joy ... I read/In all things my own deadness') is rendered all the starker by the interspersed cheeriness of the over-heard snatches of Callicles' songs from below. Eventually, Empedocles talks himself into a positive, even a happy position ('the numbing cloud/ Mounts off my soul'); but it is this very happiness, paradoxically perhaps, that prompts him to suicide.

– Ah, boil up, ye vapours!
Leap and roar, thou sea of fire!
My soul glows to meet you.
Ere it flag, ere the mists
Of despondency and gloom
Rush over it again,
Receive me, save me!   [*He plunges into the crater*]

The text concludes, ironically, with a cheery hymn of praise to 'the Father/Of all things', from Callicles, below.

Endymion: A Poetic Romance (1818), by John Keats. 4050 lines, heroic couplets. This was Keats's first and last completed attempt at the long poem (his *Hyperion* remained unfinished). Its inventive sometimes florid style did not endear it to reviewers: the savage review in the *Quarterly* was popularly thought at the time to have hastened Keats's death (a tradition memorialized in Shelley's *Adonais*), although this rather oversimplifies matters. Certainly it cannot have been easy for Keats to read that the poem embodied (to quote Lockhart's review in *Blackwood's*) a 'calm, settled, imperturbable, drivelling idiocy'.

Book 1. The poem begins with a paean to beauty ('A thing of beauty is a joy for ever;/Its loveliness increases; it will never/Pass into nothingness'). The scene is then set in Latmos, in the 'gloomy shades, sequestered deep' of a forest. A group of shepherds dances into view, and then Endymion, the shepherd-prince who rules over them: 'His youth was fully blown,/Showing like Ganymede to manhood grown'. The Shepherds sing a 'Hymn to Pan' ('O thou, whose mighty palace roof doth hang/From jagged trunks ...'). Yet Endymion is not happy, a 'cankering venom' has 'riven his fainting recollections'. His beloved sister, Peona, can tell that something is wrong: 'thou dost know of things mysterious,/Immortal, starry; such alone could thus/Weigh down thy nature.' Endymion tells her about a recent dream in which he communed vividly with the moon goddess: 'she did soar/So passionately bright, my dazzled soul/Commingly with her argent spheres did roll.' The dream is intimate ('madly did I kiss/The wooing arms which held me'), and after it real existence seems an 'ebbing sea/Of weary life'. Prompted by a mysterious voice ('"Endymion! The cave is secreter/Than the isle of Delos. Echo hence shall stir/No sighs but sigh-warm kisses"') he resolves to seek the deity of his dream, the Moon goddess Cynthia. *Book II.* Endymion meets a naiad (or water nymph) who tells him that he must 'wander far/In other regions' before he can find his way 'into the gentle bosom' of his love. Accordingly he travels underground:

> Dark, nor light,
> The region; nor bright, nor sombre wholly,
> But mingled up; a gleaming melancholy;
> A dusky empire and its diadems;
> One faint eternal eventide of gems.
> Aye, millions sparkled on a vein of gold,
> Along whose track the prince quick footsteps told.

In this strange kingdom Endymion sees the sleeping form of Adonis (an attendant cupid tells the story of Venus and Adonis), and he travels on 'through caves and palaces of mottled ore,/Gold dome, and crystal wall, and turquoise floor'. An eagle carries him to a 'jasmine bower', where he dreams another erotic encounter with the Moon ('stretching his indolent arms, he took – oh, bliss! –/A naked waist'). She confesses her love for him, a love she must hide or sacrifice her reputation for chastity ('And I must blush in heaven'). Endymion wakes up alone. *Book III*. Wandering bereft, Endymion encounters Glaucus, who tells him the story of his love for Scylla. Endymion helps bring the two together, and then looking on their happiness feels his own pain ('Oh shall I die! Sweet Venus, be my stay!/Where is my lovely mistress?'). He sees a message from Cynthia written in starlight that addresses him as *'my entire love'* and tells him to *'awake, awake'*, which he does, finding himself again in the 'forest green'. *Book IV*. Endymion meets an Indian Maiden forlorn in the woods; she sings a roundelay to Sorrow. Endymion decides to give up his ideal, unreal love and live instead with this actual woman. He resolves that 'never more/Shall airy voices cheat me to the shore/Of tangled wonder, breathless and aghast', says goodbye to 'my daintiest dream, although so vast/My love is still for thee' and instead prizes 'one human kiss!/One sigh of real breath' from his Indian maid. She, however, refuses his suit ('no, no, that shall not be. Thee will I bless,/And bid a long adieu'). Peona meets and greets the two of them, but Endymion bitterly promises his sister that 'a hermit young, I'll live in mossy cave' away from humanity. Not discouraged, Peona leads them both through the woods to the temple of Diana, where the Indian Maid reveals herself to be none other than the Goddess Cynthia. She kisses Peona, and Endymion and she 'vanished far away!'. The poem concludes with Peona going 'home through the gloomy wood in wonderment'.

English Bards and Scotch Reviewers (1809), by Lord Byron. 1070 lines, heroic couplets. This satirical attack on the literary scene began life as a satire called *British Bards*, of which no copy survives. Byron augmented it following a swingeing review of his volume *Hours of Idleness* in the *Edinburgh Review*.

Byron begins 'Fools are my theme, let satire be my song' and goes on to attack the editor of the *Edinburgh Review*, Jeffrey, and then the great authors of the day: Scott ('Think'st thou, Scott! by vain conceit per-chance/On public taste to foist thy stale romance?'), Southey ('Oh! Southey! Southey! Cease thy varied song!/A bard may chant too often, and too long:'), Wordsworth ('Who, both by precept and example, shows/That prose is verse and verse is merely prose'), Coleridge ('Shall gentle Coleridge pass unnoticed here,/To turgid ode and tumid stanza dear?'), and various other minor poets. The second half of the poem is concerned with praising the virtues of classical eighteenth-century verse, as embodied by Dryden, Pope, Burns, Crabbe and others.

Enoch Arden (1864), by Alfred Tennyson. 911 lines, blank verse. The story was suggested by Tennyson's friend, Thomas Woolner.

Annie Lee is a young girl in a small seaside port, and is loved by both Philip Ray and Enoch Arden. As they grow up Enoch wins Annie's heart, and the two are married. After the wedding 'merrily ran the years/ ... seven happy years of health and competence'. The couple have children. During a period of relative poverty, Enoch takes a job as boatswain on a 'vessel China-bound'. On this voyage, however, Enoch is shipwrecked, and nothing is heard of him for ten years. Annie is again courted by Philip, who tries to convince her that Enoch is dead. Uncertain what to do, Annie consults the Bible at random, and comes across the text 'under the palm tree'.

> she closed the Book and slept:
> When lo! her Enoch sitting on a height,
> Under a palm-tree, over him in Sun:
> 'He is gone,' she thought, 'he is happy, he is singing
> Hosanna in the highest: yonder shines
> The Sun of Righteousness'.

Convinced of Enoch's death, Annie marries Philip. 'And where was Enoch?' The narrator describes his shipwreck, and his life, Robinson-Crusoe-like, on a desert island. In a gleaming passage Tennyson describes life on the island.

> The myriad shriek of wheeling ocean-fowl,
> The league-long roller thundering on the reef,
> The moving whisper of huge trees that branched
> And blossomed in the zenith.

Eventually, Enoch is rescued and returns home: but when he discovers that Annie has remarried, and is apparently happy, he chooses not to reveal himself or disturb the domestic contentment. Instead he lies down and dies. The poem's concluding lines ('So passed the strong heroic soul away./And when they buried him the little port/Had seldom seen a costlier funeral') have been mocked by some, but defended by others as catching the strikingly ambiguous attitude of the poem to conventional pieties.

Epic. The textbooks define epic as a long poem, usually celebrating the adventures (war or travel) of a great hero in continuous narrative. In practice, epic poetry has built upon the achievements of Homer and Vergil, and the term is used to refer to a canon of poems, consisting broadly of the *Odyssey* and *Iliad* of Homer, the *Aeneid* of Vergil, the *Divine Comedy* of Dante, the *Lusiad* by Camoens, *Geruselem Liberata* by Tasso and Milton's *Paradise Lost*. Standard criticism sees epic poetry as being either primary, secondary or tertiary. The original, primary epics (Homer, the anonymous *Epic of Gilgamesh*, or *Beowulf*) derived from an oral tradition, and are wholly externalized narratives. Secondary epics, of which the chief example is Vergil's *Aeneid*, are written rather than oral, and set themselves up as conscious and even reverential imitations of the primary model. Tertiary epics, finally, are literary epics existing in a culture where 'the epic' has become a venerable literary tradition; their relationship to the primary and secondary epic is a more complex one, inflected by (for instance) an ironic reappropriation of the tropes of Homer. One critical argument asserts that epics are no longer possible; that the epic form can no longer be plausibly inhabited by contemporary writers, because an epic depends above all on aesthetic and cultural *unity*. This argument, broadly, is that Romantic and post-Romantic literature, and indeed culture, sees a fragmentation and disintegration of cultural norms and aesthetic criteria; and that nowadays it is only possible to write fragmented pastiches of epic, poetry like Eliot's *The Waste Land* or Pound's *Cantos*. According to this view, epic is a cultural form that has flourished and had its day.

Whether you agree with this assessment is going to depend upon how you define 'epic'. In contemporary parlance, epic is little more than a synonym for 'very lengthy'; any film longer than two-and-a-half hours is liable to be tagged 'epic' whether or not it invokes any of the conventional attributes of the mode. Rather than being dismissive of this as vernacular debasement, it is worth considering its implications. It suggests, for instance, that in place of the elaborate generic conventions associated with epic, culture has focused on three – subject, style and length; and that the greatest of these is length. The nineteenth century was an age especially enamoured of length, of course. Coleridge may have argued that long poems strained patience (and Edgar Allen Poe, in

1845's 'The Poetic Principle', denied their legitimacy altogether); but Coleridge himself planned a number of long poems. The belief that length equates to weight, and weight to worth, dies hard in human culture. Aristophanes' *Frogs* is only half-comic in judging the respective merits of Aeschylus and Euripides by weight – the two playwrights' plays are actually weighed in scales, with Aeschylus winning because his work is *heavier* – and contemporary life abounds with instances of lengthophilia. Where Romantic writers sometimes baulked at the length required (and most Romantic epics are fragments of a larger project), the Victorian poets were able to fully indulge their love affair with length. Two poems from this period – Bailey's *Festus* and Morris's gargantuan *Earthly Paradise* constitute to this day the longest single-author written poems in literature.

Nonetheless, we cannot entirely ignore the traditional trappings of epic definition, not least because nineteenth-century authors played complex and allusive games with readerly expectations of epic convention. It is possible, then, according to the 'rules' over which rhetoricians and scholars have sweated and debated for thousands of years (and which are more or less irrelevant to contemporary life) to outline a standard or paradigmatic epic. So –

- It should be in either twelve or twenty-four books (as are the Vergillian and Homeric epics respectively), and it should be written in the same metre and style throughout – preferably whichever metre and style is considered by the culture of the day to be the most 'noble' or 'high'.
- It should start *in medias res* ('in the middle of things'), and include some portion of narrative flash-back to explain how things have reached this position.
- It should, nonetheless, tell a continuous narrative about the adventures of a heroic figure, and these adventures should involve war (in which the hero battles bravely and demonstrates extraordinary strength and skill, as in the *Iliad*) or lengthy travels (in which the hero goes through many bizarre and distant places and overcomes adversity on his way home, as in the *Odyssey*) – or both war *and* travel, as in the *Aeneid*.
- It should involve supernatural machinery: gods or spirits.
- It should include what is known as a 'catalogue of the ships', after the long list of Greek ships and where they have sailed from that occurs in Book 2 of the *Iliad*.
- It should include a visit to the underworld (*Odyssey* Book 11, *Aeneid* Book 6).
- It might (although this is optional) contain one of the following: a

recognition scene, in which the hero (disguised) is recognized by an old nurse or some such figure; a repeated fascination with 'home' and in particular 'coming home' (by extension, you may wish to style your epic as a myth of provenance, explaining the origins of a particular nation or tribe); a love story, preferably a doomed one.

- You may wish to include epic similes. Your epic should also begin with an address to whichever Muse you have decided is your inspiration.

A supple sense of these sorts of rules, either established by the scholars or derived from the epics of the past that have most influenced the particular poet, is a crucial feature of epic from Milton onwards. The games poets play with the expectations of the epic genre that these rules create are part of their effect, and the invocation of a number of the features I list is one of the ways a poem will single itself out as 'epic'. So, Milton includes a sort of 'catalogue of the ships', when he itemizes all the devils in hell as they assemble around the fallen Satan; and he finds ways to insert grandiose battle sequences into the plain Biblical story by having an archangel come down to tell Adam and Eve of the battles in heaven between the angels and the demons. By doing this, Milton is deliberately playing with our expectations of the epic mode.

This sort of intertextual 'game' becomes a central and even perhaps defining feature of the epic in the nineteenth century. *Byron makes cheerful mock of convention at the beginning of *Don Juan ('My poem's epic, and is meant to be,/Divided in twelve books ...'), and there is a witty playfulness in his use of, say, the notion of the Muse ('Hail Muse, etcetera'). But at the same time, it is clear that his eventual plans for his masterpiece envisaged a Homeric twenty-four books, and that the finished article would contain battle, odyssey, a notion of heroism redefined as erotic (but nonetheless valid), a 'catalogue of ships' in Russian generals' names and so on. We do a sort of violence to Byron's vision by calling Don Juan mock-epic. In Pope's mock-epic The Rape of the Lock, heroic convention is miniaturized as a means of trivializing the mode; but Don Juan takes place on a splendidly vast stage, and at an epic length. Simply being comic or satiric is not in itself enough to undermine the epic aesthetic (throughout the nineteenth century, Homer was believed to have authored a lost comic epic, Margites).

*Wordsworth's epic *Prelude is, similarly, sometimes put forward as anti-epic, or at least as a symptom that epic qua epic was becoming invalid. Nonetheless, although the thirteen (or fourteen) books of Wordsworth's long work seem deliberately to avoid epic convention, what we find in fact is that they are internalized. Supernatural machinery becomes the spot of time, the perceptual sense of numinous spirituality breaking through into the everyday; the descent into the underworld becomes the battle with despair and despondency; the catalogue of ships becomes a catalogue of books. On the other hand, it is the very fact that *The Prelude* is an internalized work (the life of the mind), where Homer is entirely externalized (the actions of men, into whose minds we are not permitted to glimpse), that is the actual marker of collapse of the point of epic. Coleridge's *Table Talk* for 23 October 1833 was of 'the Homeric epics, in which all is purely external and objective, and the poet is a mere voice'. Few Romantic authors would be comfortable with being 'a mere voice'. Even so devout a classicist as *Landor, whose epic *Gebir* is the most faithful adaption of the Vergillian model in English, could not sacrifice the distinctiveness of his poetic voice. Nonetheless, epic in the nineteenth century becomes less and less concerned with historically or mythically distanced subject matter, and more fascinated with expressing the personal tone and voice of the poet.

It would be closer to the mark, then, to say that nineteenth-century epic marks not so much an internalization as a personalization of the epic medium. This personalization was less confessional (even *The Prelude* is not a piece of confessional work) but rather a platform for exploring the personal responses of the author to his or her epic tradition. One of the legacies of Romantic fascination with the epic is a renewed theoretical fascination with the intertextual way the mode worked. In *The Defence of Poetry*, *Shelley distinguished epic from drama (rather than, as we might expect, from lyric). The difference for Shelley was that the true epic poem (he instances Homer, Dante and Milton) constitutes 'a bridge thrown over the stream of time', where drama is 'a prismatic and many-sided mirror, which collects the brightest rays of human nature and divides and reproduces them from the simplicity of these elemental forms'. In other words, Shelley saw the epic poet as writing not merely to express the concerns of his or her own time, but also in dialogue with the past and even as an articulation of the future (poets, as Shelley memorably defined them, being the 'mirrors of the gigantic shadows which futurity casts upon the present'). In practice, this notion of epic as 'bridge' manifested itself chiefly in terms of a specific dialogue with specific epic antecedents; Milton is the most frequently invoked precursor in nineteenth-century epic writing, but Homer, Vergil, Dante, Chaucer, Spenser and Ariosto are also invoked by many nineteenth-century writers. Indeed, some critics have seen in the Romantic period a revivification of the primary epic, with a poem like *Don Juan* being, in Donald Reiman's terms, as externalized, as caught up in 'the only present' and as encyclopaedic of its time, as Homer.

Shelley's metaphor of the bridge is a useful one to us; partly because it suggests division in a mode that contemporary critics almost all defined in terms of its unity. *Browning is perfectly comfortable invoking the gamut of epic convention (his Muse becomes his dead wife, his battle-ground the formalized conflict of the courtroom, his odyssey internalized, and so on); yet his vision is essentially fragmented, broken between ten separate speakers, each with a particular view that is sometimes incompatible with the other narrators. *Tennyson's attempt at an epic cycle observes all the conventions, but cannot maintain the unity of a consistent narrative line. The very longest epic productions of the age – *Bailey's *Festus and *Morris's *Earthly Paradise – break their frame-stories into a thousand pieces. Generically, too, the form of epic blurs and distorts in the nineteenth century (shifting into verse-novel, narrative poem, brief epic, lyric-epic, elegiac epic and so on). It is hard to avoid the sense that the form is actually fragmenting before our eyes and that the trail leading into the shattered poetic experiments of the Modernists is clear to see. Victorian poets, of course, tried to work in unified terms: Tennyson had a single body of myths, a single national identity, behind his Idylls of the King; Browning had a real-life murder mystery as the point of focus for all his different speakers in The Ring and the Book. But the centripetal forces inherent in both of these constructions pull them apart more forcibly than these structures can hold them together. Other poets substitute other qualities – sex for *Swinburne in *Tristram of Lyonesse, geology for *Montgomery in *Greenland – but the effect is always to overstrain the unifying trope, and so to distort the poem as a whole (although, I should add, these distortions are often fascinating and brilliant).

Later poets have, more or less, abandoned the notion that a consistent, unified, epic vision is possible at length in poetry today. The nineteenth century, then, comes down to us as the last period of literary history when poetry was being written by poets who believed that it was possible. For all that the fault lines of post-Romantic culture make themselves plain, it remains a brilliant body of writing.

Epic of Hades, The (1876, 1877), by Lewis Morris. Not actually a long poem, more a collection of various inter-related dramatic monologues put into the mouths of figures from Greek myth. Book 2 was published in 1876, the whole thing in 1877. It enjoyed a remarkable popularity and had sold 50,000 copies by the century's end.

Book 1. Tartarus (the deepest and most hopeless level of the Greek underworld) consists of four monologues, *Tantalus, Phaedra, Sisyphus* and *Clytemnestra*, all spoken by people who had committed terrible crimes and been harshly punished by the gods. Tantalus hears voices commanding him to kill his own son; he is punished by being unable to satisfy his hunger and thirst, despite having food and drink just out of reach. The narrator comments that he knows 'the undying worm of sense, which frets and gnaws/The unsatisfied stained soul'. Phaedra conceived a quasi-incestuous passion for her husband the king's son Hippolytus, but spurned by him she convinces her husband that he made improper advances upon her, and the king prays to Poseidon to destroy Hippolytus; in Tartarus she is not permitted to forget, 'always before [her] eyes, the one dread scene/Of horror'. The tyrant Sisyphus has to push a great stone up a hill, only to have it 'crash,/A horrible thunderous noise, as down the steep/The shameless fragment fell.' The murderess Clytemnestra is also there, 'and on her side/An ancient stain of gore, which did befoul/The royal robe'. *Book 2. Hades*. The narrator encounters *Marsyas*, flayed to death by Apollo for daring to challenge him to a contest of song; beautiful *Andromeda*, chained to the cliff as a sacrifice to a fearsome sea-monster until rescued by Perseus; *Actaeon*, turned into a stag by Diana and torn to pieces by his own hounds; *Helen*, the cause of the Trojan war; *Euridice*; *Orpheus*; *Deianeira* the tragic wife of Hercules; *Laocoon* crushed to death by sea-serpents at Troy; self-loving *Narcissus*; snake-haired *Medusa*; the handsome youth *Adonis*; *Persephone*; *Endymion* and *Psyche*. *Book III. Olympus*. The epic concludes with monologues by various divinities: virgin huntress *Artemis*, the semi-divine *Herakles*, goddess of love *Aphrodite*, grey-eyed *Athene*, Zeus's wife *Here*, god of poetry *Apollo* and King of Heaven *Zeus*. The work ends on a more Christian note, when the narrator understands that the Greek gods are merely parts of 'the prime Source ... in those fair forms/Which are but part of Him ... the Soul of the World'.

Essay On Mind, An (1826), by Elizabeth Barrett. 1262 lines, heroic couplets. Another derivatively Popian piece of work, as was Barrett's first publication *The Battle of Marathon*, this philosophical and abstract meditation on the nature of mind does at least mark a significant improvement over its forerunner.

Book I. Mind, says the poet, naturally wishes to investigate itself; but there are different sorts of mind. Byron ('the Mont Blanc of intellect') is contrasted with the 'soft-eyed Fancy' of Campbell. Four elements of mind are distinguished: Invention, Judgement, Memory and Association. The products of mind are in the first instance 'Philosophy', which comprises History, Science and Metaphysics. The importance of 'History' is underscored; England needs to learn from the decline of the

Roman Empire to avoid a similar fate. 'Science' is the 'search for Truth', and scientists (Archimedes, Leibnitz, Newton) are praised; but the important message is 'dwell not on parts'. Partial knowledge is dangerous, only the whole will suffice. *Book II.* The poet moves on to Metaphysics, the key to metaphysics being a correct understanding of the way language works. Words are poor means of expression, and the poet looks forward to communication after death 'where souls may see as they themselves are seen/And voiceless intercourse may pass between'. After Philosophy, the poet introduces Poetry; and various poets (Shakespeare, Milton, Byron) are discussed.

EVANS, Marian. See George ELIOT.

Excursion, The, being a Portion of the Recluse, a Poem (1814), by William Wordsworth. 8916 lines, blank verse. As its title suggests, this discursive work is a fragment from Wordsworth's grandiose, unfinished epic *The Recluse*: his other completed long poem, *The Prelude*, being a prelude to the same unfinished work. This, Wordsworth's first published long poem, was not universally praised on first appearance (a review by Jeffrey in the *Edinburgh Review* began with the sentence: 'This will not do'); and as poetry it is generally considered inferior to *The Prelude*.

Book First. The Wanderer. The narrator is walking out in the countryside on a sunny day; he comes to a ruined cottage and meets with his old pal, the Wanderer, 'a man of reverend age,/But stout and hale'. The Wanderer used to be a pedlar, and saw much of life in his youth. After making enough money peddling, he 'then resolved/To pass the remnant of his days, untasked'. Accordingly 'he lived at ease', but 'still he loved to pace the public roads'. He and the narrator rest from the sun under a shady tree, and the Wanderer tells the history of the ruined cottage. Margaret, 'a woman of a steady mind/Tender and deep in her excess of love' is abandoned by her husband. She continues to hope that he will return; indeed, this hope takes over her life, to the detriment of her children and the upkeep of the cottage. Eventually she dies, 'last human tenant of these ruined walls'. The narrator is moved by the story, but reflects 'that consolation springs/From sources deeper far than deepest pain'. *Book Second. The Solitary.* The Wanderer and the narrator move on, travelling into the mountains to meet another friend, the Solitary. This latter invites them into his humble cottage ('this is my domain/My hermitage, my cabin') and feeds them. They discuss the local funeral arrangements. *Book Third. Despondency.* The three wander among the mountains, and the Solitary tells his life story. Falling in love and marrying, he was thrown into gloom by the death of his young wife. He was roused from this by the French Revolution ('Thus was I reconverted to the world;/Society became my glittering bride') but the disintegration of the rising into the Terror disgusted and disillusioned him. He travelled to America in search of a new life, but could not rid himself of his depression. *Book Fourth. Despondency Corrected.* The Wanderer addresses each of the reasons for the Solitary's depression one by one, stressing the importance of Faith in God and belief in humanity; the narrator is very struck by this, although the Solitary remains unmoved. The three return to the Solitary's cottage for sleep. *Book Fifth. The Pastor.* Next day, the three descend into a valley and rest in a churchyard, where they debate the possibility of progress and the validity of hope. The Pastor arrives, and argues that feeling is more important than intellect. Various instances are mentioned of simple men and women who have a better sense of God and who have lived better lives than learned or sophisticated men. The Pastor is invited to elaborate with reference to the people buried in his churchyard. *Book Sixth. The Churchyard Among the Mountains.* The Pastor begins with a tale of an unrequited lover who died; and continues with a Miner who refused to give up his search for gold who also died, but not before wearing a path from his cottage to the mine known to this day as 'the PATH OF PERSEVERANCE'. By contrast is the tale of a Prodigal, who wasted his talents and opportunities. Various other examples are given. *Book Seventh. The Churchyard Among the Mountains (continued).* The Pastor tells various other tales connected with the graves in the churchyard, before the Wanderer stops proceedings ('But enough;/ – Thoughts crowd in upon me – and 'twere seemlier now to stop, and yield our gracious teacher thanks'. *Book Eighth. The Parsonage.* The Pastor invites the three men into his house; inside which are introduced the Pastor's daughter, wife and son. *Book Ninth. Discourse of the Wanderer and an Evening Visit to the Lake.* Moved by the sight of the children, the Wanderer discourses upon the '*active* Principle' that informs the Universe, and how it is particularly evident in youngsters. Everybody goes off together to the other side of the Lake to climb up Loughrigg Fell. From this eminence, the Pastor praises God ('Eternal Spirit! universal God!'). The book closes with a prose footnote in which Wordsworth expresses the hope that the effect of all this on the gloomy Solitary will some day be related.

: *F* :

Faithful for Ever, by Coventry Patmore. See *Angel in the House.*

Farmer's Boy, The: a Rural Poem (1800), by Robert Bloomfield. 1513 lines, heroic couplets. Bloomfield's pastoral poem, authenticated by his genuinely rustic background, was the hit of the 1800–01 season, and had sold 26,000 copies by 1803.

Spring. The scene is laid in Euston is Suffolk, and we are introduced to the 'meek, fatherless, and poor' farm labourer, Giles. He is described ploughing a field, and various aspects of the rural scene are mentioned: rooks, lambs at play, the activities of Mary the milkmaid and so on. The tone varies from simple and rather affecting descriptions of country matters ('the woods and groves in solemn grandeur rise,/Where the kite brooding unmolested flies') to the occasional startling narratorial interjection:

> Unrivall'd stands thy country CHEESE, O *Giles!*
> Whose very name alone engenders smiles ...
> Hence Suffolk dairy-wives run mad for cream.

Summer. Giles is described working contentedly ('Come HEALTH! come, *Jollity!*') at the tasks of Summer. A storm is described, and the harvest is brought home. *Autumn*. Hogs wander the woods. 'The poor distracted young Woman', lovely Poll, who 'ere her *twentieth* Summer could expand' had lost 'her mind's serenity' is described, although we are not given the cause for her madness. The canto closes with a fox-hunt. *Winter*. The farmer's Christmas fire, winter turnips, a sheep-killing dog, and various other wintry elements of the countryside are described. A ghost, 'grisly SPECTRE, cloth'd in silver-gray' affrights Giles, but turns out to be an Ash-Tree. The poem ends with an invocation to the 'ETERNAL POWER! from whom these blessings flow'.

Fate of Adelaide, The: A Swiss Romantic Tale (1821), by Letitia Landon ('L.E.L'). 1037 lines, blank verse.

Canto 1. Adelaide and Orlando are lovers among the romantic scenery of the Swiss Alps. But:

> Again the sound
> Of arms recall'd Orlando to the field;
> And he will go; not Adelaide's the love
> That would enchain him to her witchery –
> No; she would bid her lover from her arms,
> E'en though her heart were breaking.

The first canto dwells on the parting of the lovers, with lengthy descriptions of 'summer's mildest reign', 'fragrant sighs', 'airy notes of fairy minstrelsy' and the like. *Canto 2.* Orlando does not return, and Adelaide's soul 'held but one feeling, desolate,/The recklessness of cold and fix'd despair'. In fact, he is not dead, but rather the hero of the crusades, and betraying his faith with Adelaide he has married Zoraide ('the dark splendour' of whose 'glancing eyes' tell us 'she was the child of eastern climes'). The couple return to Italy where they are hospitably received. Chance brings Orlando back into Adelaide's presence ('her faded cheek/Wore a strange ghastly hue; her eye was dim') but she does not recognize him, and when he tries to kiss her, she dies. Orlando is stricken with grief and guilt. Zoraide senses his alienation from her, fades and dies herself; she is buried next to Adelaide. The remainder of Orlando's life is 'a fiery page,/Traced with unreal characters', until he too expires.

Festus. A Poem (1839), by P. J. Bailey (the subsequent editions of the poem added considerably to the bulk of this poem, such that by the eleventh 'Jubilee' edition in 1889 it amounted to nearly 40,000 lines of blank verse).

Inspired by Goethe's *Faust* which Bailey read as a law student (and which prompted him to pursue a career in poetry rather than in law), *Festus* enjoyed a remarkable and, to some critics, bewildering popularity. It ran through eleven official editions in Bailey's life, selling many hundred of thousands of copies; in the USA thirty unauthorized editions appeared before 1889; and there were a number of selected and abridged versions published before 1900. The different editions vary considerably (although the general shape of the poem remains the same). Summarized here is the 'seventh enlarged edition' of 1864. Its massive length makes detailed precis of its 54 scenes unmanageable, but the general drift of the poem is easily represented.

The action begins in Heaven, where the Seraphim hymn 'God! God! God!', and God and Lucifer converse. With a more obvious echo of the legend of Job than Faust, God allows Lucifer to tempt Festus, a sensitive and poetical young man ('I know him,' says God, perhaps superfluously. 'He is thine/To tempt'). Lucifer appears to Festus in the countryside, and promises him knowledge and power, an offer Festus accepts on the grounds that '[God] will not let thee harm me. He I love/ And thee I fear not'. Festus tells Lucifer of his unhappy life, most particularly of his love for Angela ('I loved her for that she was beautiful', he says, '... and that she never schooled within her breast/One thought') and her death ('She whom I once loved died./The lightning loathes its cloud – the soul its clay'). Lucifer carries Festus off to the country town to see Angela's funeral procession, and allows him to see her spirit. Here Festus meets Clara, with whom he plights a troth ('I know that thou dost love me ... Thou art my first, last, only love'). He uses his new supernatural powers to impress her, although she is not sure that they are 'innocent'. Festus prays to God to be again 'pure', but hears nothing ('it may be,' he ponders, 'Silence is the voice of God'). When Lucifer refuses to grant this wish, Festus quarrels with him. Lucifer whisks Festus around the world in an hour and then on to a Village Feast, where Festus encounters a Student, who seems impressed by the bargain Festus has struck:

> STUDENT: I should like to see the world
>   And gain such knowledge which is –
> FESTUS: Barrener
>   Than ice; possessing and producing nought
>   But means and forms of death or vanity.
>   The world is just as hollow as an eggshell.
>   It is a surface, not a solid, mind:

Lucifer then takes Festus to the centre of the earth ('Behold us in the fire-crypts of the world'), to a ruined temple ('once sacred to the sun') and a metropolis. Then he frees Festus from his body, so that his spirit can float up to a nearby, better planet, Venus ('a world where every loveliest thing/Lasts longest; where decay lifts never head/Above the grossest form'), where he meets and is blessed by the spirit of Angela. Thence to the 'immarbled madness' of the moon, and back to Earth and his body. Here, with another female friend (Helen) Festus makes merry for a while, but is saddened by his memories of Angela. He also neglects Clara, who has renamed herself Marian, and who accordingly takes her leave of Festus. Lucifer takes Festus on another disembodied trip, this time to Heaven (where Lucifer introduces him to God, although Festus can only see the supreme being as 'dazzling darkness') and, on the return trip, to various intervening worlds. Back on Earth again, Festus expounds at length to Helen and the Student on the other spheres he has visited, his visions, and the 'Poem of my Life'. After an interlude with another woman, Elissa, Festus renews his travels through the cosmos (observing that, 'Space, though void of things, feels full of God') and addresses the stars ('What are ye, orbs?/The words of God –

the scripture of the skies?'). He tells Lucifer of an apocalyptic dream he
had of 'general doom', in which he saw the myriad souls of men
'cursing' as 'to hell/They hied like storms'. Lucifer confirms that 'the
world/Is full of me as ocean is of brine' and shows Festus around Hell.
Here the Son of God appears, and reveals that in fact it is Hell that is
doomed to destruction, at which Festus rejoices ('Be it soon!'). Back on
earth, Festus, evidently feeling amorous, tries to push his love for Elissa
into impropriety ('Now, Festus!' she admonishes him, 'this is wrong')
but is saved by the intrusion of Lucifer. He has a vision of the passage
of Angela's soul moving from higher to higher spheres. Elissa dies, and
Festus reflects on his life so far. He is reconciled with Clara, who has (it
turns out) never stopped loving him. It transpires that he has seen his
name among a roll of the elect: 'I have beheld my name writ on the
book/Of life eterne'. Safe in this knowledge, he accepts Lucifer's temp-
tation of 'a throne at which earth's puny potentates/May sue for
slavedoms – and be satisfied', even though he knows that this enthrone-
ment will coincide with the end of the world. He is crowned at a huge
gathering of kings and people, conceding that it is 'enough/That I am
monarch of the world', urging them to 'all acknowledge loyally my
laws ... It will be best/No rise against me can stand. I rule of God:/And
am God's sceptre here'. The kings resist ('Tyrant, we love thee not'), but
the issue seems academic, since this is the end of the world. Lucifer
points out to Festus 'the death groan of the sons of men – Thy subjects
– King!'. The entire earth dissolves, and Festus himself dies, expressing
his faith in God.

> Open thine arms, O death! thou fine of woe
> And warranty of bliss! I feel the last
> Red mountainous remnant of the earth give way.
> The stars are rushing upwards to the light;
> My limbs are light, and liberty is mine.
> My spirit's infinite purity consumes
> The sullied soul. Eternal destiny
> Opens its bright abyss. I am God's!

God and the angels celebrate the end of the 'age of matter'. At the
conclusion of the millenium Festus awakes again. On the day of judgement, the Son of God appears and announces 'The Book of Life is
opened. Heaven begins'. The final scene is set in 'The Heaven of Heav-
ens', where the Recording angel announces that 'all men are judged save
one', and The Son of God replies 'he too is saved'. Festus is accordingly
grateful ('Could I, Lord! pour my soul out,/In thanks, even as a river
rolling ever,/It would be too scant for what I owe to Thee'). Lucifer is
banished from Heaven (says God: 'Evil! away for aye!'), and as he goes
he asks Festus for forgiveness ('forgive me that I tempted thee'). This is

enough for God to rescind his judgement, and Lucifer, also grateful ('the humblest I of all/The beings thou hast made, Eternal Lord') is permitted to stay in Heaven. The poem ends with an elaborate hymn to God.

Fifine at the Fair (1872), by Robert Browning. 2463 lines, iambic hexameter, rhymed couplets. A lengthy, complex and often baffling dramatic monologue wherein a narrator (identified with the mythic philanderer Don Juan), in conversation with his wife Elvire, constructs a defence of his adulterous desire for a gypsy girl, Fifine, encountered at the Pornic Fair that morning. This work, long neglected on the grounds of its stylistic and formal 'obscurity', has recently been resurrected by Browning scholars and studied as one of his most rewarding and sophisticated texts.

The narrator is a contemporary French version of the eternal philanderer, Don Juan. He invites his wife Elvire to walk with him through the annual Fair of the northern French town of Pornic. He is particularly struck by the gypsy good-looks of one of the rope-dancers, Fifine: ('complete the creature trips/Our way now, brings sunshine upon her spangled hips,/As here she fronts us full, with pose half-frank, half-fierce'). As they walk on, Don Juan defends his attraction towards Fifine by articulating his sense of the polarity of womankind: some women are pure and ethereally beautiful (such as his wife); some are darkly sensual (like Fifine). Both, it seems, are 'necessary' for man. Coming across an old druidic monument, he is moved to contemplate pagan nature-worship, and the fluidity of the Vital Force it deified:

> 'All's change, but permanence as well.'
> Grave note whence – list aloft! – harmonics sound, that mean
> 'Truth inside, and outside, truth also'; and between
> Each, falsehood is that change, as truth is permanence.
> The individual soul works through the shows of sense,
> (Which ever proving false, still promise to be true)
> Up to an outer soul as individual too;
> And, through the fleeting, lives to die into the fixed,
> And reach at length 'God, man, or both together mixed.'

(This last is a quotation from Aeschylus.) Don Juan draws his argument to a close by suggesting that, after all, inconstancy cannot be justified, since it is a function of immaturity ('Inconstancy means raw, 'tis faith alone means ripe'), and he promises that in future he will remain faithful to Elvire. But, at the poem's close, he creeps away to return to the Fair for an assignation with Fifine (he had put some gold coins into her tambourine at the fair by way of advance payment), and returning much later he finds his wife has finally left him (or so we infer from the epilogue).

Firmillian, or The Student of Badajoz: a Spasmodic Tragedy (1854), by 'T. Percy Jones' [W. E. Aytoun]. 2147 lines, mostly blank-verse. Aytoun originally wrote a cod-review for *Blackwood's Magazine* in 1851, in which he quoted at length from the absurd poetry of poetic-drama called *Firmillian* by the imaginary poet Jones. He was moved to do this, as a parodist, by the great popularity of a certain sort of poetic production, exemplified by *Bailey's *Festus*, *Smith's *Life Drama* and *Dobell's *Balder*. Aytoun's ridicule of this poetic school as 'spasmodic' was devastating, and he capitalized on the success of his review by actually writing the original text. But what began as parody of a (now largely forgotten) poetic style grew into something much greater, a Pythonesque articulation of the absurdity of life and art. *Firmillian*, witty, hilarious, trenchant and in its way profound, may be one of the most neglected long poems of the Victorian period.

Scenes I–III. Firmillian, a student, is writing a poem that designs 'to paint the mental spasms that tortured Cain'. But, he realizes, he has done this 'feebly', because 'what we write/Must be the reflex of what we know' and he has never murdered anybody. He resolves to correct this state of affairs, by killing three of his drinking companions. *Scenes IV–VI.* Firmillian has killed his friends, but he feels no remorse. Uncertain as to whether remorse is 'a mere invention, as the Harpies were' or whether he has 'mista'en the ready way to track her down' he resolves on further crime. He overhears a hotheaded Graduate (a character modelled on John Ruskin) in conversation with a Priest; the Graduate declares he would like to blow up the churches of the city (the 'marble garments of the ancient Gods'). Firmillian can use him as a scapegoat; he plants dynamite in the Cathedral of St Nicholas, and the sixth scene ends with the stage-direction: [*The Cathedral is blown up*]. *Scenes VII–IX.* Firmillian is pleased with the explosion ('Twas a grand spectacle! The solid earth/Seemed from its quaking entrails to erupt/The gathered lava of a thousand years'), but still feels no remorse. Deciding that he has 'been too coarse and general in his business' he decides to murder someone closer to home, his best friend Haverillo. He lures him up to the top of a tower, the Pillar of St Simeon Stylites, and pushes him off. *Scene X.* Apollodorus, a critic, is standing beneath the Pillar. He exhorts the god Apollo:

> I do beseech thee! send a poet down!
> Let him descend, e'en as a meteor falls,
> Rushing at noonday –
>   [*He is crushed by the body of HAVERILLO*]

Scenes XI–XV. Firmillian wanders the mountains, and decides that he does not want to write a poem on the subject of 'Cain' after all. Instead he will pursue 'love, love, love!' To this end he assembles his three girlfriends (two white, one black) for a *menage-à-quatre*; but all three women walk out in disgust. Finally, Firmillian runs from justice across a barren moor; a chorus of Ignes Fatui lead him on through the darkness until he falls to his death in a quarry.

First Book of Urizen, The (1794), by William Blake. 517 lines, short unrhymed lines of various stress. An early, short version of the mythological material Blake was to elaborate at greater length in *Vala, *Milton and *Jerusalem. For the personal mythology of which this work is an expression, see the headnote to Blake's life.

The poem concerns two of the four eternal principles, which are aspects of each individual but also quasi-gods in their own right. Urizen (the controlling will) separates himself from the other eternals, and then tries to seize control through his laws; but by entering the realm of time he has made himself susceptible to death. Los (imaginative energy) is horrified at Urizen's chaotic form, and comes down to watch over him:

> And Los round the dark globe of Urizen
> Kept watch for the Eternals, to confine
> The obscure separation alone;
> For Eternity stood wide apart,
> As the stars are apart from the earth.

Urizen's single manifestation breaks into a male and a female, Los and Enitharmon; their offspring is Orc, who completes the fall. Waking from his sleep, Urizen explores his new world of restrictions, laws and tyranny, and encounters much misery; but the physical distress of hunger and cold is as nothing compared to the 'the Net of Religion' – 'so twisted the cords, and so knotted/The meshes, twisted like to the human brain'. Some of the children of this world follow Fire (Fuzon), which they take to be a god, and leave the world they know (Egypt). This is where the poem ends; it is likely Blake intended to continue it, although no continuation exists.

Forest Sanctuary, The (1826), by Felicia Hemans. 1537 lines, 9–line stanzas. Mrs Hemans's favourite among her own works, this poem constitutes a sort of lengthy proto-'dramatic monologue'.

The narrator describes both his inward mental anguish and his external adventures, having fled from sixteenth-century Spain to escape religious persecution, and come for refuge to the wilderness of the North American forests. *Part One.* The poem begins voicing the narrator's homesickness for Spain ('Yet art thou lovely! – Song is on thy hills –/O Sweet and mournful melodies of Spain'), and promising his young son (whom he has brought with him) a better life than the persecution he himself endured. He recalls the day in Spain when he witnessed a parade of heretics and realized that some of his dearest friends were being marched along ('my Alvar! – making/The might of truth; and be thy memory cherished ... sweet Inez!'). He watches them burnt at the stake, and afterwards, 'amidst the stillness rose my spirit's cry,/Amidst the dead ... Saviour! ... Give light!' *Part Two*. The narrator is then imprisoned for his newfound beliefs, and tortured (he declares 'shall not Truth's high name/Bear up her martyrs with all-conquering sway?') until he is eventually released. He returned to his father's home ('I had brought sorrow on his grey hairs down') and collected his wife and son. Together they fled 'o'er the blue deep' to America; but Leonora (his wife) sickens and dies on the voyage, and the narrator and his boy are left alone to strike out into the wilderness.

Four Zoas, The, by William Blake. See *Vala, or the Four Zoas*.

FRERE, John Hookham (1769–1846). More a politician than a poet, Frere is remembered today as the author of *Whistlecraft, which in turn was a major influence behind Byron's *Beppo and *Don Juan. The son of a wealthy London merchant, Frere attended Eton and Caius, Cambridge. A friend of Canning from his youth, he entered parliament as the member for West Loue in Cornwall (a rotten borough) in 1796. His political career (during, of course, the Napoleonic wars) included undersecretary of state in the foreign office, and a number of prestigious diplomatic appointments to Lisbon, Madrid and Berlin. He wrote a number of parodies and imitations, many of which were published in the *Anti-Jacobin*. He married in 1816, and published the first two cantos of *Whistlecraft in 1817 (the final two appeared in 1818). But his wife's health was not good and the couple retired to Malta for that reason, where they spent the rest of their life together. From Malta Frere learned Hebrew and Maltese, and translated a great deal, including some highly regarded versions of Aristophanes' plays.

Fudge Family in Paris, The (1818) by Thomas Moore. 1815 lines, various metres. A satirical and amusing verse-novel in which (Moore later claimed) 'of various forms of cockneyism and nonsense I endeavoured, in the personages of the Fudge Family, to collect the concentrated essence'. In twelve letters, and selections from personal journals, the preposterous Fudge Family describe their experiences of the Paris of 1817, shortly after the restoration of the Bourbon dynasty. The self-serving Mr Fudge writes anapests to Castlereigh ('At length, my Lord, I have the bliss/To date to you a line from this/ "Demoraliz'd" metropolis'). His daughter Biddy Fudge writes mindless letters to a friend in Ireland, mostly about French fashions; his son, Bob Fudge, reveals a veritable obsession with food. The closest the work comes to seriousness is expressed in the revolutionary letters of young Roman Catholic Phelim Connor, a third-cousin of the Fudges ('For charity made private tutor to Bob').

Moore was inspired by Christopher Anstey's *New Bath Guide* (1766), which also comprises a series of verse-letters relating various burlesque adventures. He later published a sequel, *The Fudges in England.

Fudges in England, The: being a Sequel to 'The Fudge Family in Paris' (1835), by Thomas Moore. 1388 lines, various metres. Mr Fudge is dead, Bob Fudge grown tremendously fat, and Biddy Fudge (who in the previous volume was seen 'in full blaze of bonnets, and ribands, and airs – /Such a thing as no rainbow hath colours to paint') is now reduced 'to wrinkles and prayers'. The plot has four chief actors: Biddy Fudge, her beautiful young niece Fanny Fudge, the handsome young Patrick Magan, and O'Mulligan, an unscrupulous Irish priest turned evangelical Protestant (for temporizing reasons), the chief butt of Moore's satire. Biddy Fudge is drawn to Patrick, but he has fallen in love with Fanny (despite her prolific production of dreadful poetry, in the 'Keepsake' style of the 1830s), and Biddy ends up marrying the fortune-hunting Mulligan. Patrick and Fanny elope together, fully expecting to live a penniless life, but in a final twist Bob dies and leaves all the Fudge property to Fanny, bypassing Biddy and thwarting O'Mulligan's desires.

: G :

Gebir (1798), by Walter Savage Landor. 1881 lines, blank verse. Faced with charges of obscurity by reviewers, Landor took the unusual (and possibly unique) step of translating his own epic into Latin (*Gebirus* was published in 1803) to elucidate matters.

Book 1. Gebir, King of the Gadites, has invaded Egypt. Charoba, the Egyptian Queen, is anxious ('What should the damsel do? should royal knees/Bend supplicant? Or defenceless hands engage/Men of gigantic force, gigantic arms?'). Dalica, Charoba's nurse, advises her to dissemble ('Rather than fly him, stoop thou to allure'). When Charoba meets Gebir she actually falls in love with him, although Dalica assumes it is all show, and plots the vengeance on the conqueror she (wrongly) thinks her mistress desires. Meanwhile Gebir's brother, Tamar, has met and fallen in love with a sea-nymph. *Book 2.* Gebir has decided to settle in Egypt and has begun rebuilding the ancient city of Sidad. His men work all day, but every night the work is mysteriously demolished. Gebir disguises himself as his brother Tamar and wrestles with the sea-nymph, defeating her. He reveals himself, and the nymph (who loves Tamar) is shocked. He asks her the reason why his architectural plans have been failing, and she replies that 'this land of Egypt is a land/Of incantation; demons rule these waves;/These are against thee'. If Gebir undertakes some propitiatory sacrifices, the demons will let him build. The ground suddenly opens, and Gebir and the nymph descend into the underworld. *Book 3.* In the underworld Gebir meets an ancestor, Aroar, who reveals various spirits in agony (mostly Kings, including thinly veiled portraits of British monarchs such as George III). *Book 4.* The Queen's nurse, Dalica, suggests a festival to celebrate the arrival of Gebir's people. Charoba, unaware of Dalica's bad intentions, agrees. *Book 5.* Dalica visits her evil sister, Myrthyr, in the city of Masar, and obtains from her a magical shirt that has been dipped three times in deadly poison ('twas a dark purple; and its dye was dread'). *Book 6.* Tamar and the sea-nymph marry. She tells him that Gebir is doomed, and then carries him away over the Mediterranean. At Corsica she prophesies the rise of Napoleon Bonaparte, one of Tamar's descendants ('From Tamar shall arise, 'tis Fate's decree,/A mortal man above all mortal praise'). Tamar is taken to within sight of Spain, and told that 'his countrymen will have justice, and Egypt enjoy liberty and equality'. Then the two of them fly off to Rhine to enjoy private connubial bliss. *Book 7.* The day of festivities dawns to cheering crowds as the newlyweds mount joint-thrones. Dalica appears with the deadly shirt, and 'round his shoulders drew the garb accurst'. The blood 'mantles in his manly cheeks', and Gebir staggers from the throne, makes a final speech, and dies.

Geraint and Enid (1886), by Alfred Tennyson. See *Idylls of the King*.

Gertrude of Wyoming (1809), by Thomas Campbell. 838 lines, Spenserian stanzas. Based on a historical event ('the desolation of Wyoming, in Pennsylvania, which took place in 1778, by an incursion of Indians', as Campbell's introductory note has it), this was the poet's most popular work.

Part 1. Albert, having emigrated to Susquehana, from Scotland ('green Albyn!') is the patriarch of a Pennsylvanian community. One summer an Oneyda warrior, Outlassi, brings him a small boy, the only survivor of a massacre by Huron Indians. Albert recognizes the child as the grandson of an old friend, and determines to rear him as the happy playmate of his own daughter, the beautiful Gertrude. *Part 2.* Henry reaches young manhood and goes off to travel in Europe, where he spends eight or nine years in search of improvement. Meanwhile, Gertrude grows into a beautiful woman. One day, while reading Shakespeare in 'a deep untrodden grot,/Where oft the reading hours sweet Gertrude wore', she meets a handsome stranger, who turns out to be Henry Waldegrave. He vows never to leave again; the two declare their love. *Part 3.* It is now the time of the American War of Independence ('the year, by proud oppression driven,/When Transatlantic Liberty arose,/Not in the sunshine, and the smile of heaven,/But wrapt in whirlwinds'). Gertrude and Henry have married, and Henry has determined to fight for 'the cause of freedom's holy band'. Outlassi, the Huron warrior, arrives, and reports that his tribe has been destroyed by Mohawks, led by the half-Native half-German figure of Brandt ('the monster Brandt,–/ With all his howling desolate band'). Brandt attacks again and there is a battle, in which both Gertrude and her father perish. Henry and Outlassi sing a dirge over the corpses.

Goblin Market (1862), by Christina Rossetti. 567 lines, short irregularly rhymed verses. Rossetti's sing-song fairy tale has been subject to a great many critical and allegorical interpretations, often concentrating on the erotic suggestiveness of the vivid verse. Rossetti herself always said that 'she did not mean anything profound by this fairy tale'.

Lizzie and Laura, two sisters, live in a cottage by themselves. From time to time they hear the call of the goblin merchants: 'Come buy our orchard fruits/Come buy, come buy'). Lizzie is sensible, and advises the more skittish Laura not to listen to them, but Laura is tempted by the luscious fruits. She creeps out and meets the Goblins, and because she has no money buys their fruit with a 'golden curl' of her hair. She experiences an intense delight on tasting the fruit: 'She never tasted such before/How should it cloy with length of use?/She sucked and sucked and sucked the more'. Returning home, she hopes to eat again the following night, but she can no longer hear the goblin-men's cry 'with its iterated jingle/Of sugar baited words'. She sickens, and fades away until on the point of death. Lizzie puts a silver penny in her purse and goes out to meet the goblin men.

> Laughed every goblin
> When they spied her peeping:
> Came towards her hobbling,
> Flying, running, leaping,
> Puffing and blowing,
> Chucking, clapping, crowing
> Clucking and gobbling,
> Mopping and mowing,
> Full of airs and graces,
> Pulling wry faces,
> Demure grimaces.

Lizzie gives them her penny, but they will not let her carry any of the magical fruit away; when she refuses to eat there and then they become violent, 'elbowed and jostled her/Clawed with their nails'. They squeeze the fruits over her face in an attempt to make her taste some, but Lizzie is firm. Eventually they give up, and Lizzie runs home to her sister with the fruit still smeared over her: 'Laura ... hug me, kiss me, suck my juices ... eat me, drink me, love me'. Laura, tasting the fruit a second time, recovers. They live on, happier and wiser: 'for there is no friend like a sister'.

: *H* :

HEMANS, Mrs Felicia Dorothea, *née* Browne (1793–1835). Remembered today, if at all, as the author of two lines of poetry ('The boy stood on the burning deck/Whence all but he had fled', from 'Casabianca', 1829), Felicia Hemans was a prolific and wide-ranging poet of considerable contemporary reputation. Many of her readers saw her as a sort of female – and virtuous – Byron (whom she often outsold).

She was born in Liverpool, her father a merchant and her mother of Italian descent. Financial difficulties marked her childhood, forcing the family to move from Liverpool to the Welsh village of Abergele, Denbighshire. Her precocity (much remarked upon by her contemporaries) was marked by a poem written on the occasion of her mother's birthday when she was eight years old:

> Clad in all their brightest green,
> This day the verdant fields are seen;
> The tuneful birds begin their lay,
> To celebrate thy natal day.

Even so early a lyric demonstrates both the strengths and weaknesses of Hemans's versifying – an imitative skill that veered sometimes towards feeble pastiche.

Welsh scenery and folklore formed a lasting passion and subject for her poetry. Another – Spain – derived from a fascination with the Peninsular war that was raging in 1809 when Browne met her future husband, Captain Hemans of the 4th Regiment. They married in 1812 and went to live in Daventry, Northamptonshire, where Felicia gave birth to the first of her five sons.

Her first collection (*The Domestic Affections, and Other Poems*) appeared in 1812, and the theme of happy domesticity was to recur again and again in her work. Ironically, an increasing literary reputation based chiefly on this theme ran parallel with the deteriorating domestic circumstances of the poet herself. On the literary side we see success: from 1816 a volume of her verse appeared virtually every year until her death in 1835 (and afterwards if we include *Poetical Remains*, 1836, and *Early Blossoms* in 1840). But the private side of the equation was sliding further and further into misery.

1816 saw *The Restoration of the Works of Art to Italy, A Poem.* *Modern Greece*, which brought comparisons with Byron, came out in 1817; *Translations from Camoens and other Poets* (1818) was highly thought of in its day. Her 'Ode: On the Death of the Princess Charlotte' from the same year was one of several royal and patriotic pieces. In 1818 Captain Hemans left her, ostensibly to travel to Southern Europe for medical reasons, in fact never to return. Hemans was left to bring up five sons single-handedly, and she relied heavily on her writing to provide her with income to this end. *Tales and Historic Scenes* came out in 1819 (including *The Abencerrage*), and in 1821 *Dartmoor, A Poem* won a prize from the Royal Society of Literature. *Welsh Melodies* appeared in 1822, and 1823 saw the (unsuccessful) staging of her first play, *The Vespers of Palermo*, at Covent Garden (the play was successfully revived at Edinburgh later in the year). *The Forest Sanctuary, and Other Poems* first appeared in 1826; and a second edition of this volume, including 'Casabianca', came out in 1829. 'The Forest Sanctuary' remained Hemans's own favourite among her works.

Hemans made many literary friends, among them Wordsworth (whom she particularly admired), Scott, Joanna Baillie and Dean Milman; she enjoyed a huge popularity in England, and an even bigger one in America (a Boston publisher tried to entice her over the Atlantic with the offer of a periodical to edit). The *Edinburgh Review* adjudged her work 'infinitely sweet, elegant, and tender ... informed with a purity and loftiness of feeling'. Byron, on the other hand, wrote to his publisher from Ravenna on August 12, 1820, instructing him to send 'no *more modern* poesy – I pray – neither Mrs Hewoman's – nor any female or male Tadpole of Poet Turdsworth'. Byron thought Hemans's writing a 'false stilted trashy style, which is a mixture of all the styles of the day – which are all *bombastic*'. Hemans, it might be added, was equally disappointed with Byron, especially after reading Moore's *Life of Lord Byron* in 1829: 'alas! the best part of that fearfully mingled character is but ruin – the wreck of *what might have been*'.

After the death of her much-loved mother, Hemans lived mostly in Dublin, and continued her prodigious poetic output. Religious poems featured more prominently in her later work (for instance, the devotional collection *Scenes and Hymns of Life* and *Hymns for Childhood*, both 1834). Her health, never strong, suffered a series of blows in 1834: scarlet fever gave way to a cold, which was in turn succeeded by 'ague, a hectic fever and symptoms of dropsy'. She died on 16 May 1835 at the age of forty-one, and was buried in St Anne's Church, Dublin. Wordsworth mentions her death in his 'Extempore Effusion upon the Death of James Hogg'.

The bulk of Felicia Hemans's output consisted of short lyrics, odes and sonnets but her longer narrative poems, never exceeding 1600 lines in length, are of considerable competence and interest. She has been little studied in recent years, but there are signs of a revival in interest.

Human Life: a Poem (1819), by Samuel Rogers. 1622 lines, heroic couplets. A contemplative poem, expressing many commonplaces ('Such is Human Life! ... It glimmers like a meteor and is gone!', 'Man is born to suffer' and so forth). Rogers begins by considering each of the four stages of a man's life: birth, coming of age, marriage and death. He then goes on to trace the life of a representative (and genteel) Everyman, from his nativity onwards:

> The child is born, by many a pang endear'd.
> And now the mother's ear has caught his cry;
> Oh grant the cherub to her asking eye!
> He comes! – she clasps him. To her bosom press'd,
> He drinks the balm of life, and drops to rest.

He grows up, marries, becomes a father, goes off to fight for his country, returns a hero, enters politics, is accused of treason against the State ('Alone before his judges in array' he 'stands for his life') is acquitted, and returns to his idyllic hearth, grows old and finally dies.

Human Tragedy, The (1862, much revised and expanded 1876), by Alfred Austin. 7240 lines, ottava rima. Austin declared his rationale for this poem in a preface added to the third edition of 1889 – namely, his belief that human life is tragic, and 'the tragedy is due, not to man's vices, but to his virtues'. According to Austin, 'Sexual Love, Religious Sentiment, Patriotism, and Humanity' necessarily lead human lives towards their doom. He maintained that this belief was not Pessimism ('Pessimism is a false and unworthy doctrine'), and that though 'a tragedy Life is, and a tragedy it must ever remain' nevertheless 'it is a noble tragedy; ennobled by action, struggle, conflict ... and ever and anon illuminated by joy, exultation, and happy pathos'.

Act 1. The scene is England, the time June–November 1857. Noble Godfrid meets the innocent and beautiful Olive at her father's country estate. The two fall in love, although Godfrid convinces himself that his feelings are 'but a fancy'. Prompted by honour, Godfrid leaves; and Olive, on the rebound, marries the decent but boneheaded Gilbert. *Act 2.* It is March 1858, and Godfrid has exiled himself to Spiaggiascura on the Italian coast, nursing what he now recognizes as a broken heart. He befriends the saint-like Olympia, and she exhorts him to travel with her to Milan to meet a certain holy man, that she might 'win [him] back, lost sheep, to Christ's dear fold'. The trip is unsuccessful, Olympia (nursing her own tender passion) leaves to become a nun, and Godfrid retires to Florence. By May 1859, with Napoleon III's invasion of Piedmont, Godfrid is ready to enlist as a soldier in the cause of Italian freedom when he bumps into Olive, who begs him to come with her.

Gilbert is ill with a fever, and Godfrid goes to help nurse him. He returns to health, and secretly realizes that there is an unconsummated passion between his wife and Godfrid. But then, Olive falls sick and swiftly dies. At Olive's funeral, Godfrid announces "'This is no time for tears./Farewell ... At last, at last, a godlike Cause is found".' Gilbert agrees to go with him ('"Now wherefore should I stay?"'). *Act 3.* It is eight years later, and Godfrid and Gilbert are fast friends and heroes of the Italian cause. Gilbert, apparently recovered from the death of his wife, is in love with Miriam, a beautiful Italian orphan; and she, in turn, promises to marry him as soon as Rome is liberated. In the subsequent battles Gilbert is badly wounded. Miriam drags his dying body to a church to marry him ('The trembling friar took up the clammy hand,/Whose pulse beat faint, and laid it within hers'). Godfrid has also been severely injured, and he is nursed back to health by Olympia, now a nun. *Act 4.* It is 1871; Rome has been freed. Gilbert, it turns out, is not dead – he has been nursed back to health by a devoted Miriam ('Dragged from the clutches of tenacious death/By Miriam's love'). Gilbert, Godfrid, Olympia and Miriam all, by various routes, end up in Paris during the siege by the Prussians. With an act of heroism, Godfrid and Olympia sacrifice themselves (killed simultaneously, it seems, by French and Prussian forces), while allowing Gilbert and Miriam to escape:

> And Godfrid had but time, – at last! – to fling
> His arms around the form he had loved so well,
> Thinking to save, and she to him to cling,
> When, 'twixt the madness of the twain they fell
> He pierced by ball that fought for faith of old,
> She by the shaft who 'gainst all faith rebel;

The Mother Superior of Olympia's order allows the two bodies to be buried together, and 'Gilbert and Miriam live, and strive to cope/With grief in tutoring a baby mind,/Named after Godfrid'.

Hyperion: A Fragment (1820), by John Keats. 884 lines, blank verse. Keats worked on his unfinished epic project between September and December 1818, but abandoned it in April 1819. It was published, as a fragment, in *Lamia, Isabella, the Eve of St Agnes and Other Poems* in 1820.

Book I. The Titans, the elder gods of Greek mythology, have been defeated by the newer race of gods called the Olympians. The poem begins among the Titans, in the gloom of their fallen state 'deep in the shady sadness of a vale'. Saturn, brother of Hyperion, and leader with him of the Titans, consoles himself with his wife (and, as it happens, sister) Thea. Thea encourages him to meet with the other fallen Titans. Meanwhile, Hyperion remains, as yet not overthrown, in his splendid palace in the sky, 'bastioned with pyramids of glowing gold,/And touched with shade of bronzed obelisks'. But he is worried: 'Saturn is fallen, am I too to fall?' He hears the voice of his father Coelus, urging him 'to the earth!/For there thou wilt find Saturn and his woes'. *Book II*. Saturn addresses the other fallen Titans: 'Tell me, all ye brethren gods,/How we can war?' Oceanus replies that they shouldn't, because their fall was an inevitable part of universal progress ('We fall by course of nature's law'); but others think that Hyperion can provide them with a hope for overthrowing the Olympians: 'Hyperion,/Our brightest brother, still is undisgraced'. Hyperion appears among them. *Book III*. The scene shifts to Delos, where Apollo 'wandered forth/Beside the osiers of a rivulet'. An 'awful goddess' (Mnemosyne) approaches, and the poem breaks off with Apollo being transformed by her into something extraordinary:

> Soon wild commotions shook him, and made flush
> All the immortal fairness of his limbs,
> Most like the struggle at the gate of death....
>   At length
> Apollo shrieked – and lo! from all his limbs
> Celestial ...

Between July and September 1819 Keats tried reworking this unfinished poem, starting over again and producing one and a half cantos of *The Fall of Hyperion: A Dream* (eventually published in 1857); but this too was unfinished.

Idylls of the King (various publishing dates, 1842–91), by Alfred Tennyson. 10,289 lines, 12 books, blank verse. Tennyson's Arthurian epic has a complex publishing history, in that it was not composed in one go, but accumulated over half a century. Tennyson wrote a 272–line blank-verse 'Morte D'Arthur' in 1833, partly as a result of the death of Arthur Hallam, and this was published in 1842 with a framing poem called 'The Epic', in which an unnamed poet admits that he had 'burnt/ His epic, his King Arthur, some twelve books' because 'nothing new was said in it'. Tennyson had written some other short Arthurian poetry ('The Lady of the Lake' 1832, 'Sir Lancelot and Queen Guinevere: A Fragment' 1842), but he did not follow up his mooted plan for an Arthurian epic at that time. In 1859 he published a volume called *Idylls of the King*, which contained four poems, *Enid*, *Vivien*, *Elaine* and *Guinevere*. In 1862 this volume was reissued, with a verse-dedication in memory of the Prince Consort (who had died December 1861). In 1869 *The Holy Grail and Other Poems* appeared, and in 1872 *Gareth and Lynette and Other Poems*. The Imperial Library Edition of Tennyson's Complete Poetry also appeared in 1872, and it brought together all the *Idylls* written by that date (with the addition of a new Epilogue, *To the Queen*); the old 'Morte D'Arthur' of 1842 (augmented at beginning and end), appeared as *The Passing of Arthur*. The only remaining section of the poem to appear was *Balin and Balan*, written in 1874 but not published until 1885. The sequence as we now have it was first published in 1891.

1. *The Coming of Arthur* (1869). Leodogran, one of the petty kings of strife-torn England, is suffering under the attacks of a 'heathen horde,/Reddening the sun with smoke and earth with blood'. He hears tell of 'Arthur newly crowned' and asks for his aid. The young king comes, and immediately falls in love with Leodogran's daughter, Guinevere. Arthur defeats the horde, and asks for Guinevere's hand in marriage, but Leodogran is unwilling to marry his daughter to any except a king. Arthur's origins are in doubt, but 'Lot's wife, the Queen of Orkney, Bellicent' confirms that Arthur is indeed Uther's son, and explains the role of Merlin and the Lady of the Lake. Leodogran is satisfied, and Arthur and Guinevere are wed. Arthur announces that he will no longer pay tribute to Rome ('Seeing that ye be grown too weak and old/To drive the heathen from your Roman wall'), and in 'twelve

great battles' he unifies the kingdom. Tennyson's main source was Malory's *Morte Darthur*.

2. *Gareth and Lynette*. Gareth, a young prince (son of King Lot of Orkney) yearns to become a knight at Arthur's new Court. Despite his mother's objection he travels to Camelot, where he works in the kitchens for a year. Lynette, a lady of noble blood, comes to Camelot to ask for aid: her sister, Lyonors, is besieged in her castle (Castle Perilous) by four evil knights. Gareth begs for the honour of rescuing the maiden, and Arthur grants it. Lynette (who had wanted a proper knight) does not hide her disgust: 'Dish-washer and broach-turner, loon! - to me/ Thou smellest all of kitchen'. Gareth overcomes various obstacles on their journey together, eventually defeating three of the knights (the knights of the 'Morning-Star', 'Noon-Sun' and 'Evening-Star') before finally taking on the fourth, the 'Death-knight'. But inside the fearsome, skeletal armour of this last is nothing but a boy, the younger brother of the other three knights ('Fair Sir,' he whines, 'they bad me do it'), and he is easily defeated. The ending of the Idyll leaves it uncertain as to whether Gareth marries Lynette, or Lyonors. Tennyson's main source was Malory.

3. *The Marriage of Geraint*. Sir Geraint has married Enid (the 'e' is pronounced short, as '*Ennid*'). The bulk of the Idyll describes the meeting of the two of them – how Geraint, on a quest to avenge an insult that a strange knight had perpetrated in Guinevere's presence, received hospitality with the dilapidated Earl Yniol ('Once rich, now poor, but ever open-doored'). The insulting knight (known as 'the sparrow-hawk') turns out to be Yniol's wicked nephew, and Geraint defeats him and wins the hand of Yniol's daughter, Enid.

4. *Geraint and Enid*. Geraint moves away from the court at Camelot, uncertain as to the virtue of Guinevere. He misunderstands a remark of his wife's, and believes her also to have been faithless. He insists that she put on a ragged dress and follow him round the countryside as he undertakes various adventures, forbidding her to speak to him. She remains devoted to him, even when she thinks him slain by the evil Earl Doorm, and as a result they are eventually reconciled. The sources for these two Idylls (originally published as one) were *The Mabinogion* (which had been translated by Lady Charlotte Guest, 1838–49) and the *Erec* of Chretian de Troyes.

5. *Balin and Balan*. Balin and Balan are brothers, the first hot-tempered, though fiercely loyal, particularly to Queen Guinevere. Balan goes on a quest to destroy a terrible wood-demon, but before he goes he warns Balin to curb his temper ('Let not thy moods prevail, when I am gone'). Balin asks permission to have Guinevere's symbol on his shield, but one day in the garden he overhears Lancelot and Guinevere

together. Distraught he leaves Camelot, 'nor stayed to crave permission of the King/But, mad for strange adventure, dashed away'. He meets Sir Garlon, who mocks the tokens of Balin's devotion to Guinevere ('hast thou eyes, or if, are these/So far besotted that they fail to see/This fair-wife worship cloaks a secret shame?'), and Balin kills him. He has to flee the vengeful posse of Garlon's father, and takes refuge in a forest. There, Vivien meets him, and she maliciously invents a story apparently proving Guinevere's adultery. 'She lied with ease; but horror-stricken he,/ Remembering that dark bower at Camelot,/Breathed in a dismal whisper "It is true".' He destroys the tokens of his devotion to the Queen with 'a weird yell,/Unearthlier than all shriek of bird or beast', and Balan (thinking 'The scream of that Wood-devil I came to quell!') rides in. The two brothers fail to recognize one another, fight and are both killed. Tennyson took some details from Malory for this Idyll, but also claimed that 'the story of the poem is largely original'.

6. *Merlin and Vivien*. Tennyson's Vivien seems motivated for her evil by revenge ('My father died in battle against the King,/My mother on his corpse in open field; She bore me there, for born from death I was'.) She comes to Camelot, and begs protection from Guinevere as an orphan. This granted she tries to subvert the working of the court. An attempt to seduce Arthur backfires ('It made the laughter of an afternoon/That Vivien should attempt the blameless King') and Vivien instead focuses on Merlin.

> Then fell on Merlin a great melancholy;
> He walked with dreams and darkness, and he found
> A doom that ever poised itself to fall,
> An ever-moaning battle in the mist,
> World-war of dying flesh against the life,
> Death in all life and lying in all love,
> The meanest having power upon the highest
> And the high purpose broken by the worm.

Merlin leaves Camelot and crosses the Channel to Broceliande, with Vivien following him. There she uses her feminine wiles upon him, eventually learns from him a magic charm, and uses it to imprison him forever inside a giant oak. 'Then crying "I have made his glory mine",/ And shrieking out "O fool!" the harlot leapt/Adown the forest'. Tennyson drew on Malory for the tale of Merlin's enchantment, although the character of Vivien is largely his own.

7. *Lancelot and Elaine*. The story of 'Elaine the fair, Elaine the loveable,/Elaine the lily maid of Astolat' and her unrequited love for Lancelot was based by Tennyson on the French prose *Lancelot* and the English stanzaic *Le Morte Arthur*. Lancelot, wishing to joust anonymously, borrows a shield from the Lord of Astolat, leaving his own

shield at Castle Astolat. There Elaine sees and falls in love with him. She guards Lancelot's shield in her tower, and eventually ventures out to declare her love, but she is rebuffed (Lancelot: 'Had I chosen to wed,/ I had been wedded earlier, sweet Elaine:/But now there never will be wife of mine'). Elaine pines and dies, her body drifting downriver in a barge, with a letter in her hand explaining her plight and asking for burial. Arthur orders the building of a costly tomb.

8. *The Holy Grail*. A vision of the holy grail ('the cup, from which our Lord/Drank at the last sad supper with his own') comes to a nun, sister of Sir Percivale; she tells her brother that, if retrieved, the grail would heal 'all the world'. Galahad, the purest of Arthur's knights, sits in the 'Siege Perilous' (a magical chair built by Merlin before his disappearance) and Arthur's knights have a vision of the grail. The quest commences, and Percivale (the narrator of this Idyll) sets out. He encounters many elusive temptations on the way, all of which crumble into dust and ashes when he tries to encompass them, and eventually reaches the Grail castle, where he sees the grail itself but is unable to retrieve it. Back in Camelot Arthur laments that only a tenth of the knights who set out on the quest have returned: and Percivale leaves to become a monk.

9. *Pelleas and Ettarre*. Pelleas is one of the new generation of knights made by Arthur to fill the gap left by the search for the grail. He falls in love with the proud and haughty Ettarre, and offers her the prize won at the tournament, but she rejects it ('I cannot bide Sir Baby' she says). She returns to her castle and refuses to see Pelleas, even to the point of sending out her three finest knights to kill him. Pelleas defeats these, and camps before Ettarre's castle ('There he watches yet,' she says, scornfully, 'There like a dog before his master's door'). Gawaine chances by and promises to help Pelleas in his suit, but on gaining entrance to the castle he falls in love with Ettarre himself and betrays Pelleas's trust. Pelleas rides sorrowfully away, and becomes embittered and disillusioned when he learns (via a chance meeting with Percivale) of Guinevere's faithlessness with Lancelot. When he comes across Lancelot he wildly attacks him (announcing 'a scourge am I/To lash the treasons of the Table Round'). Lancelot defeats Pelleas, but returns unhappily to Camelot, where 'the Queen/Looked hard upon her lover, he on her;/ And each foresaw the dolorous day to be'.

10. *The Last Tournament*. The glory is fading from Arthur's Court. Lancelot rescues a baby wearing a ruby necklace from an eagle's nest, but Guinevere's ministrations are not enough to prevent the death of the child. The ruby is used as the prize for a 'Tournament of Dead Innocence', but Arthur is unable to preside over the jousts (he has to go off and reassert his order in rebellious parts of the country) and Lancelot

deputizes with a guilty heart. The prize is won by Sir Tristram, but (symptomatically) he does not want it for his lady, but for his lover Isolt, King Mark of Cornwall's wife. Tristram rides to Cornwall and presents his lover with the gift. They talk of the direful state of the realm, but Mark surprises them and kills Tristram. Arthur returns to discover that Guinevere has left him

11. Guinevere. In Arthur's absence, a guilt-filled Guinevere begs Lancelot to leave the court. Modred, in league with Vivien, surprises the lovers in their final meeting, and Guinevere flees. She enters a convent at Almesbury, and discovers that her infamy is known even by the novice nuns. Arthur visits the nunnery, first speaking bitterly to her ('Well is it that no child is born of thee./The children born of thee are sword and fire,/Red ruin and the breaking up of laws') but afterwards forgives her, rather high-handedly ('Lo! I forgive thee, as Eternal God/ Forgives') and goes off to fight the final battle. Guinevere stays in the nunnery as Abbess and eventually dies there.

12. The Passing of Arthur. Sir Bedivere is the narrator. As Arthur prepares for the final battle, the ghost of Gawain is blown past on the wind howling 'Hollow, hollow, hollow all delight'. The battle lasts all day, until every knight has fallen except Arthur, Modred and Bedivere. Arthur slays Mordred, but receives a fatal wound in the process. He orders Bedivere to throw his sword, Excalibur, into the mere, and Bedivere goes twice and twice is unable to give up so powerful a weapon. On the third time, he does throw it, and the Lady of the Lake catches it. Bedivere carries the King down to the shore, where a mystic barge takes him away to 'the island valley of Avilion'. The 1833 'Morte D'Arthur' included in this Idyll almost without change, ends on a rather bleak note.

> Long stood Sir Bedivere
> Revolving many memories, till the hull
> Looked one black dot against the verge of dawn,
> And on the mere the wailing died away.

For the 1869 printing, Tennyson added (as well as a lengthy passage at the beginning) a few lines at the end giving a rather different cast to events. Bedivere climbs a cliff to get one last glimpse of the ship.

> Thereat once more he moved about, and clomb
> Even to the highest he could climb, and saw,
> Straining his eyes beneath an arch of hand,
> Or thought he saw, the speck that bare the King,
> Down that long water opening on the deep
> Somewhere far off, pass on and on, and go
> From less to less and vanish into light.
> And the new sun rose bringing the new year.

Improvisatrice, The (1824), by L.E.L [Letitia Landon]. 1578 lines, octosyllabic couplets with interspersed lyrics and other metres. This melancholy confection of sentiment and romance is based on Madame de Stael's *Corinne*.

The Improvisatrice is a beautiful, talented young female poet who lives in a palace in Florence. She paints and extemporizes poetry of great beauty, winning much praise thereby, but nonetheless she is sad; in words that look forward to her own early death she announces 'I ever had from earliest youth/A feeling what my fate would be'. She falls in love with the handsome Lorenzo ('Raven curls their shadow threw,/Like the twilight's darkening hue,/O'er the pure and mountain snow/Of his high and haughty brow'). He returns her love, but then goes off to marry another woman, Ianthe. The Improvisatrice is heartbroken and pines away. But Lorenzo has not really been untrue – he only married Ianthe out of duty, because he had been betrothed to her since his youth. She conveniently dies soon after the marriage, and Lorenzo hurried to the Improvisatrice to claim her as his bride. But it is too late, she has sunk too far, and she dies in his arms.

Within this frame narrative are various examples of the Improvisatrice's art, including three fairly lengthy verse-tales: 'Leila and Abdalla' (a 'Moorish Romance' telling of the doomed love of the title couple, who elope together over sea but are shipwrecked and drowned, their bodies being cast up on the shore of Italy in one another's arms); 'The Indian Bride' (a tale of suttee) and 'Leades and Cydippe' (Leades waits to long to marry his beloved Cydippe, and she pines away and dies; he returns to find her buried under a cypress tree, and soon after dies himself).

INGELOW, Jean (1820–97). Born 17 March 1820 in Boston, Lincolnshire, the daughter of an East Anglian banker. Ingelow lived her early life in Boston (the English Boston, that is) and afterwards in Ipswich, and her lyrics are full of the scenery and the atmosphere of the fenland. Her first volume of poetry, *A Rhyming Chronicle of Incidents and Feelings* (1850) was little noticed, although Tennyson privately admired some of its lyrics. With the publication of her most famous volume, *Poems*, in 1863 Ingelow moved to London, where she remained for the rest of her life. The lyrics and dramatic monologues of *Poems* were much admired for their graceful and plain style, their close observations of nature and life, and for a (very Victorian) tone of high pathos. The volume went through four editions in the year of its publication, and had gone through twenty-three editions by 1879. An illustrated edition, with engravings from the greatest artists of the day, was published in 1867. A Biblical epic, *A Story of Doom (published in A Story of

Doom and Other Poems) came out in 1867, and less successful volumes followed, *Poems, Second Series* (1876) and *Poems, Third Series* (1885). Ingelow diversified her literary production, producing novels (such as the four-volume *Off the Skelligs* in 1872), and numerous children's stories and poetry. She died in 20 July 1897, and is buried in Brompton Cemetery. While piety and pathos often cramp the effects of Ingelow's verse, there are great beauties in her lyrics, and she possessed a fine, self-taught, technical ability.

In Memoriam A.H.H. (1850), by Alfred Tennyson. 2900 lines, in stanzas of four octosyllabic lines rhyming abba. The death of Arthur Hallam in 1833 was, in many ways, the central event of Tennyson's life; and this colossal elegy, composed piecemeal between 1833 and 1850, was his attempt to come to terms with his bereavement. Its publication was a key factor in the choice of Tennyson as Poet Laureate in 1850; Queen Victoria kept a copy beside her bed after the death of Prince Albert. It remains one of the central poetic documents of the Victorian period.

The poem consists of 131 separately numbered elegies, with a Prologue and Epilogue. Some critics have denied that the whole achieves any particular unity or coherence (T. S. Eliot, for instance, argued that its only unity was the unity of the diary), yet Tennyson himself claimed a tripartite structure (apparently modelled on Dante's *Divine Comedy*), punctuated by three successive Christmases, at lyrics 28, 78 and 104. On another occasion he suggested a more elaborate nine-part structure. The numbers that follow are numbers of individual lyrics.

Prologue. Sets the religious tone of the whole, with a hymn to 'Strong Son of God, immortal Love'. *Part One*. 1–8: these lyrics detail the most despairing phase of Tennyson's grief over Hallam, a grief in which his Sorrow denies the existence of God, and refuses hope ('The stars blindly run ... From out waste places comes a cry,/And murmurs from the dying sun'). *Part Two*. 9–20: Tennyson claimed these lyrics were 'all connected – about the Ship', which is to say, the ship bringing back Hallam's remains from Vienna, where he had died. The mood is calmer, less bitter.

> Fair ship, that from the Italian shore
> Sailest the placid ocean-plains
> With my lost Arthur's loved remains,
> Spread thy full wings and waft him o'er.

Part Three. 21–27: The narrator loses his calm resignation, and tries instead to convince himself that 'it is better to have loved and lost/Than never to have loved at all'. *Part Four*. 28–49: The narrator increasingly enquires into the state of life after death – 'How fares it with the happy dead?' – and wonders if dying is like a 'second birth', whether souls in heaven have to learn everything anew as babies do, or whether they are not changed out of recognition. *Part Five*. 50–58: The mood shifts back into a negative cast, the narrator wondering whether men are 'the flies of later spring' that 'weave their petty cells and die'. *Part Six*. 59–71: A new tone of acceptance enters the poem, characterised by a looking-forward, and a consideration of how the narrator will live the rest of his life. 'O Sorrow, wilt thou live with me/No casual mistress, but a wife,/My bosom friend and half of life?' *Part Seven*. 72–98: The narrator is shaking off his more morbid inactivity, and contemplates 'so many worlds, so much to do/So little done'. He asserts that 'Doubt is Devil-born'. *Part Eight*. 99–103: These four lyrics have to do with Tennyson's move from Sommersby in 1837. *Part Nine*. 104–31. The mood swings from mature acceptance of loss ('Love is and was my Lord and King') to a wild, even frenetic, energy:

> Ring out, wild bells, to the wild sky,
>   The flying cloud, the frosty light:
>   The year is dying in the night;
> Ring out, wild bells, and let him die.

Epilogue. The occasion for the epilogue is the wedding of Tennyson's sister, Cecilia, to Edward Lushington. The poem ends, therefore, with a sort of epithalamium, and on a positive note.

Inn Album, The (1875), by Robert Browning. 3079 lines, blank verse. Browning based this narrative on a true story associated with the Baron de Ros.

A gentlemanly adventurer had, several years previously, seduced a motherless girl, thinking her too simple to resent his actions. Surprised by her bitter resentment into proposing marriage, he was doubly surprised when she rejected his offer with contempt. She went off to live a secluded life as the wife of a poor and narrow-minded clergyman, whose peace of mind she did not disturb with the truth of her past. Meanwhile, the elderly *roué* took up with a young and inexperienced gentleman, hoping to fleece him of his wealth. This young man had also been connected with the woman, and had even proposed marriage to her, an offer she had rejected for his own sake. The narrative opens in a country inn, near the woman's country home; it is morning, after a night in which the two men have been playing cards. The vicissitudes of luck have meant that the older rake owes the younger man £10,000. He obliquely offers the unwitting younger man the woman in lieu of payment, an offer he makes by writing a message to her in the inn album, threatening to expose her to her husband unless she agrees to the younger man's advances. When the woman visits the Inn she takes poison rather than capitulate, but before dying reveals the full situation; the younger man, outraged, flies at the older man's throat and kills him. The woman spends her last breath writing a message in the Inn album to exonerate the young man from this crime ('he would have outraged me,/So, my defender slew him') and dies.

Island, The: or, Christian and his Comrades (1823), by Lord Byron. 1425 lines, heroic couplets. Byron based his version of the *Mutiny on the Bounty* story on Bligh's *Narrative of the Mutiny and Seizure of the Bounty, in the South Seas, in 1789*. He did not think particularly highly of his own poem.

Canto the First. Captain Bligh is sleeping while the mutiny takes place ('Awake, bold Bligh! the foe is at the gate!/Awake! Awake! – Alas! it is too late!'). He and his followers are put into a small launch and set adrift, 'but tis not mine', says the poet, 'to tell their tale of grief ... We leave them to their fate'. *Canto the Second.* The *Bounty* sails to the Tonga islands, which are lavishly and beautifully described. We learn of the love between the islander Neuha ('in growth a woman though in years a child') and a sailor 'the blue-eyed northern child' Torquil. Life is idyllic for a time. One evening, a cigar-smoking figure emerges from the wood: it is Ben Bunting, bringing news of 'a strange sail in the offing'. The sailors board the *Bounty* and make ready to fight with the intruder. *Canto the Third.* The fight is over, 'the mutineers were crush'd, dispers'd, or ta'en'. A remnant gather by a jutting rock, amongst them Fletcher Christian 'with his arms across his chest', and Torquil. Hostile sailors come to capture the remaining mutineers, but they escape in canoes paddled by Neuha and other natives. *Canto the Fourth.* The mutineers are taken to a forbidding black rock, and Neuha leads Torquil in an undersea swim, through a submerged entrance and into a cave. Under this 'self born Gothic canopy' the lovers are able to hide from the pursuers. Christian and the rest are not so lucky: they die in battle.

: J :

Jerusalem, The Emanation of The Giant Albion (written 1804–07, engraved 1804–20), by William Blake. 4299 lines, Blakean long line. Blakes last great epic, a more coherently elaborated version of his personal mythic schema (for which see the note to Blake's life) than *Vala*. It connects myth, biography, the Bible and Blake's idiosyncratic perspective on British (or more particularly English) history and culture in the figure of the giant Albion. *Jerusalem* shares much of the symbolism and method as *Milton*, such that some critics see the two epics as a connected piece of work. Summary of this work is difficult; there is little plot as such (Albion is fallen at the beginning, and at the end he rises again), and iteration of all the particular detail of the poem would involve more space than we have here. I limit myself to giving the broad movements of the separate chapters.

Chapter 1. The poem begins with an invocation to Albion: 'awake, awake, O sleeper of the land of shadows, wake, expand/I am in you and you in me, mutual in love divine'. This fallen giant is the personification of England (and all English people, present, past and future), but also an eternal reality, a spiritual aspect of Eternity. He has a lover, mate or 'emanation', a female principle to match his male. This emanation is Jerusalem, although in this fallen state she is Vala, a lower more sensual version of the same eternal principle. Vala, who is presented in Blake's work as something of a seductress (see *Vala*) draws Albion away from the beautiful rural landscapes of Beulah to the land of Ulro, which is chaos. This is the fall of Albion. It behoves another of the eternal principles or quasi-gods of Blake's mythology, Los (who represents imaginative energy) to try and rescue the giant. He decides to do this by creation: 'I must create a system, or be enslaved by another man's;/I will not reason & compare, my business is to create'. Los battles his own evil self, creates Erin (Ireland) 'in perfection lovely' to watch over the sleeping Albion, and builds a beautiful city Golgonooza to guard against the chaos of Ulro. However Albion's children (instanced by various historical and contemporary individuals), are doing evil in the world, and prompted by them Albion comes to believe that his love for his emanation (Jerusalem/Vala) is a great sin. He renounces her. But Vala is able to spread 'her scarlet veil over Albion', gaining power over him. *Chapter 2.* Albion weakens, and lays upon his couch. The poem explores the connections between ancient druidic culture and the Old

Testament ('Your ancestors derived their origin from Abraham, Heber, Shem, and Noah, who were druids ... Albion was the parent of the druid'). Albion is identified with Israel. Los continues his attempts to save Albion, by rallying his 'friends' (the great cities of England, London, Bath, York and so on). *Chapter 3*. The narrative line of this chapter is particularly fragmented. Albion has fallen into the power of his Spectre, and the consequences are evil. Jerusalem is separated from Albion and carried in captivity to Babylon. The children of Albion (now apparently identified with the twelve tribes of Israel) have become enslaved by Vala; they build Stonehenge, the embodiment of error ('a building of eternal death, whose proportions are eternal despair') – error not because of its pagan associations, but because it represents an attempt to 'enchain' the splendours of the universe in a narrow, rational, scientific labyrinth. We are given many particular instances of Albion's fallen state, and of Los's fiery attempts at redemption. *Chapter 4*. The chapter begins with a lament by the imprisoned Jerusalem ('God hath forsaken me;/The arrows of the Almighty pour upon me & my children'). The daughters of Albion continue their nefarious activities, and Los continues to battle against them. Finally, the giant Albion begins to awake:

> Time was finished! The Breath Divine breathed over Albion
> Beneath the furnaces & starry wheels and in the immortal tomb;
> And England, who is Brittania, awoke from death on Albion's
>   bosom.
> She awoke pale & cold;

Albion fires his arrows of intellect, whereupon 'the innumerable chariots of the Almighty appeared in Heaven' and a multitude of spirits moves over the earth. Albion is reunited with his emanation, Jerusalem.

Joan of Arc (1796), by Robert Southey. 5442 lines, blank verse. A product of Southey's youthful, revolutionary period; 'it was written,' he later wrote, 'in a republican spirit', under the belief that 'a happier order of things had commenced with the independence of the United States, and would be accelerated by the French Revolution'. The first edition of this work contained allegorical and supernatural machinery, including a long passage called 'the Vision of the Maid of Orleans'; this was all omitted from the second edition, 'the Vision' being printed separately in Southey's Complete Works.

First Book. Sir Robert of Vaucouleur, convinced by his vassal Claude of the divinely appointed mission of the young Joan, agrees to take her to see the King. On the journey, Joan tells the Duke of Orleans, also travelling with them, the story of her youth, and how her village was blighted by the war with England. *Second Book*. The travellers rest at a poor cottage, and swap tales of the horrors of the Hundred Years War, and the defeats at Agincourt and Roan in particular. Joan prophesies 'woe to the Mighty Ones who send abroad/Their ministers of death'. *Third Book*. Joan is presented to Charles, King of France, and wins him over ('This is indeed the agency of Heaven!') despite the attempts of theologians to prove her diabolically inspired. *Fourth Book*. Charles and Joan (now dressed in her suit of armour) resolve to relieve the siege of Orleans. *Fifth Book*. They march to Orleans. Isabel (a woman sent out of the starving city) tells them of how, and with what brutality, the English made war upon them. *Sixth Book*. The siege is raised: 'swift as the affrightened herd/Scud o'er the plain, the English hasten to their sheltering forts'. *Seventh Book*. Joan pursues the English with battle and defeats them roundly. *Eighth Book*. After a night of respite, battle is joined again; now the French are besieging the English inside their fort. Descriptions of the engagement become more graphic ('a huge stone, thrown from some petrary/Smote him upon the breast ... as it shattered him/His blood besprinkled them, and they beheld/His mangled lungs lie quivering'). *Ninth Book*. The English withdraw under cover of darkness. Joan wins her title of 'Maid of Orleans'. *Tenth Book*. The retreating English meet a new English force; together, this troop engages the pursuing French army. After a mighty battle, the French are victorious. Joan crowns Charles undisputed King of France.

: K :

KEATS, John (1795–1821). Born at Finsbury, London, 31 October 1795, Keats came from comfortable lower-middle-class stock. His father was head ostler at the Swan and Hoop Inn. Keats Senior died in 1804 after a fall from a horse, and Keats himself (aged only 14) nursed his mother through her last illness (she died in 1810). As with his two brothers George and Tom, and his sister Fanny, Keats knew that he had to make a living. In 1811 he left school to train as a physician. He was apprenticed to a surgeon and in October 1815 enrolled as a medical student at Guy's Hospital. But Keats's first love was poetry, which he had read avidly ever since school. (A fellow student recalled later that Keats used to sit in the lecture theatre 'in a deep poetic dream: his mind was on Parnassus with the muses'.) Keats published his first poem in Leigh Hunt's *Examiner* ('O Solitude', 5 May 1816), and went on to publish more. With Hunt's encouragement, Keats gave up medicine, and devoted himself to poetry, writing many shorter pieces and planning a long poem, *Endymion. His first collection, *Poems* (1817) was mostly ignored until Lockhart picked on Keats, along with Hunt and various others, as examples of what he deplored as the 'Cockney' school of poetry. According to legend, it was the savagery of this review (and later of Croker's 1818 review of *Endymion*) that lead indirectly to Keats's ill-health and early death – Shelley's 'Preface' to his elegy for Keats, *Adonais*, set this ball rolling. But the reviews, though undoubtedly painful, had no part in the infection by the tubercular bacillus, which probably happened late in 1817 and 1818.

Keats met Wordsworth several times, and disagreed with what he saw as 'the egotistical sublime' of his poetry (he believed the poet should be ego-free, 'the poetical character ... it is not itself – it has no self – it is everything and nothing'. Rather, Keats was influenced by three poets whose reputations were based on long poems, and accordingly he held it as a central poetic tenet that the test of a truly great poet was epic. As a boy he was enamoured of Spenser (his very first poetic production was an 'Imitation of Spenser'), and he took some of the lushness of description of *The Faerie Queene* and enhanced it in his own writing. Secondly, Keats read Mary *Tighe's *Psyche*, and drew many features from that work. Milton, finally, exerted a lasting and profound influence upon him; the severe classicism of *Paradise Lost* as a dialectical opposition to the excesses of Spenser. Despite lacking the Classical education of the public school of the day (he read the Classics only in translation) he returned again and again to Greek myth. Partly this was conventional, but there was a part of Keats where an aesthetic of pure beauty shaded into a pantheism that went beyond Christianity. Wordsworth, hearing the poet read his 'Ode to Pan' (from *Endymion*) dismissed it as 'a very pretty piece of paganism'; but the jibe was close to the truth. Keats's two long poem projects were attempts to establish a pagan life-religion, rather than Christianity, as the proper subject of poetry: and *Hyperion* was a deliberate attempt to reconfigure *Paradise Lost* as a pagan poem.

Keats worked on *Endymion* throughout 1817 and published it in 1818. Some favourable reviews (and an ecstatic response by *Shelley) were balanced by some severe and even swingeing notices later in the year. In December 1818 Keats's brother Tom died, and Keats moved into his friend Brown's house in Hampstead. During the winter of 1818–19 he met and fell profoundly in love with Fanny Brawne; and despite a series of sore throats (presaging his final illness) he began work on *Hyperion* and his famous Great Odes. He worked through 1819, but his ill health was increasing. He became engaged to Fanny Brawne but what was now unmistakably 'consumption', or tuberculosis, was effectively ending his poetic career. His final volume of poetry, *Lamia, Isabella, The Eve of Saint Agnes, and Other Poems* was published in July 1820, to better reviews. Keats was now bleeding from the lungs and, following doctors' advice, travelled to Italy (Shelley had invited him to come). He worsened on the journey, and settled in Rome, where he died painfully on 23 February 1821. A postmortem examination revealed no lung left; Keats had coughed it all away.

Keats is sometimes seen as the archetypal poet of beautiful moments (of which there are a great many in his work) rather than a writer skilled at constructing larger patterns. Yet, within the constraints of the dense poetic texture he worked with there is a great deal of artistry about the architectonic of *Endymion*, and *Hyperion* promises to work interesting intertextual variations on *Paradise Lost*.

King Arthur (1848–49), by Edward Bulwer Lytton (Lord Lytton). 12 books, 9550 lines in sesta rima. The first large-scale Victorian attempt at Arthurian epic. Lytton combined what he calls in his preface 'the three cardinal divisions of Epic Fable ... the Probable, the Allegorical, and the Marvellous'. Probability dictated a certain reliance on historical sources, such that Arthur is king of Siluria, or Cymri (Wales), defending his kingdom against encroachment by English Saxons. The Marvellous involved the use of epic machinery from various Norse fables, and the

Allegorical aspect of the poem (whereby the quest of Arthur represents the passage of the soul through life) was much remarked upon by contemporary reviewers.

Book 1. Arthur is granted a vision of his kingdom being overrun by the Saxons. The king consults Merlin, who tells him that only by obtaining three items can he save his throne: he must search for a magic sword 'hid in the Lake of Argent Music-Falls', 'the silver Shield in which the infant sleep/Of Thor was cradled' and 'the virgin guide' who sits before 'the Iron Gate' of the underworld'. Arthur departs on his quest. *Book 2.* Arthur has landed on the continent, guided across the ocean by a mystic dove. He enters the court of the wily King of the Vandals, Ludovick, who greets him with seeming hospitality. But in fact, Ludovick plots with the Saxons to deliver Arthur up to them, and only a warning from the mystic dove saves the Cymrian king. He leaves the Vandal court, and is pursued by the Saxons. *Book 3.* A would-be assassin from a primitive forest cult is prevented from slaying Arthur when he is attacked by a wolf. Arthur slays the wolf and saves the savage's life, preaching the Christian doctrine of forgiveness. Later, the savage repays the compliment, riding in with 'a wild barbarian band' to save Arthur from the pursuing Saxons. Arthur travels on into the Alps, and comes across a hidden valley, the home of a lost Etruscan tribe. The male line of their royal family has died out, and they plan to marry Arthur to the royal maiden Ægle. *Book 4.* Arthur falls in love with Ægle. A raven brings Arthur news from Merlin, and he resolves to quit the Etruscans. *Book 5.* In Cymri Merlin speaks of the coming Saxon invasion and warning beacons are lit. Ægle, love-lorn, follows Arthur as he attempts to navigate the stream out of the hidden valley, but she drowns in the 'foaming rapids'. Arthur mourns, until the mystic dove brings him a bitter herb to rub on his eyes: 'And straight the film fell from his heavy eyes'. *Book 6.* The raven appears in Cymri, and Merlin tells Gawaine that he has been selected to join the quest. He sets out, led by the raven. After a series of adventures, he lies down beneath an oak only to discover it to be a Fairy tree ('the hollow oak of demon race/ Blithe Gwyn ab Nudd's elfin family').

> The tiny people swarm around, and o'er him,
>   Here on his breast they lead the morris dance,
> There, in each ray diagonal before him,
>   They wheel, leap, pirouette, caper, shoot askance,
> Climb row on row each other's pea-green shoulder,
> And point, and mow upon the shock'd beholder.

Tied to the spot by 'charms, cramps and torments', Gawaine is tempted by the displayed wealth of the fairies: but when he reaches for them he is rebuked by choruses of 'preaching' and 'pinching' fairies alternately

('Fairy treasures are not rated/By their value in the mart'). Suddenly the fairies vanish. Gawaine continues on his way, but only to fall prisoner of a band of Vikings. *Book 7.* The Lady of the Lake appears to Arthur and transports him to a 'meteor-isle' that sinks beneath the waves to reveal caves full of treasures. Wandering through subterranean caves, he encounters the 'Lords of Time' who reveal to him 'WHAT HAS BEEN, WHAT IS, AND WHAT SHALL BE'. We are treated to a potted history of Britain, up to the reign of 'Crowned Liberty'. Arthur wins the sword, the first object of his quest. *Book 8.* Gawaine is to be sacrificed at the shrine of Freya (he and a dog are both to be roasted alive and eaten). He gets the dog to chew through their ropes during the night, and they escape. *Book 9.* Arthur, meanwhile, has sailed north in search of the Shield of Thor. He encounters, and saves, the crew from an icebound Norwegian ship. They travel together across the 'world of winter', are attacked by a band of 'Esquimaux' and carried back to their ice-huts. There they meet Gawaine, whose various adventures had resulted in him befriending the Esquimaux. *Book 10.* Arthur approaches the Polar lair of the Demon Dwarf ('At once a dwarf and giant – trunk and limb/ Knit in gnarl'd strength'). He follows the Dwarf into a cave, past the remains of dinosaurs ('Lurid skeletons of vanished races,/They who, perchance ere man himself had birth/Ruled the moist slime of uncompleted earth'). They come eventually to the Cave of Lok where Arthur retrieves the Shield. The Dove now leads Arthur back to northern England (ancient Cimmeria), where he falls asleep among some Ancient Druidic ruins. The dove disappears. *Book 11.* Carduel is under seige by Saxon forces. Lancelot fights in single combat with the Saxon king, Harold. Caradoc fights and dies. His soul appears to Arthur as a 'Shadow', and leads him through the Cimmerian ruins to the Realm of Death. The Virgin sitting before the Gates of Iron bears a strange resemblance to the mystic dove. Taking ship, Arthur and Gawaine lead the Virgin back to Carduel. Encountering the seige, he leaves the Virgin in the care of a nearby Convent. We discover that this Virgin is actually Genevieve, the eldest daughter of Harold, the Saxon King. *Book 12.* The Saxons, driven back from Carduel, resolve to sacrifice a Christian maid. Genevieve, having left the Convent, approaches the Saxon camp, where the crucifix about her neck singles her out for sacrifice. After renewed fighting, Merlin is able to save Genevieve. Eventually the two kings, Arthur and Harold, parley; Cymrian Arthur and Saxon Genevieve are to wed, and Merlin ends the poem with a prophecy: 'From Cymri's Dragon England's power shall date,/And peace be born to Cymri from the Dove'.

King Poppy: a story without end (1875 privately printed, revised version published posthumously, 1892), by 'Owen Meredith' (i.e. E. R. B. Lytton). 5311 lines, blank verse. Lytton hoped that this huge, comprehensive, anti-Utilitarian poem would crown his career; its purpose was to 'suggest what a poor tissue of human unreality human life would be if the much-despised influence of the imagination were banished from it'. To this end he attempted the synthesis of classical myths, history, nursery tales, and various theories of life and art.

Persephone, banished to the underworld, has carried her flowers with her, but all of them have died except a small, white poppy. Trying to save this flower, the goddess calls on the god Phantasos ('Sole author he of those dumb dramas play'd/In the fantastic theatres of Thought/By puppet actors'). This 'God of Whims' snatches the poppy and carries it into the world of Dreams, where another Spirit (Phrenoleptos, whose 'whisper is madness', and who used to dwell 'within the grape's dim orb') enters into it. Eventually, Poppy is returned to this world, to bring 'Consolation to a race/Else irremediably miserable', and there he falls into a stony crag, and dreams of the regal trappings that will one day be his.

From here the action shifts to a satirical version of England, 'Diadummiania', ruled by King Diadummianus. This monarchy is 'safely asleep', and does little: a law passed requires six further laws to 'undo all the mischief'. The national anthem is 'Old King Cole', the revolutionary party sings 'Cherry Ripe', the central symbol of the National Religion is the Flying Horse, and the highest honour is to be dubbed 'Knight Commander of the Uncatchable Carp'. The heiress to the kingdom is Princess Diadema, but her nurse has a vision of Diadema giving away the crown of the kingdom, and when the King learns of this he consults the Court Wizard, Pilgram. Pilgram builds a secret island to which Diadema is transported (to keep her out of the way of harmful influences until she is of age), and in the meantime Pilgram constructs a sort of robot princess to take her place at court. The robot princess does well enough to escape detection, and is even sent to school in Diadema's place. There, a mistake in arranging the mechanical cylinders by which her 'intelligence' is controlled results in her writing an essay on alcohol, instead of answering the set question on Peter the Great. The confusion results in the blowing up of the 'Russian Question', and school is discontinued.

The real princess, meanwhile, grows sad on her island, and sings a song; a reply comes from a Shepherd boy, the 'voice of Love', and the two are united 'in song and dream'. Diadema is now 'alone as she had never been before,/Alone and conscious of her loneliness'. Poppy, still in his stony crag, also sings a song that Diadema hears, promising the princess love in return for her crown. Diadema lets the crown drop from her lap (onto the head of Poppy), and she falls into a deep sleep, 'a maiden princess sleeping/Forever in a palace by the sea'. The Shepherd boy, missing her song, goes in search of her. After many adventures, he arrives at the magic island badly wounded, to die by her side. His blood drops onto King Poppy, giving him his regal colour.

In Diadummiania, the King abdicates and Pilgram sets up robot, or 'puppet', ministers, who do the job rather better than the real ones (Pilgram's advice to the real rulers of the realm is 'Leave the People's honest faith/In salutary error undisturb'd./Never reveal the unreality/Of puppets who are popular'). In the other realm, however, the Realm of Imagination (or Realm of Consolation), King Poppy rules.

> Feaster of famisht hearts, rebuilder bright
> Of ruin'd fortunes, pain's victorious foe,
> Grief's comforter, Joy's guardian, good King Poppy.

: L :

Lady of the Lake, The (1810), by Walter Scott. 4960 lines, octosyllabics with interspersed songs. Despite its title, this work (the third of Scott's highly successful long poems) bears no relation to Arthurian legend. It is set in the 1530s.

Canto First. The Chase. The poem opens with a vigorous description of a stag hunt:

> The antlered monarch of the waste
> Sprung from his heathery couch in haste.
> But, ere his fleet career he took,
> The dew-drops from his flanks he shook ...
> A moment snuffed the tainted gale,
> A moment listened to the cry,
> That thickened as the chase grew nigh;
> Then as the headmost foes appeared,
> With one brave bound the copse he cleared,
> And, stretching forward free and far,
> Sought the wild heaths of Uam-Var.

The hunter leads his dogs against the prey, but his horse is worn out and dies. Standing beside the lake (Loch Katrine) and admiring its beauty, he sees a handsome woman come to the shore in a little boat: 'A chieftan's daughter seemed the maid'. The hunter introduces himself (as a knight called James Fitz-James) and is invited back to a hall beside the loch, the home of the fierce highland chief Roderick Dhu. She herself is Ellen, the daughter of the outlawed Lord James of Douglas. *Canto Second. The Island.* Fitz-James is greatly struck with the beauty of Ellen; but it becomes clear that he is not alone in desiring her. Both the chieftain Roderick Dhu and the young Malcolm Graeme are similarly besotted. Roderick arrives (to the strain of a now-famous 'martial ditty': 'Hail to the chief who in triumph advances'), Malcolm Graeme and Douglas (Ellen's father) with him. Roderick announces that the king (James) is preparing an assault upon them ('The King's vindictive pride/Boasts to have tamed the Border-side'). Douglas decides that he is the cause of this, and sets out for Stirling to give himself up. *Canto Third. The Gathering.* Roderick presides at a sacrificial offering of a goat while a monk carrying a burning cross utters dire warnings ('woe to the wretch who fails to rear/At this dread sign the ready spear'). He sends a messenger to muster the clans, and they rally to the Cross of Fire (the Ku Klux Klan drew much of their iconography from this poem). *Canto Fourth. The Prophecy.* The hermit monk informs Roderick of his prophecy: 'WHICH SPILLS THE FOREMOST FOEMAN'S LIFE/THAT PARTY CONQUERS IN THE STRIFE'. Her father gone, Ellen sits forlorn. James Fitz-James approaches and declares his love: 'Near Bochastle my horses wait;/They bear us soon to Stirling gate./I'll place thee in a lovely bower,/I'll guard thee like a tender flower.' But Ellen rejects his suit, and reveals her love for Malcolm Graeme. Gallantly, James withdraws, giving Ellen a ring which (he says) the king himself will recognize, and grant the wish of the bearer. Fitz-James makes his way back towards Stirling, and on the way encounters Roderick Dhu, with whom he immediately quarrels ('"Art thou a friend to Roderick?" – "No" –/ "Thou darest not call thyself a foe?" –/"I dare!"'). *Canto Fifth. The Combat.* Roderick Dhu and Fitz-James fight; 'thrice the Saxon blade drank blood'. Fitz-James' eventual victory fulfils the prophecy of Canto 4. He carries the badly wounded highlander off to Stirling Castle a prisoner. Meanwhile, Douglas (Ellen's father) arrives at Stirling, where he has an audience with the king and is imprisoned. *Canto Sixth. The Guard Room.* Ellen arrives at Stirling, and presents her signet ring to the King. It turns out that Fitz-James is none other than the King himself, James. He grants Ellen's wish, to free her father, and her marriage to Graeme is blessed by the royal hand. Roderick dies of his wounds.

Lalla Rookh (1817), by Thomas Moore. An 'eastern romance' consisting of four separate verse tales, with a connecting prose framework. A sort of oriental *Canterbury Tales*, the work was tremendously popular, and had gone into 20 editions by 1840.

The framing story concerns the journey of the beautiful Lalla Rookh (the name means 'Tulip Cheek') from Delhi to Cashmire, where she is to marry the King of Bucharia. On the way, the handsome young poet Feramorz relates various oriental tales, which the staid Great Chamberlain, Fadladeen, severely criticizes.

Veiled Prophet of Khorassan. (2138 lines, heroic couplets). Mokassa is the evil prophet of the title, who wears a silver veil to hide (he says) the blinding radiance of his holy face from his followers, although in fact his face is hideously deformed. Under a banner of 'Liberty' Mokassa recruits a huge following for a war against the Caliph, including a young warrior of renown called Azim. The beautiful young Zelica was once the lover of Azim, but had thought him dead in the Greek wars, and had joined Mokassa's harem in grief. Mokassa intends to use Zelica to seduce Azim, thereby binding the warrior to him, but instead of this she reveals to him Mokassa's true and evil identity. Later, battle is joined with the Caliph, and Mokassa is about to triumph ('the Orient World's Imperial crown/Is just within his grasp'), when Azim rides in with his followers, turns the tide, and enables the Caliph's victory. A beleagured Mokassa poisons all his followers and hurls himself into a vat of acid, in the hope that people will believe his body has been apotheosized ('In one bold plunge commences Deity!'). Azim breaks through the gate of Mokassa's citadel, and attacks a figure wearing Mokassa's silver veil, but in doing so he inadvertently kills Zelica.

Paradise and the Peri (521 lines, various metres). A Peri, one of the children of the fallen angels, mourns the fact that she cannot enter Paradise; the guardian angel tells her 'The Peri may yet be forgiven/ Who brings to this Eternal gate/the Gift most dear to Heaven'. The Peri first brings a drop of blood from the veins of a warrior who died defending liberty, but this is not enough. Next she brings the sigh from an expiring maiden, who died with her lover rather than be separated, but again is denied. Finally, she brings the tear of repentance from the eyes of a hardened criminal, and with this 'The Gates are pass'd, and Heav'n is won!' The Great Chamberlain dismisses this work ('this flimsy manufacture'), but Lalla Rookh, much to her dismay, discovers that she is falling in love with the young poet.

The Fire-Worshippers (2226 lines, various metres). The Ghebers, or Fire-worshippers, have been conquered by the Muslim Emir al Hassan, but maintain a covert resistance. Hafed, a young Gheber, is in love with Hinda, the daughter of the Emir; but at the beginning of the poem they must part, prompting Hinda's famous words:

> Oh! ever thus, from childhood's hour,
> I've seen my fondest hopes decay; ...
> I never nurs'd a dear gazelle,
>   To glad me with its soft black eye,
> But when it came to know me well,
>   And love me, it was sure to die!

Walking by the ocean one day, the disconsolate Hinda is captured by a pirate crew and transported over the sea to their base. There she discovers that her lover is in fact the Chief of the Ghebers, and they are joyfully reunited. However a traitor has betrayed the Ghebers to Al Hassan, and a surprise attack leads to a bloody battle ('vainly hundreds, thousands bleed'). Hafed is killed, and Hinda drowns herself in grief.

The Light of the Haram. (741 lines, various metres). Selim is the Caliph of Cashmire, Nourmahal his beautiful wife (the 'light' of his harem). They have quarrelled over 'something, light as air – a look/A word unkind or wrongly taken'. Nourmahal summons the enchantress, Namouna, who teaches her a magical song with which to charm her husband. Nourmahal sings the song at a banquet, 'the charm is wrought', and Selim's love is rekindled. After this tale, the Grand Chamberlain sums up his attitude to such poetry ('frivolous – inharmonious – non-sensical'). The group arrive finally in Cashmire, and it is revealed that the young poet Feramorz is in fact the King of Bucharia in disguise. He and Lalla Rookh are happily married.

Lady Holland is reputed to have met Moore at a dinner party and declared: 'Mr Moore, I have not read your Larry O'Rourke; I don't like Irish stories.'

Land East of the Sun and West of the Moon, The, by William Morris. See *The Earthly Paradise.*

LANDON, Letitia Elizabeth (1802–38). Known on her title-pages by her initials ('L.E.L'), Landon enjoyed a brief period of contemporary success, and then married into misery and suicide. Her mournful life story functioned as a sort of melancholy ideal of the doomed poetess throughout the nineteenth century; Elizabeth Barrett *Browning and Christina *Rossetti (to name two) wrote elegies for her.

Landon wrote poetry from her early girlhood on, of a twee dreadfulness ('The command of language is really surprising ... ' gushed Dorothy Wordsworth of one fairy poem; 'I could have kissed her for giving the fairies a cake'.) Her first collection appeared in 1809, at the age of seven. The collapse of her father's business plans gave her reason to write for money, and from the age of fifteen onwards she did just that: a great many poems appeared in magazines and annuals, and another collection (*On the Domestic Affections*) appeared 1820. She began to be known for her occasional pieces (Disraeli called her the 'snub-nosed Brompton Sappho'). *The Fate of Adelaide* was published in 1821. In 1822 she published *The Improvisatrice*, which went through six editions by the end of the year. After her father's death, her mother (to whom she was never close) moved to the country; but Landon stayed on in London by herself. *The Troubadour* (1825) repeated the success of *The Improvisatrice.*

Estranged from her mother, and living by herself in London she found herself in a socially dubious position. Rumours circulated of her love affairs (with *Bulwer Lytton, and with the writer and editor William Maginn), and an air of genteel scandal surrounded her. She continued writing poetry for money (her collection *The Golden Violet*, 1827, earned her £1000); and also wrote a number of novels (*Romance and Reality* 1831, *Ethel Churchill* 1837, among others). An engagement with John Forster (the future biographer of Dickens) was broken off, apparently because of the increasing scandal surrounding Landon. In 1838 she married George Maclean. He worked in the colonial office and was stationed on the Gold Coast. It seems that Landon did not particularly love this man, but her tarnished reputation meant that she had to grab whom she could. She travelled with her new husband to West Africa, where she was very miserable. Unhappy with Maclean, who seems to have taken a mistress, suffering from poor health and feeling isolated and abandoned in a far-flung part of the British Empire, she took an overdose of prussic acid and died in 1838.

Laon and Cythna (1817), by Percy Shelley. See *Revolt of Islam*.

Lara (1814), by Lord Byron. 1272 lines, heroic couplets. A sort of sequel to *The Corsair*.

Canto the First. Lara is a man (despite his name) who has been absent from his ancestral lands in Spain for many years, and who returns suddenly accompanied only by a young page boy called Kaled. His household strive to make him welcome, but he acts peculiarly, staying up at all hours, having a fit and gabbling in an unknown tongue that only Kaled is able to understand. Indeed, Lara seems the archetypal, alienated and stormy Byronic figure: 'He stood a stranger in this breathing world,/An erring spirit from another hurl'd;/A thing of dark imaginings'. At a festival hosted by a neighbouring nobleman called Otho, another noble, Ezzelin, appears to recognize Lara ("Tis he! how came he here?') and accuses him of some fearful crime upon which he declines to elaborate; Lara takes exception and Ezzelin agrees to reveal all the following day at noon. *Canto the Second*. Noon arrives, Ezzelin does not appear, and Lara gets into a fight with Otho, a friend of the accuser. Otho is wounded, but not fatally. But the matter is not cleared up, and 'strange suspicion, whispering Lara's name,/Now daily mutters o'er his blacken'd fame'. Lara is suspected of having had Ezzelin murdered, and his expertise with the sword (demonstrated in the fight with Otho) seems to bespeak a violent past. The Serfs, long oppressed, revolt; and Lara leads a band of proles, although he cares little for their liberty ('What cared he for the freedom of the crowd?/He raised the humble but to bend the proud'). There is a battle between Lara's band and Otho's forces in which Lara is badly wounded. He dies in Kaled's arms, although Kaled turns out to be not a page boy but a girl. In fact, Lara's true identity is the former pirate Conrad from *The Corsair*, and Kaled is Gulnare, the Turkish slave girl.

Lay of the Last Minstrel, The (1805), by Walter Scott. 3167 lines, irregular ballad metres. This was the work that launched Scott's career as a writer of long poems. Based on Scottish legends (such as the story of the goblin apprentice Gilpin Horner), border ballads and in part plagiarized from the (as yet unpublished) *Christabel* of Coleridge, the work was extremely successful. Loved alike by critics and public, it sold 15,000 copies in five years and laid the foundations for the commercial success of the nineteenth-century long poem.

The framing device of the poem concerns the last travelling minstrel or bard, travelling the Scottish lowlands in the seventeenth century during that time of persecution of such figures by the Puritans. Our minstrel recites a last poem for a noblewoman, a story set during the 1500s. *Canto First.* The Lady of Castle Branksome, in the Scottish borders, repairs to her 'secret bower', where she summons her old retainer, the 'moss-trooping' William of Deloraine. William is to ride to the tomb of Michael Scott, the semi-legendary wizard; there a monk will give him something – 'Be it scroll or be it book,/Into it, knight, thou must not look;/If thou readest it thou art lorn!/Better thou had'st ne'er been born'. *Canto Second.* Deloraine rides to Melrose and meets the Monk; they open Michael Scott's tomb ('there he lay/As if he had not been dead a day') and take his 'mighty book', which Deloraine carries back to his lady. Meanwhile, the Lady's daughter Margaret is receiving a suit from a young knight, Lord Cranstoun: but there is a blood feud between the Cranstouns and Branksome that renders the love hopeless. *Canto Third.* Lord Cranstoun, leaving the castle, meets William of Deloraine arriving; they engage in single combat, and Deloraine is wounded. Cranstoun orders his page (a goblin in the shape of a boy) to carry Deloraine into the castle for treatment, and rides off. The goblin boy tries to open the magic book Deloraine is carrying (but the iron clasps 'would not yield to unchristened hand'), steals it anyway, and eventually conveys the wounded knight into the castle. Once inside, he (out of a spirit of goblin mischief) carries away the 'fair young child' and heir to the house.

> He led the boy o'er bank and fell,
> Until they came to a woodland brook;
> The running stream dissolved the spell,
> And his own elvish shape he took.

The goblin considers throttling the boy, but instead delivers him into the hands of the English enemy, whose troops (under the command of Lord Dacre) are camped preparatory to an assault on Branksome (under the pretext that Deloraine is a cattle thief). Meanwhile, in the castle the Lady tends the wounds of Deloraine. Made aware of the English threat, the Scots prepare for the defence of the castle: 'Mount, mount for Branksome, every man!' *Canto Fourth*. The English attack, and Scottish feuds are forgotten as the different clans rally to fight the invader. A huge battle threatens, until it is agreed that the dispute will be settled by single combat between the (still wounded) William Deloraine and the English Sir Richard Musgrave (whose lands Deloraine is accused of harrying); the prize for this combat will be the young boy, the Branksome heir. *Canto Fifth*. The combatants fight: 'to the axe the helms did sound/And blood poured down from many a wound'. With a mighty blow the Englishman is felled ('Brave Musgrave, no!/Thence never shalt thou rise again!'). But it turns out that the victor is not Deloraine, but Lord Cranstoun dressed in his armour (which his goblin page had stolen for him). Having won the day, and rescued the boy, the blood feud between the Cranstouns and Castle Branksome is healed. *Canto Sixth*. The minstrel comes over all mock-bashful at the marriage of Lord Carnstoun and Margaret ('Me lists not at this tide declare/The splendour of the spousal rite'). The goblin tries to make mischief among the wedding guests, but he is summoned away by a terrifying blast of lightning and a disembodied voice: 'GYLBIN, COME!'. The day is joyful, with minstrels singing various ballads.

L.E.L. See *Landon, Letitia Elizabeth*

Leonore, A Tale (1860), by Georgina, Lady Chatterton. Seventeen sections, 2572 lines, blank verse.

The scene is set in Southern France in the 1370s. Princess Leonore, daughter of the Count de Foix, is in love with an English knight, Sir Guy, Baron Anzinans; but her father wishes her to marry Prince Juan, heir of Aragon. Leonore's friend, Marguerite, is betrothed to a young sculptor, Adolphe. But Marguerite hatches a plan to enable Leonore to marry whom she wishes, and to raise her own social standing higher than would be possible as a sculptor's wife. She announces that she is to wed Baron Anzinans herself, and that the two weddings will go ahead on the same day. The marriages duly take place, each bride wearing a veil, and it is only afterwards that Prince Juan discovers he has unwittingly married Marguerite. Leonore and her new husband ride off to Castle Anzizans, but an enraged Juan follows with an army. Only Leonore's pitiful pleadings prevent full-scale war. Leonore then dies giving birth to a son, extracting from her husband a promise never to wed again. Sir Guy is distraught at her death and has a marble statue built in the church as a memorial. But some years later he meets a beautiful maiden in the woods around his castle, her face 'more fair/ Than any face on earth he e'er had seen'. Sir Guy declares his love for this mysterious woman (who tells him 'On one condition only I consent./It is, that thou shouldst not inquire my name,/Nor seek to lift the veil I wish to draw/O'er my mysterious birth'). But, meanwhile, the statue has disappeared from the church (the priests announce 'this a miracle must be!') When the mysterious maiden arrives for the wedding she declares: 'Yes! I am Leonore – thy once-loved wife;/To me the holy rite hath wed thee twice', and, climbing back on the podium, reverts to being a statue again. The plot is then wound up – Marguerite having been made miserable by her deception has absconded from her husband, Prince Juan. She spends some time in a nunnery, before eventually being reconciled with and married to (Juan having conveniently died in battle) the long-suffering Adolphe.

Life and Death of Jason, The (1867), by William Morris. 10,534 lines, heroic couplets (with occasional lyrics interspersed). Morris's first lengthy poetic work. Originally planned as one of the cycle of epic tales in *The Earthly Paradise* it grew too long in the telling and was accorded a book of its own.

Book 1. Aeson, rightful king of the Minyae at Iolchos, has been overthrown by the 'covetous and strong' Pelias. Aeson, fearful that Pelias will kill his family to secure his throne, sends his son Jason into the woods to be raised by Chiron, the Centaur. Grown to manhood, Jason encounters the goddess Juno in the forest, who tells him that he is to leave the woods and return to Iolchis. *Book 2.* Jason returns to Iolchis and makes himself known before Pelias and a crowd of the Minyae ('"Pelias," he said, "I will not call thee king,/Because thy crown is but a stolen thing"'). Pelias promises to renounce the crown once Jason has recovered the fabled golden fleece from Æa, across the ocean. Jason vows to undertake this quest. *Book 3.* The Argonauts, the crew of the Argo who will accompany Jason on his quest, assemble. *Book 4.* The quest begins. The Argo calls in for provisions at 'the Mysian land', and the youth Hylas wanders off into the idyllic landscape, only to be beguiled by a water nymph and drowned. The Argonauts search for the vanished Hylas in vain; eventually all except Hercules continue the voyage. *Book 5.* The Argonauts are given rich gifts by the Cyzican king, Cyzicus; but in a later confusion Jason kills him in battle. They sail to Thrace in search of King Phineus, but find him blinded and taunted by furies. They free him. *Book 6.* The Argo sails through the Symplegades and arrive at the town of Æa, the location of the golden fleece, where they are cordially greeted by King Aetes. He tells them that before they can have the fleece they must complete three impossible labours – yolk together two brazen bulls to plough the ground, and then sow as seeds the dragon's teeth, and finally defeat the Hydra that guards the fleece. *Book 7.* Jason meets Aetes' daughter Medea: 'while she spoke/Came Love unseen, and cast his golden yoke/About them both ... betwist them flew/With fluttering wings, the new-born strong desire'. Medea visits Jason at night and gives him a magic potion. *Book 8.* Aided by Medea's potion, Jason tames the brazen bulls and sows the dragon's teeth; a race of 'earth-born' warriors spring up, and Jason kills them all. *Book 9.* While Medea (dressed 'in thin clinging silk alone') charms the Hydra to sleep with a tune, Jason steals the fleece. The Argo, with Medea, leaves in a hurry. *Book 10.* Unable to go south, the heroes travel north. *Book 11.* The Argo continues north up a river as far as possible; then they draw the ship overland until they reach 'a river running to the northern sea'. The Argonauts are miserable in the northern climate: 'the silent snow fell till the world was white'. *Book 12.* After wintering for ten weeks, the Argo eventually makes its way to the northern sea. After various adventures in the desolate northern reaches they make their way back to the Pillars of Hercules. *Book 13.* The Argo stops off at Circe's isle, where Medea receives divine intelligence about events in Iolchis ('still the sceptre presses Pelias' hand/And Aeson is at rest for evermore'). *Book 14.* The Argonauts successfully navigate past the Sirens' isle (samples of their songs are included). *Book 15.* Wary of the evil Pelias, the Argo hides off the coast and Medea goes alone, and in disguise, to Iolchis. She slays Pelias. *Book 16.* Jason returns in triumph to Iolchis and is made king, with Medea his queen. The Argonauts disperse to their various homes. *Book 17.* This lengthy final book (1367 lines) more or less retells the story of Euripides' *Medea*. Ten years later, Jason has wearied of Medea. He marries Glauce, the daughter of Creon, king of Corinth; but Medea refuses to go quietly. She kills Glauce, and Jason's (and her own) children, before fleeing. Faced with this catastrophe, Jason thinks to kill himself, but is stopped by his aged nurse. The remainder of Jason's life labours under 'a load of shameful misery', even though he is crowned King of Corinth as well as Iolchis. He visits the now crumbling hulk of the Argo, and goes to sleep on deck; but the 'stem-post' collapses in the night and 'beneath the ruined stem did Jason lie/Crushed, and all dead of him that here can die'.

Life Drama, A (1852), by Alexander Smith. 3086 lines, blank verse with many interspersed lyric metres. One of the works (with Bailey's *Festus* and Dobell's *Balder*) that was stigmatized in contemporary criticism with the descriptive label *Spasmodic. In fact, Smith's variegated poetic collage is rather more restrained and interesting than the label suggests. Its poetry can be over-ingenious in its use of image ('the night, which, like a sea,/Breaketh for ever on a strand of stars'), but sometimes can be fairly dignified and even powerful ('To hear the soft and whispering rain, feel the dewy cool of leaves,/Watch the lightnings dart like swallows round the brooding thunder-eaves'). It also sometimes slips into the bathetic ('I shall go down to Bedfordshire tomorrow').

Scene I. Walter, an aristocratic modern-day poet, soliloquizes on his thirst for fame ('O Fame! Fame! Fame!'). *Scene II.* Walter meets a Lady in the woods, and reveals to her his plans to write a Great Poem detailing the entire history of the universe. *Scene III.* Walter is tormented by his love for the Lady. *Scene IV.* Walter tries wooing the Lady with a poetic tale, but she tells him that 'within a month my bridal bells/Will make a village glad', that she will be 'wedded to grey hair, and eyes/Of cold and cruel blue', and that she expects to be dead (presumably of unhappiness) by the following Spring. *Scene V.* Walter solus expresses gloom ('No Love! Love bringeth wretchedness'); he meets a peasant and child, his tenants, and vents his spleen: 'Black is this world, but blacker is the next'. *Scene VI.* Two year later Walter is in London and still miserable. His friend Edward tries to console him. *Scene VII.* Walter and Edward talk about things on a balcony overlooking the sea, and Walter reveals 'there was one very dear to me that died'. Edward invites him down to his Bedfordshire Manor, and describes the people he will meet, including the beautiful Violet. *Scene VIII.* At the Manor, Edward and Arthur (another young friend) both sing songs. Walter recites a mournful poetic tale, and Violet realizes that it is autobiographical. *Scene IX.* Walter and Violet watch the sunset ('the sun is dying like a cloven king/In his own blood'), and Walter tells her of his childhood in Kent. They declare their love for one another. *Scene X.* The path of true love seems to be going astray. On a bridge at midnight, Walter tells a passing Prostitute that he is 'damned' for some obscure 'sin' ('Oh, as a lewd dream stains the holy sleep,/I stain the holy night'). *Scene XI.* Walter returns to his childhood home and resolves to 'throw off his dead and useless past'. *Scene XII.* Walter's great poem has been published and accounted a huge success. Edward and a friend discuss his success, and wonder why it is he remains so unhappy. *Scene XIII.* A more mellow Walter watches the sunset with Violet, reveals the torturous path his soul has taken, and the two of them seem prepared for a happy life together.

Light of Asia, The (1879), by Edwin Arnold. 4443 lines, blank verse with occasional interspersed lyric metres. The full title of this, Arnold's most famous and successful work, makes plain its subject: *The Light of Asia, or The Great Renunciation (Mahabhinishkramana), Being the Life and Teaching of Gautama, Prince of India and Founder of Buddhism (as Told in Verse by an Indian Buddhist)*.

Book the First. Gautama is born into this world, the son of King Suddhodana; at his birth a sage announces that he is the Buddha ('Thou art He!/I see the rosy light, the foot-sole marks,/The soft curled tendril of the Swastika,/The sacred primal signs thirty and two'). He grows up as a normal Prince, except that he demonstrates extraordinary learning and compassion. *Book the Second*. The King hears a prophesy that his son will either become 'a king of kings ... trampling the neck of all his enemies', or else turn his back on all worldly delights, 'tread the sad and lowly path/Of self-denial'. Anxious to promote the former eventuality, he attempts to bind the boy to worldly pleasures. He holds a festival requiring the attendance of the most beautiful women in the kingdom, and Gautama falls in love with the lovely Yasodhara. They are married and live in a splendid palace. *Book the Third*. Growing restless, Gautama decides to travel. Outside the city he discovers for the first time poverty, misery, old age, sickness and death. He looks about with 'heavenly pity', declaring 'the veil is rent/Which blinded me'. *Book the Fourth*. The pregnant Yasodhara wakes weeping from a dream that Gautama is bound to leave. Her husband confirms that though 'I loved and love Yasodhara', he has been 'seeking to save the sad earth ... I choose/To tread its paths with patient, stainless feet'. *Book the Fifth*. Gautama lives a life of contemplation in the countryside, 'wholly wrapt from self/In keen unravelling of the threads of thought'. He does good generally and is revered by the common folk. *Book the Sixth*. Six years pass, and Buddha learns from the simple folk, until enlightenment finally dawns on him sitting beneath the Bodhi tree: he understands Karma, the wheel of life and the way towards Nirvana. 'Then he arose – radiant, rejoicing, strong' singing a song of his new wisdom. *Book the Seventh*. Buddha returns to his father's court. King Suddhodana is initially outraged by his son's humble dress and shorn head, but is won over by the Buddha's wisdom. *Book the Eighth*. This book is mostly given over to quatrains embodying 'the wisdom which hath made our Asia mild'.

Lord of the Isles (1815), by Walter Scott. 4587 lines, octosyllabics with interspersed songs. Scott's sixth, and last, long poem, before he yielded the field to *Byron and devoted his energies wholly to writing novels.

The poem is set in 1307, at the time of the return of Robert the Bruce to Scotland and the battle of Bannockburn.

Canto First. The beautiful Edith of Lorn is talking with her mother Morag about her love for Lord Ronald, the Highland Lord of the Isles. Edith and Ronald are affianced, but Ronald is actually in love with another woman: Isabel, the sister of Robert the Bruce. Meanwhile, the Bruce himself returns to Scotland from his exile (he had been driven from his country after the murder of the Red Comyn). *Canto Second.* Ronald is feasting to mark his nuptials when the Bruce presents himself, and announces that his 'first and dearest task' is to 'free Scotland from her thrall'. The marriage ceremony is broken up. Fearful that she will be married off to an English lord in a marriage of convenience by Ronald, Edith vanishes. *Canto Third.* The Bruce and Ronald muster their forces and travel from Skye through Scotland. On the way, they pick up a young boy who acts as a mute page to Ronald. The page saves Ronald from an assassination attempt. *Canto Fourth.* Ronald and Bruce discuss women: Bruce can promise nothing with respect to his sister ('But for my sister Isabel–/The mood of woman who can tell?'); meanwhile the young page boy bursts into tears ('the bitter sobs came thick and fast'). They sail round the coast, finally meeting Isabel who reveals that 'my hopes are fixed on Heaven alone;/Nor e'er shall earthly prospects win'. The page perks up at this news. *Canto Fifth.* Isabel recognizes that the page boy is in fact Edith in disguise. Edith falls into the hands of the English and is about to be executed, until saved by the Bruce. *Canto Sixth.* This canto is mostly given over to a description of the battle of Bannockburn, at which Robert the Bruce defeats the English. Edith's mute devotion has finally won Ronald's heart, and the two marry.

Loves of the Angels, The (1823), by Thomas Moore. 1821 lines, various metres. Moore's last long poem was based on the oriental tale of the angels of Harut and Marut, and the Rabbinical stories of Uzziel and Shamchaza, wherein three of Allah's angels fall in love with mortal women. Moore began it as a prose work, but put this aside when Byron published his 'Heaven and Earth'. Returning to it later, he endeavoured to turn it into an allegory of 'the fall of the Soul from its original purity'.

First Angel's Story. An angel narrates his love for Lea, 'one of earth's fairest womankind'. He promises to tell her the spell that grants entry to heaven that he might 'meet, but once, the thrilling touch' of her lips; but on repeating the spell Lea sprouts angel's wings and flies up to paradise, leaving the angel an earthbound Spirit. *Second Angel's Story.* Rubi, once a Spirit of Knowledge, loves the maiden Lilis. She combines beauty with a 'Mind, outshining clear/Through her whole frame'. He appears to her in his 'best pomp', but his brilliance is too much for her: 'I saw her lie/Black'ning within my arms to ashes!' *Third Angel's Story.* Zaraph loved Nama, and was permitted to live with her as a mortal. They must suffer the various ills that afflict all mortals, but they will eventually live in eternity.

Loves of the Plants, The (1789), by Erasmus Darwin. See *Botanic Garden.*

Lucile (1860), by 'Owen Meredith' (i.e. Edward Robert Bulwer Lytton). 8325 lines, twelve cantos in rhyming couplets of anapestic tetrameter. Lytton borrowed the plot (although not the ending) from George Sand's *Lavinia.* The third, revised edition carried a preface that distanced Lytton from the work ('an experiment so alien to my present appreciation of the nature and conditions of verse that I could now, on this ground, withdraw it'), although *Lucile* remains (as Paul Turner says) 'very readable, often recalling Byron's *Don Juan* in its witty and resourceful versification, and Oscar Wilde's *The Importance of Being Earnest* in its sophisticated flippancy'.

Part I, Canto 1. Lord Alfred Vargrave, an English gentleman, is holidaying in the French resort of Bigorre with his future wife, the childlike Matilda. He receives a letter from an old flame, Lucile de Nevers (with whom he had broken off a romance ten years earlier) requesting that he visit her in nearby Serchon to exchange their old love letters. Matilda's cousin John (also in Bigorre) advises against the visit, but Alfred feels honour-bound to go. *Canto 2.* On the way to Serchon Alfred falls in with a French gentleman, later revealed to be Eugene de Luvois. On his arrival, Alfred dines and forgets his troubles.

> We may live without poetry, music and art;
> We may live without conscience, and live without heart;
> We may live without friends; we may live without books;
> But civilized man cannot live without cooks.
> He may live without books, – what is knowledge but grieving?
> He may live without hope, – what is hope but deceiving?
> He may live without love, – what is passion but pining?
> But where is the man that can live without dining?

Canto 3. An interview with Lucile reveals her to be older but just as beautiful (in her 'soft second summer, more ripe than the first'). Alfred's feelings for her revive, but he returns the letters and resolves to leave. Luvois also visits Lucile in order to propose marriage, but her reply ('I ask you to leave me the time to reflect') convinces him that her heart has been taken by the return of Alfred. *Canto 4*. Returning to Bigorre, Alfred chances upon Lucile out riding. During a sudden thunderstorm, the two are thrown together and Alfred declares his love. Lucile does not reply to his proposal of marriage ('I cannot reply/Without time for reflection'). *Canto 5*. Lucile sends Alfred a letter containing her reply to his proposal ('No Alfred!... [your] hand and your honour are pledged to another'). *Canto 6*. Luvois visits Lucile to restate his proposal, but (enraged by the thought of his English rival) her second refusal causes him to fly into a temper – 'He had thrown, and had miss'd/His last stake'.

Part II, Canto 1. The following year, the four meet up by chance in the German spa of Ems. Alfred and Matilda are married now, although Alfred's heart still pines for Lucile. Luvois watches, embittered, as Lucile and Alfred appear to renew their friendship, and by way of revenge resolves to seduce and ruin Alfred's young wife. *Canto 2*. Cousin John writes from London with a warning that Matilda's unscrupulous uncle, Sir Ridley MacNab, is in financial difficulties, and advising Alfred to withdraw his wife's funds from MacNab's trust. But Alfred, mooning over Lucile, pays little attention. Matilda, meanwhile, upset by her husband's apparent coldness towards her, is moving towards Luvois. *Canto 3*. Matilda wanders into the hotel garden late one night ('Through the deep blue concave of the luminous air,/Large, loving and languid, the stars here and there,/Like the eyes of shy passionate women, look'd down'). Luvois meets her there, and pays suit; but Lucile herself is also present in the garden. She declares that she will do her duty, and preserve Matilda's honour; the canto ends with the two women together in Matilda's room. *Canto 4*. Cousin John arrives from London to report the news of Sir Ridley MacNab's collapse. Alfred, having omitted to withdraw his wife's funds before the disaster, is ruined. He enters his wife's room to tell her the news, and finds her at prayer ('She had put off her dress, and look'd to his eyes/Like a young soul escaped from its earthly disguise'). They reaffirm their love for one another. *Canto 5*. Lucile confronts Luvois, and insists that their respective sufferings have not been in vain ('Vulgar natures alone suffer vainly'). She promises to revisit him in the future, should events require it of her. *Canto 6*. The action moves forward twenty-five years to the Crimean war. Alfred and Matilda's only son has been dreadfully wounded at the battle of Inkerman: the only thing that can save him is the knowledge that his love for a beautiful French maid (a love which had been interdicted by the girl's stern guardian) is not in vain. The maid is the ward of Luvois, now a battle-hardened and revered French General; and Lucile (who has taken holy orders and is nursing the wounded) brings about a reconciliation between Luvois and the son of his enemy.

LYTTON, Edward Earle Lytton, Bulwer-Lytton. see BULWER-LYTTON.

LYTTON, Edward Robert Bulwer, first earl of Lytton (1831–91). The only nineteenth-century poet of any merit to have declared war on Afghanistan, Lytton was the son of the celebrated novelist Edward *Bulwer-Lytton. He wrote under the pseudonym 'Owen Meredith' (chosen because an ancestor, Ann Meredith, was the sister of Owen Tudor, the founder of the Tudor dynasty) partly to distinguish himself from his father in literary endeavours, although it is also true that Lytton's diplomatic work and his poetry constituted two separate realms in his life.

His childhood, overshadowed by the stormy break-up of his parents, was not happy; he was educated at Harrow, and with a tutor in Bonn, where he attempted suicide. He formed a close relationship with his father's friend, John Forster, nineteen years his senior, that lasted until the latter's death in 1876. His father repeatedly attempted to discourage Lytton's poetic ambitions, and to push him into a career in the diplomatic service; Lytton, ever loyal, tried to follow his father's advice. In Italy as an unpaid embassy attaché in 1852 he met and befriended Elizabeth and Robert *Browning, and fell under the literary influence of the latter in particular. Partly inspired by Arnold's *Empedocles on Etna*, he attempted a verse tragedy conforming to the rules of Attic drama, and *Clytemnestra* resulted. He and his father came to an arrangement, whereby Bulwer-Lytton agreed to countenance the publication of a volume of his son's poetry, and Lytton agreed to refrain from writing verse for a period of two years in order to concentrate on his political career. *Clytemnestra, The Earl's Return, The Artist and Other Poems* was published by Chapman and Hall in 1855. Lytton had been promoted in 1854 to a post at the Paris Embassy, and in 1856 to the Hague. It was there that he wrote the faintly Byronic *The Wanderer*, published in 1858. This collection of 101 poems traces the (semi-autobiographical) adventures on the continent of an unnamed hero, from the 'dreamland of youthful desire', through sections set in Italy, France, England, Switzerland and Holland.

Various diplomatic posts marked Lytton's upward path, and the limited success of *The Wanderer* was followed by the greater popularity of *Lucile* (1860). Posted to Vienna (1859–63) he met Julian Fane, and the two versified the libretto of Wagner's *Tannhauser* together. *Tannhauser, or the Battle of the Bards* appeared in 1861, and *Serbski Pesme*, Lytton's translations of Serbian folksongs (his interest in which dated from his time in the embassy at Belgrade), appeared in 1863. The same year saw a short prose novel, *The Ring of Amasis*; and the following year Lytton married Edith Villiers. From 1863 to 1868 he worked on an epic verse-history of the universe, influenced by Victor Hugo's *La Legende des Siècles*. *Chronicles and Characters* came out in two volumes in 1868, but was greeted with so resounding a critical and popular silence that Lytton grew despondent, and began to doubt his abilities as a poet. He was appointed Secretary of Legation at Madrid, and there supervised the publication of *Orval, or The Fool of Time, and Other Poems*, a collection of translations, adaptions and imitations of various originals.

During the 1870s Lytton put his energies into his career, his only verse being various *Fables in Song* (1874). He rose swiftly through the ranks, and in 1875 Disraeli appointed him Viceroy of India. He had been working on a verse fairy-tale, *King Poppy* (an early version of this poem was printed privately in 1875), and he had planned to make this work public but decided it 'wouldn't do for a Viceroy to publish verse'. In India Lytton worked to tackle the Indian famine, and his domestic policies (such as abolishing the hated salt tax, and attempting to lessen the 'inconvenient and deplorable gulf which unavoidably exists between English and native society') saw some success. He also entered into negotiations with the Afghani amir, Shere Ali, in an attempt to forestall Russian expansion in that area. Shere Ali, however, prevaricated, and received a Russian embassy while turning away a British one. Lytton broke off negotiations and declared war (the Second Afghan War 1878–80). With the downfall of Disraeli's government in Britain in 1880 Lytton resigned, and scandal followed when a £12 million accounting discrepancy with respect to the war was discovered. As reward for his four-year term as viceroy, Lytton was created Earl of Lytton. He returned to England, and verse. His verse-novel *Glenaveril* appeared in 1885, and *After Paradise and Other Poems*, a collection of poems written (some of them) as early as 1865, in 1887. That year, Lytton was appointed ambassador to France, and it was in Paris that he died, in 1891. Two volumes of verse were published posthumously, *Marah* (1892), a collection of lyrics, and the astonishing, much-revised *King Poppy* (1892).

Lytton's popularity, once great in high society circles, has dwindled to nullitude today: but much of his verse contradicts Swinburne's judgement of him as 'a Seventh-Rate poet' (from the title of Swinburne's parody of Lytton in *Heptalogia*). *Lucile* and *King Poppy* in particular deserve resurrection.

: *M* :

Madoc (1805), by Robert Southey. 8635 lines, blank verse. An occasionally striking but ultimately tedious yoking together of Welsh and Aztec mythologies, this work is based loosely on historical incident. Madoc was a twelfth-century Welsh Prince, son of Owen Gwyneth. He travelled over the ocean and founded a kingdom in Aztlan.

Part 1 (in eighteen sections). Madoc in Wales. Prince Madoc returns to Wales after two years in America. He arrives during the wedding celebrations of the Welsh King David and his sister Emma, and tells his tale: after a long and perilous voyage they arrived in the New World and befriended the natives. Eventually they encountered the Azteca chief Coanocotzin in his imperial city. Undismayed by the 'four towers' of 'piled human skulls' and other instances of barbarity, Madoc defied the Azteca. The Welsh and Azteca battled, and then treated for peace. Madoc resolved to return to Wales and 'tell the tidings of success/And seek new comrades'. *Part 2 (in twenty-seven sections). Madoc in Aztlan.* Madoc returns to Aztlan after an uneventful voyage. The Welsh have established themselves in the new land ('the sound/of axe and dashing oar, and fisher's net ... and pastoral pipe,/Were heard, where late the solitary hills/Gave only to the mountain-cataract/Their wild response'). Christian priests effect some conversions among the natives (particularly among the snake-god-worshipping Hoamen); but war breaks out again with the Aztecas, and Madoc is taken prisoner. Madoc is bound to the 'stone of sacrifice' and obliged to do battle with the greatest Azteca warriors. Madoc, armed with a golden shield and sword, fights the warrior Ocellopam. His sword is broken, and he only avoids death by driving 'the splinter'd truncheon of his broken sword/Full in the enemy's face' (with startling physiological exactitude, Southey tells us it entered 'where the nasal nerves/Branch in fine fibrils o'er their mazy seat'). Ocellopam is killed and, armed with a new sword, Madoc fights Tlalala ('the Tiger'). At this point the Welsh army burst into the city, and engage the Azteca in prolonged combat. Eventually the Azteca are defeated, and they resolve 'to seek another country'. 'So in the land,' the poem concludes, 'Madoc was left sole Lord', while the Aztecas set off to 'rear a mightier empire' elsewhere, 'till Heaven ... sent among them/The heroic Spaniard's unrelenting sword'.

Marmion; a Tale of Flodden Field (1808), by Walter Scott. 6194 lines, irregular ballad metres. Very highly regarded in its own day (it sold 13,000 copies in six months and went through six editions by the end of the year), this poem perhaps stands as an emblem of the fate of all such nineteenth-century poetic endeavours. Thomas Hardy once declared that he thought *Marmion* superior to Homer's *Iliad*, but it is little read today. Each canto is prefaced with a verse epistle to a prominent friends of Scott's, rather in the manner of Dryden.

Canto First. The Castle. The scene is set in 1513. An English knight and his company enter Norham castle and distribute largess. This is Marmion, a favourite of Henry VIII, and a man whose character is a mixture of heroism and caddishness. Marmion, it seems, is travelling on an embassy to the Scottish court; and he asks the lord of the castle (Sir Hugh the Heron) for a guide to take him into Scottish territory. Sir Hugh offers him a 'holy Palmer' coming back from the Holy Land ('"Gramercy!" quoth Lord Marmion'). The narrator notes, however, that this Palmer, for all his humble estate, was taller and had 'a statelier step withal' than all the other nobles present. *Canto Second. The Convent.* Meanwhile, a boat bearing the Abbess of the convent of Saint Hilda (including a Novice called Clara de Clare: 'she was young and fair ... betrothed to one now dead') is arriving at the convent of Saint Cuthbert. The Abbess is to judge an 'inquisition stern and strict/Of two apostates from the faith,/And, if need were, to doom to death'. One of these is a nun, although dressed as 'a page' ('her cloak and doublet, loosely tied/Obscured her charms, but could not hide'), the other a hired assassin. Both are condemned to be walled up alive. Before this grisly death, the nun (Constance de Beverley) reveals that she perjured her vows for love of a man: 'I listened to a traitor's tale/I left the convent and the veil,/For three long years I bowed my pride/A horseboy in his train to ride', but he (clearly Marmion) had grown bored of her charms: 'He saw young Clara's face more fair ... And Constance was beloved no more'. She also announces that when Marmion realized he had a rival for Clara's hand, the noble De Wilton, he 'attainted' the rival's fame (which is to say, he accused De Wilton, falsely, of treason), afterwards apparently killing him in single combat. But Clara ran away, so as not to fall into Marmion's clutches, and joined a nunnery. The Canto ends with the rather grisly 'shriekings of despair' and 'stifled groans' of the two malefactors, walled up to die. *Canto Third. The Hostel.* 'The livelong day Lord Marmion rode:/The mountain path the Palmer showed'. They stop off at a village inn (for 'cheerful fire and hearty food'), where Marmion's page sings a song. Its melancholy tone prompts remorseful feelings in Marmion ('Well might he falter!' observes the narrator, 'by his aid/Was Constance Beverley betrayed'). The inn's landlord tells a ghost story, concerning a joust between a knight of old and an elfin warrior. The story strangely affects Marmion. *Canto Fourth. The Camp.* Marmion and his mysterious Palmer guide arrive at the Scottish camp, where they are met by Sir David Lyndesay, 'Lord Lion King-at-Arms'. Lyndesay has been commanded by the Scottish King (King James) to distract Marmion, 'he would not foeman's eye/ Upon his gathering forces pry/Till full prepared was every band/To march against the English land'. Lyndesay tells Marmion that a 'ghostly wight' had appeared at the court of King James and warned him against going to war. Marmion goes pale at this news. He reveals how affected he had been by the story he had heard in the inn (in Canto 3), and how afterwards unable to sleep he had ridden into the night and done battle with a supernatural foe, who had bested him and had been on the point of killing him, only desisting when Marmion had prayed to St George ('the first time e'er I asked his aid'). Marmion is taken to Blackford Hill, where he sees the massed Scots armies preparing for war. *Canto Fifth. The Court.* Marmion and Lindesay pass through the Scottish camp, and travel to Holyrood to meet the king. 'The Monarch's form was middle size ... And, oh! he had that merry glance,/That seldom lady's heart resists'. He is carrying on an affair with the wife of Sir Hugh the Heron (from Canto 1), who sings the famous song beginning 'O, Young Lochinvar is come out of the west'. King James taunts Marmion with his plans to invade England, and Marmion responds in kind. We then discover that Lady Clare, the novice nun (who had become a novice nun precisely to escape Marmion's attentions after he had slain her lover De Wilton) has been captured by King James. The Palmer is given proof by the Abbess (also captured by James) of Marmion's perfidy: namely, forgeries by Marmion, 'letters that claimed disloyal aid/And proved King Henry's cause betrayed'. A vision appears on the battlements at Holyrood and issues a supernatural summons ('I cite you by each deadly sin,/That ere hath soiled your hearts within'), beginning with James and including all the nobles, Marmion not excepted. Marmion leaves Holyrood, still in the company of the Palmer, and carrying Clare with him. *Canto Sixth. The Battle.* The party rest at Tantallon Castle. Wandering the battlements, Clare comes across the lover she had thought dead: De Wilton. It transpires that he had survived his combat with Marmion, and had been disguised as the Palmer all along. The following day, Marmion's troop arrives at the camp of the English commander Surrey. Battle is joined, and described with much bloodthirsty relish. Marmion is struck down, and is dragged from the field: 'his hand still strained the broken band;/His arms were smeared with blood and sand:/Dragged from among the horses' feet,/With dinted shield, and helmet beat'. He lives long enough to learn that Constance has been killed, but he dies, tended by Clare. Meanwhile, the English win the battle, crushing the Scots and killing King James. De Wilton and Clare marry.

Maud: a Monodrama (1855), by Alfred Tennyson. 1325 lines, in a variety of lyric metres. Tennyson's alternate title, 'The Madness', accurately sums up the topic of this elaborate, ornately constructed and often very beautiful dramatic monologue. Its germ was a brief lyric written after the death of Arthur Hallam, but the story Tennyson wove around this kernel was quite removed from his own life. The narrative is only ever obliquely alluded to, and is therefore sometimes difficult to follow; the chief interest of the work is its precise delineation of a morbid consciousness descending into insanity.

Part I. The narrator's father has committed bloody suicide ('O father! ... was it well? – /Mangled, and flattened, and crushed, and dinted into the ground?') after having been ruined in financial speculation. The unnamed speaker rails against the corruption and misery of his age. We then learn 'of the singular beauty of Maud', the daughter of a local landowner. The narrator and Maud were betrothed as children, and although no passion has grown up between them during their childhood it seems to blossom now.

> She came to the village church,
> And sat by a pillar alone;
> An angel watching an urn
> Wept over her, carved in stone;
> And once, but once, she lifted her eyes,
> And suddenly, sweetly, strangely blushed
> To find they were met by my own.

The romance continues, but seems doomed when the narrator learns that Maud's hot-headed and rather tyrannical brother (they nickname him 'the Sultan') disapproves of the match, and wishes to see her married to a young lord. The section ends with the famous lyric beginning 'Come into the garden, Maud', which tells of the narrator waiting for his beloved to come to him in the garden at dawn, after an all-night Ball at her house. *Part II.* The tone changes dramatically. It transpires that Maud was followed to her garden rendezvous by her brother and the 'babe-faced lord'; a quarrel breaks out, and the brother strikes the narrator 'over the face ... struck for himself an evil stroke'. The two fight a duel, and Maud's brother is killed (as he dies he whispers 'the fault was mine ... fly!'). The narrator escapes to the North French coast, where he learns that Maud has died of grief that her lover has killed her brother. On receiving this news the narrator himself loses all touch with sanity. Section 5, the Mad Scene (which Tennyson claimed to have written in 20

minutes) is apparently set in a French asylum, although the narrator
believes himself to have died and been buried in a shallow grave:

> Only a yard beneath the street
> And the hoofs of the horses beat, beat,
> The hoofs of the horses beat
> Beat into my scalp and my brain.

The section ends with his pitiful request 'to bury me, bury me/Deeper,
ever so little deeper'. *Part III*. This brief (50-line) section acts as a sort
of coda to the poem. In it, the narrator claims to have regained his
sanity, although he adds that a vision of the dead Maud has appeared to
him in the night sky, and instructed him to join the army for the coming
war in the Crimea. He himself sees this as a positive conclusion to his
saga: 'It is better to fight for the good than to rail at the ill ... I embrace
the purpose of God and the doom assigned'. Critics have seen the
conclusion as either reprehensible jingoism, or (more frequently) as a
finely balanced Tennysonian irony.

Mazeppa (1819), by Lord Byron. 869 lines, octosyllabic couplets. This
intriguing work is based on a passage from Voltaire's *Histoire de Charles
XII*.

The Swedish king Charles has just been defeated at the battle of
Pultowa, and has only just escaped with his life. He sits down with his
(much reduced) band of chiefs, one of whom, Mazeppa, tells a tale of
his youth to help the king nod off. As a young lad he had served a
certain Count, and had carried on an affair with the Count's young
and beautiful wife. (He describes their mutual attraction as 'young
hearts and minds/Conveying, as the electric wire,/We know not how,
the absorbing fire'). Discovered by the wrathful Count, Mazeppa is
bound naked onto the back of a horse, and sent on his way ('They
loosed him with a sudden lash–/Away! – away! – and on we dash!') The
exhausted rider is carried through various exotic landscapes, through a
'wild wood' where he is lashed by the boughs as they pass, through a
river, over a 'boundless plain', until eventually horse and rider reach the
Ukraine. The horse collapses dead under him, and Mazeppa falls into a
swoon; he awakes to discover himself being tended back to health by a
beautiful Cossack maid. Mazeppa concludes his tale with a moral ('let
none despair!'), but discovers 'the king had been an hour asleep'.

Milton (written 1804–08; plates etched 1809–10), by William Blake.
1748 lines, Blakean long line. Unhappy with the sprawling synthetic

epic of *Vala*, upon which he had been working for many years, Blake strove in *Milton* to create a brief epic, after the manner of Milton's *Paradise Regained*. The poem is an expression of Blake's personal mythology (see the general note to Blake), and was occasioned by events in Blake's own life, although this inspiration is far from obvious in the poem itself. Partly this had to do with Blake's doubts as to his epic vocation, doubts prompted by the lack of cohesion in *Vala*; partly it had to do with Blake's two-year habitation of a cottage in Felpham (on the South coast), where a soldier called Scholfield had publicly accused him of sedition. The courts found Blake not guilty of this charge, but the whole business shook him badly, and Scholfield appears demonized in various forms in his later poetry. The poem begins with a prose preface exhorting artists to throw of their fetters, and containing the famous lyric beginning: 'And did those feet in ancient time/Walk upon England's mountains green?'.

Book the First. John Milton is walking about in eternity. He hears the song of a bard retelling the fall of Satan (which had been the subject, of course, of Milton's own *Paradise Lost*) but the Bard gives the true version of this symbolic fall. There follows a debate with Palamabron (a version of an argument Blake had had with a friend, Hayley). Milton realizes that he had been in error to assume Pity and Love were part of the Divine Countenance, instead (the reality) of being Human Abstractions. This realization rouses his poetical fervour, and he becomes bored of his Miltonic heaven, where he has nothing to do but wander about 'pondring the intricate mazes of Providence'. He decides to travel to this world – 'I go to Eternal Death!' (which is to say, to our life as seen from the perspectives of eternity). Blake sees him come down: 'Then first I saw him in the zenith as a falling star,/Descending perpendicular, swift as a swallow or swift;/And on my left foot, falling on the tarsus, entered there'. The book closes with a powerful, sustained passage of descriptive poetry in which Milton/Blake apprehends the mortal world with eternal perceptions. *Book the Second.* The book opens with a beautiful description of Blake's pastoral near-paradise, Beulah (Blake's mythic geography places the actual paradise, Eden, at the centre, surrounded by the near-paradise of Beulah, which is in turn surrounded by the chaotic non-entity of Ulro). Milton/Blake is then carried to the cottage in Felpham by Los (the spirit or quasi-god that, in Blake's mythological scheme, embodies Imagination). Here he encounters the virgin Ulolon, who is Milton's ideal partner or mate (in Blake's terms, his emanation). Milton tells Ulolon of his mission to regenerate Albion, this land and our land: 'to bathe in the waters of life; to wash off the not-human ... To cast off the rotten rags of memory by inspiration;/To cast off Bacon, Locke & Newton from Albion's covering;/To take off his filthy garments & clothe him with imagination'.

Modern Greece (1816), by Felicia Hemans. 1010 lines, 10–line stanzas. The comparisons with Byron's *Childe Harold's Pilgrimage* are perhaps inevitable, but (as Byron himself was quick to notice) Mrs Hemans had never visited Greece. If her poetic description of the state of the country draws on her reading rather than her experience, the contemporary response to the poem was positive. The theme is a sort of *ubi sunt*: the glories of Greece's past are contrasted with the feeble state of the present: 'And thou art desolate – thy morn hath passed/So dazzling in the splendour of its way,/That the dark shades the night hath o'er thee cast/Throw tenfold gloom around thy deep decay'. The poet then uses her imagination to resurrect the 'bright age of Pericles' and the 'City of Theseus'. The work ends with an address to England: 'O England ... thou hast power to be what Athens e'er hath been'.

MONTGOMERY, James (1771–1854), Scottish poet and radical, re-membered mostly for book-length poems rich in geological description, and an evocative power of description that may have influenced Tennyson.

Montgomery's upbringing was joyless: his parents all but washed their hands of him by putting him in a community run by the radical religious sect called the Moravians, and then going off on missionary work to the West Indies where they both died. Despite the efforts of the Moravians to dissuade him from such dubious endeavours, Montgomery composed two epic-length poems before his sixteenth birthday – one on Alfred, the other ambitiously entitled 'The World' (the central incident in this latter was the Archangel Gabriel ambushing Satan and slicing off one of his wings). Apprenticed to a baker, Montgomery ran away in 1787 with three-and-six in his pocket, and tried to make his way in London as a poet. This plan did not meet with much success, and Montgomery eventually wound up editing a newspaper in Sheffield, the *Sheffield Iris*. His radical politics and aggressive editorial line had him sent to prison on several occasions, the first time for publishing a ballad praising the storming of the Bastille, 1794. After release from his sec-ond prison term (1796) Montgomery published the cheerily titled *Prison Amusements* (1796), as well as a four-volume novel, although he was later to try to destroy all copies of these early productions.

Sheffield had something of a reputation for political radicalism at this time, and Montgomery's brushes with the law seem rather to have strengthened his popularity than otherwise. The publication, in 1806, of *The Wanderer of Switzerland brought him his first touch of national fame; the volume ran swiftly through three editions, and a swingeing notice in the Edinburgh Review (January 1807) served actually to augment his reputation. The Wanderer brought Montgomery literary cachet – he became a reviewer on the Eclectic Review and met several of the literary names of the day. His next work, *The West Indies (1809), was directed against the slave trade, and displayed his radical politics to advantage. This was followed by the giant composition *The World Before the Flood (1812), which took the Biblical theme of the battles between the Giants and the Patriarchs. Montgomery's two most famous works came next. The first, *Greenland (1819) was founded on the records of Moravian missions to Greenland, but is most notable in its elaborate and often striking descriptions of the rocks and other geological manifestations of the landscape. His next work, *The Pelican Island (1826), was even longer, and the human interest is even less, although the blank verse descriptions of the scenery are sometimes extremely impressive.

Above all else, Montgomery was a religious man, and he wrote hundreds of hymns, many of which are still sung today. He devoted the latter portion of his life to religious work, lectures on poetry (to the Royal Institution 1830–31, published in 1833) and other scholarship. A civil list pension of £50 a year awarded him by Robert Peel's administration was more a reflection of his political reputation than his poetic one. He died suddenly on 30 April 1854, and was given a public funeral. The monument designed by John Bell and paid for by Sheffield public subscription can still be seen today in Sheffield cemetery. Montgomery was far from being the strongest poet of his age, but his resolute sense that anything was fit matter for poetic elaboration, and his geological poetry in particular, single him out as quintessentially nineteenth-century.

MOORE, Thomas (1779–1852). Moore was born in Dublin, Ireland, the son of a grocer. Though a Catholic, he was able to attend Trinity College, Dublin, and in 1799 he moved to London to study law. His literary career took precedence over subsequent official posts (he used an appointment as Admiralty Registrar in Bermuda, 1803, as an opportunity to take an extended holiday throughout North America). His more serious poetic endeavours sold well enough, although they were poorly reviewed in some quarters: 1806's Epistles, Odes and Other Poems was particularly badly reviewed by Francis Jeffrey in The Edinburgh Review. Moore challenged him to a duel, and only the intervention of the authorities prevented bloodshed; as a result of this occasion, Moore and Jeffrey became firm friends. Moore began reviewing for the *Edinburgh*, and was later even offered the position of editor.

Trading on his Irishness, Moore produced what was to become a series of ten volumes of pleasant Celtic lyrics, putting words to traditional Irish airs (*A Selection of Irish Melodies*, which appeared between 1808 and 1834). These publications assured Moore's reputation, which became world-wide. Moore's first major excursion into comical light verse, *Intercepted Letters: or the Twopenny Post Bag, by Thomas Browne the Younger* (1813) signalled his talent in this area. And from 1811 onwards, Moore established a deep friendship with *Byron. He was later to edit Byron's 'Memoirs'.

1814 saw a commission from the publisher Longman to write a romantic poem. Moore drew on the possibilities opened up by Byron's successful oriental verse tales to fashion the stories in *Lalla Rookh*. The mixture of oriental romance and the comedy of the interspersed prose connecting passages (in which Moore had his revenge on Jeffrey and the *Edinburgh Review*) made it immensely popular. It was published in 1817 to huge sales.

Moore had need of the money. A deputy in Bermuda had misappropriated £6000, and the buck stopped with Moore. He left England in 1819, and travelled in Europe, staying mostly in Italy until the debt had been repaid. He only returned to England in 1822. Meanwhile he continued to publish. *The Fudge Family in Paris* (1818) was a delightful comic exploration of English prejudices, in which Moore's Catholicism asserted itself. The oriental *The Loves of the Angels* (1823) was almost as great a success as *Lalla Rookh*. A sequel to the *Fudge Family in Paris*, *The Fudges in England* came out in 1835. Moore towards the end of his long life remained popular, although he succumbed to Alzheimer's disease in 1849. He was awarded a civil list pension in 1850 and died two years later.

MORRIS, Lewis (1837–1907). No relation to the more famous William, Morris had become an eminent enough poet by the 1890s as to be disappointed that he was not appointed laureate. His poetry is mostly very feeble, but Morris became one of the most eminent Welshmen of his age, and contributed a great deal to the emerging University of Wales.

The eldest son of a Carmarthen shipowner and merchant, Morris took a first-class degree from Jesus, Oxford, and was called to the bar in 1861. But literature was a greater love than law, and his first collection of lyric poems, *Songs of Two Worlds*, appeared in 1871. This met with enough success for a second series of lyrics, under the same title, in 1874; and a third in 1875 (the three volumes were published as one in 1878). Inspired by Tennyson's 'Tithonus', Morris conceived the plan to write a series of connected dramatic monologues, the speakers of which would be characters from Greek myth. *The Epic of Hades was the result (Book 2 appeared in 1876, Books 1 and 3 the following year). The public responded well to these subterranean poems (which had been mostly written 'amidst the not inappropriate sounds and gloom' of the London Underground); it went through 45 editions and 50,000 copies in the author's life. The Times compared Lewis to Dante, and the Spectator announced that it would 'live as a poem of permanent power'. But Morris was never again able to reach the heights (or depths) of his Hades. His 1883 collection Songs Unsung announced its author on the title page as 'Lewis Morris of Pembryn', and critics made unflattering comparisons with what they called 'William Morris of Parnassus'. Gwen: a drama in monologue in six acts (1879) owed more than a little to Tennyson's *Maud; and the tragedy Gycia (1886) was stillborn. Throughout the 1870s and 1880s Morris was putting his energies into the nascent University of Wales. He was made Secretary of University College of Wales at Aberystwyth in 1878, and held various senior positions in the University of Wales proper when it was established in 1893. It was for these services, and his vigorous support of the Liberal party (he stood for election, unsuccessfully, as a Liberal candidate several times in the 1890s) that he was knighted in 1895. His last significant poetic production, the pious and dull A Vision of Saints (1890) was an attempt to write a Christian version of the pagan Epic of Hades.

MORRIS, William (1834–96). Morris stands as the greatest of exceptions to the rule that a jack of all trades must be a master of none. He was a poet, designer, craftsman and fantasist of genius, and his paintings and engravings are of high quality. He worked in almost all fields of artistic endeavour excepting only music and sculpture, and he excelled in most. Although it is his narrative poetry that concerns us here, analysis of his achievement in that field (and he was one of the supreme Victorian narrative poets) cannot be divorced from his immersion in the visual arts. He adored *Keats, despised *Wordsworth, and declared that only the fact that *Shelley had 'no eyes' stood in the way of Morris truly admiring his poetry. The stress on the visual is apropos. Morris's poetry is some of the most colourful (literally as well as figuratively) in English literature; and although this is a feature that encourages critics to identify him with the Pre-Raphaelite movement (which certainly included many of his friends, Dante Rossetti and Edward Burne-Jones in particular), Morris's own poetry is always too much in motion to be truly Pre-Raphaelite. It is because Morris's genius was for a poetry of movement, of flow, that he was so well suited to the demands of narrative verse.

Born of well-to-do bourgeois parents, Morris was educated at Marlborough School and Exeter College, Oxford. He was articled to an Oxford architect, and worked with his new friends Rossetti and Burne-Jones on some frescoes in the Oxford Union. He wrote short poems and essays throughout the 1850s, many of which appeared in the *Oxford and Cambridge Magazine*, which he helped found in 1856. His first collection of poetry, *The Defence of Guinevere and Other Poems*, appeared in 1858 and garnered him an immediate reputation, although few sales. Its powerful lyrics and brief narratives balanced finely between beauty and violence, and were all rendered with a Keatsian precision of visual image. In 1859 Morris married the beautiful Pre-Raphaelite model, Jane Burden. They moved to the famous Red House (in Bexley), which had been designed for Morris by Philip Webb. Unable to find suitable furniture for their new home, Morris began designing and creating his own pieces. This lead to the creation of a firm, Morris, Marshall, Faulkener and Co., to produce high-quality fittings that were beautiful and functional: furniture, textiles, wallpaper and stained glass. But his marriage to Jane, although it produced two children, was not happy. She began a long-term affair with Rossetti (and later with another of Morris's friends). Morris was almost certainly aware of this circumstance.

A large (and from time to time frankly fat) man, Morris was hugely kind-hearted, gentle and civilized, but he was also prone to mania. Stories from university have him flying into apoplectic rages, banging his head so hard against the walls of his room as to leave a large dent in the plaster, biting through the wood of his window-ledge. In less extreme form, this mania manifested itself as a titanic enthusiasm, and a remarkable capacity for sustained creative work. At the same time as putting tremendous amounts of energy into his firm, Morris was, throughout the 1860s and 1870s, writing good verse at a rate exhausting to contemplate. Some days he managed to turn out 1000 lines of poetry; 600 and 700–line days were not uncommon (as his biographer Fiona MacCarthy points out, most serious writers are content with 1000 *words* of *prose*). He liked to compose on railway journeys, where the motion of travel soothed him into a sort of writing trance. If the poetry were poor, or padded out, we might understand this prolixity; but (despite what some critics assert) the poetry is never less than adequate to the tasks of the poem and is more often than not striking, beautiful, perfectly cadenced and timed. He fashioned a sweeping, onward-moving poetic voice ideally suited to the sweep of epic narrative, inventing a distinctive style that was (to quote Swinburne) 'so broad and sad and simple'.

Through the 1860s Morris was working on a large-scale collection of long poems, a sort of modern-day *Canterbury Tales*: *The Earthly Paradise*, that Morris hoped to publish with 500 of his own woodcuts (this plan was eventually abandoned). In 1867 he published his first long poem, *The Life and Death of Jason*. This had originally been intended for *The Earthly Paradise*, but had grown too long for inclusion. The work was a great success. The publication of *The Earthly Paradise* followed, the twenty-five connected long poems emerging in four volumes between late 1868 and early 1870; taken together, it remains the longest poetical production of the century. Length is no guarantee of merit, of course, but Morris is long to a purpose. The crucial thing is to understand the importance of this length, and accordingly we need not to be distracted by the less crucial aspects of the poetry. Morris's escapism, archaic diction, familiar stories, emphasis on unhappy love (a reflection of his own life) and colourful, vividness of description are actually not the point of his poetry (although these are the features most often discussed by contemporaries and modern critics). His verse is actually about moving onwards, about the joy of travel and the stagnation and depression of arrival, even arrival at the wished-for destination. The length of the works enacts this journey-aesthetic.

With Rossetti (who by now had been Jane's lover for some years) Morris took a joint tenancy of Kelmscott Manor in 1871. This was later to be the site of Morris's own, famous printing press. In 1872 he published a work based on the form of the medieval masque, *Love is Enough*; this was also the year in which he journeyed to Iceland for the first time. This visit (others followed in later years) aroused Morris's passion for the sagas and legends of Icelandic literature. With the help of Eirikir Magnusson he worked at translating some of these (including *Grettis Saga* and *Laxdaela Saga*), also publishing translations of the *Aeneid* (1875), the *Odyssey* (1887) and *Beowulf* (1897). This work also informed his creative writing. His epic treatment of the Volsung saga, *Sigurd the Volsung* (the same material Wagner treated in *Der Ring des Nibelungen* – an opera which Morris rightly despised) appeared in 1876. Morris regarded this work as his masterpiece, a judgement with which few critics have concurred. But although the archaisms can strike a modern reader as ugly, and although we are generally not as familiar with the legends behind the poetry as would be good for the aesthetic effect of the whole, *Sigurd* is indeed a powerful and muscular work. It is a saga (in the genuine sense) of war and love located in convincingly realized landscapes of huge scale, and with the freshness of the created myth of, say, Tolkien.

The lukewarm reception of *Sigurd* disappointed Morris; he wrote no more of his own long poems, and largely moved away from writing poetry at all (his two remaining collections of short verse excepted, *Poems by the Way* in 1891 and *Chants for Socialists* in 1884–85). From the late 1870s onwards Morris became more and more involved in the burgeoning socialist movement. His membership of the newly formed Social Democratic Federation in 1883 saw him arguing passionately and effectively for a utopian socialist vision that saw necessary connections between a more just society, the dignity of work and a less hideous world (in his essay 'Why I Became A Socialist' in 1894 Morris wrote: 'apart from the desire to produce beautiful things, the leading passion of my life has been and is hatred of modern civilisation … this sordid, aimless, ugly confusion'). He headed the breakaway Socialist League in 1884, and remains one of the founding fathers of British socialism. His later novels often carry socialist morals, and many of the tricks (including the fondness for archaism) of the poems re-emerge in strange, symbolist prose rhapsodies that prefigure twentieth-century Fantasy writing: *The House of the Wolfings* (1889), *The Roots of the Mountains* (1890), *News from Nowhere* (1891), *The Wood Beyond the World* (1894) and *The Sundering Flood* (1898) all have their admirers today. Morris's work in printing and binding with his Kelmscott Press, mostly from this period, is also famous.

Critical dismissal of Morris's long poetry, most often on the grounds that it is too 'trance-like' and 'flabby' is profoundly misguided. To characterize the mood of Morris's poetry as flabby is inappropriately to apply the criteria (concision, epiphanic intensity, epigrammatic focus) of the lyric and short poem; the twentieth-century popularity of such modes of writing does not give them universal application. Neither is 'trance' a necessarily pejorative description of the flowing, moving, travelling but never restless quality of Morris's narrativity. His is an unjustly neglected aesthetic: a poetics of becoming.

Paracelsus (1835), by Robert Browning. 4151 lines, blank verse with interspersed songs. This philosophical dramatic-poem represents Browning's attempts at a more objective poetic style, following the introspection of *Pauline*. It is based loosely on the life of the historical alchemist.

Part 1, Paracelsus Aspires. We begin at Wurzburg in 1512, where Aureole Paracelsus is telling his friends, Festus and Michal, of his ambitions; which are, modestly, 'to comprehend the works of God,/And God himself, and all God's intercourse/With the human mind'. The path to this absolute knowledge lies in alchemy, and although his friends warn him of the possible consequences of his hubris, the scene ends with him readying to 'plunge' into his studies. *Part 2, Paracelsus Attains.* We are now at the house of a Greek conjurer in Constantinople, 1521. Paracelsus has not uncovered the ultimate secret he was searching for, and he is in gloomy mood ('Time fleets, youth fades, life is an empty dream'). He encounters a young poet, Aprile, and the two exchange perspectives on the world:

PARACELSUS: I am he that aspired to KNOW: and thou?
APRILE: I would LOVE infinitely, and be loved!

Aprile later dies, telling us that 'God is the perfect poet,/Who in his person acts his own creations'. Although at first contemptuous of Aprile's position, Paracelsus gradually becomes aware of its fundamental truth. *Part 3, Paracelsus.* It is now 1526. Paracelsus has returned to Basle to work as Professor at the university. In conversation with his old friend, Festus, he reveals that he detests the students he has to teach, and despite the outward trappings of success feels he has utterly failed. *Part 4, Paracelsus Aspires.* 1528. Paracelsus again aspires, although his aims are now modified by his sense of the necessity of both knowledge and love ('I have tried each way singly: now for both'). *Part 5, Paracelsus Attains.* It is 1541, and Paracelsus is on his deathbed in a Salzburg hospital, oblivious to the solicitude of his ever-watchful Festus. Just before dying, Paracelsus awakes from delirium and delivers a lengthy monologue in which is summarized the wisdom of his life (and which, Browning was later to claim, foreshadowed Darwin's doctrine of evolution by thirty years). Finishing he asks, 'I have said enough?' and his friend instructs him 'Now die, dear Aureole!', which he duly does.

Parisina (1816), by Lord Byron. 586 lines, octosyllabic couplets. Byron based this poem on a circumstance mentioned in Gibbon's *Antiquities of the House of Brunswick*.

The Italian Prince Azo is married to the beautiful Parisina; his only son is Hugo, a bastard Azo had fathered on a woman called Bianca. One night, in bed with Parisina, Azo hears her murmur the name 'Hugo' in her sleep; he realizes that his wife and his son have been carrying on a semi-incestuous affair. Azo has Hugo beheaded (in front of a large crowd who had gathered 'to see the Son fall by the doom of the Father!'); Hugo dies nobly ('without display, without parade ... as not disdaining priestly aid'), but from that moment Parisina is seen 'no more in palace, hall or bower'. Azo finds another bride ('and goodly sons grew by his side'), but he remains wretched throughout his life.

Parleyings with Certain People of Importance in their Day, to wit: Bernard de Mandeville, Daniel Bartoli, Christopher Smart, George Bubb Doddington, Francis Furini, Gerard de Lairesse, and Charles Avison (1887), by Robert Browning. 3495 lines, variously rhymed blank verse. Browning's last major poem is a powerful meditation on a variety of themes, but its density and obliqueness meant that it baffled its original audience. In it Browning deliberately resurrects a variety of obscure figures from various walks of life to provide himself with the opportunity of exploring a wide range of subjects.

Prologue: Apollo and the Fates. The scene is set in the underworld of Greek myth, at the moment when Apollo is negotiating with the three Fates (Clotho, Lachesis, Atropo) for the life of his mortal friend, Admetus (the same myth is the premise of Euripides' *Alcestis*). In Browning's version, Apollo attempts to bribe the fates with 'Man's invention of – WINE', of which they are unaware. Drunk (and dancing), the Fates seem about to comply, but a mysterious 'explosion from the earth's centre' startles them back to sobriety, and they compromise by announcing that they will let Admetus live if somebody can be found who will voluntarily die in his place. *With Bernard de Mandeville.* This parleying concerns ethical questions, although de Mandeville (the early eighteenth-century Dutch doctor and author of the satirical *Fable of the Bees*) is invoked chiefly as a foil to the unnamed figure of Carlyle, whose gloomy worldview is challenged. Carlyle complains that God never intervenes to help suffering humanity or prevent evil ('No stirring of God's finger to denote/He wills that right should have supremacy'). To contradict such pessimism, we are given a version of the myth of Prometheus, the Titan who helped mankind by giving them fire. In this retelling of the myth, the fire is created by a lense, 'an artifice whereby he drew/Sun's rays into a focus' which in turn represents the power of poetry to convey the 'infinitude' of God into finite, mortal minds. *With Daniel Bartoli*. Bartoli was a seventeenth-century Jesuit, and in this Parleying the narrator contrasts his worship of the Madonna with his own contention that 'the divinest women that have walked/Our world were scarce those saints of whom we talked'. As illustration, we are given the story of the beautiful, honourable and dignified Marianne Pajot, jilted by Charles of Lorraine but later happily married to the Marquis de Lassay. *With Christopher Smart*. Browning praises this minor eighteenth-century poet for one work, 'The Song of David' among a career of otherwise dull publications (he was unaware of the madder productions, such as *Jubilate Agno*, for which Smart is now more famous). To do this he invokes a metaphor: exploring a large house, he goes from room to room finding everywhere a decent but moderate taste in decor. Suddenly he enters the chapel, and is overwhelmed by the gorgeous perfection of its rich styling; but passing from it he enters another suite of rooms of decent mediocrity. So it seems to him that the mediocre imagination of Smart was suddenly transfigured by the flames of madness into the genius that composed the 'Song of David'. *With George Bubb Dodington*. Dodington was an eighteenth-century politician, and this Parleying is a meditation on political double-dealing and knavery. *With Francis Furini*. The longest of the Parleyings, this is a defence of nudity in painting, occasioned in part by the troubles Browning's own son, a professional artist, was having painting nude figures for the Victorian art market. Furini was a seventeenth-century Florentine painter of nudes who also became a priest. Nudity is defended as something not lewd, and the image of the naked Andromeda, painted by Furini, is invoked as an image with profound religious significance. *With Gerard de Lairesse*. De Lairesse was the seventeenth-century Dutch painter, invoked here as the author of a treatise on 'The Art of Painting' that had influenced the young Browning. In that book, an imaginary 'walk' is undertaken through the sorts of subjects viable for painting, and this Parleying reproduces it. In effect, Browning discusses the uses and relevance of classical myth, ultimately pointing up its limitations beside Christian belief. *With Charles Avison*. Avison was an eighteenth-century Newcastle organist. Browning had always nursed a lifetime passion for music, and it is here invoked (along with a section of musical score, from one of Avison's marches) as a form of art that goes further than the written word. *Epilogue: Fust and his Friends*. Browning collapses together the stories of Johann Fust (a German banker connected with the invention of the printing press) and Faust, the character who sold his soul to the devil. Seven 'friends', prominent citizens of Mayence, prepare to lecture Fust on the danger of what they assume has been his compact with the Devil (as evinced by his miraculous ability to copy text). The tone is comic, and the misunderstanding is swiftly cleared up, although the implications of Fust's printing device, that (for instance) heretics and schismatics will be able to distribute their tracts more efficiently, crosses the minds of the friends. The poem ends with Fust foreseeing the coming of Luther.

PATMORE, Coventry (1823–96). His middle names ('Kersey Dingham') were just as odd as his Christian name.

Born in Woodford, Essex, Patmore was educated privately by his well-to-do family, with no particular career in mind. He thought of taking holy orders, but instead published a slim volume of poetry in 1844. His life was disrupted when, in 1845, his father lost all his money in an unfortunate railway speculation. For a while Patmore earned a scanty living translating foreign books and writing articles for respectable journals, until in 1846 his friends secured him a position as assistant in the printed books department of the British Museum. He felt secure enough in this post to marry Emily Augusta Andrews in 1846. He continued supplementing his income with articles for the *Edinburgh Review* and *North Briton*, and in the 1850s was working on his magnum opus. The first part of this, *The Betrothal* appeared in 1854, and the second (*The Espousals*) in 1856 (together these works constitute *The Angel in the House*). The bourgeois conventionality of these works, together with their romantic love-story plot, conspired to make them a big hit with the public. The narrative is tangentially continued in *Faithful for Ever* (1860) and *The Victories of Love* (1862), known collectively as *The Victories of Love*. With his wife, Emily, he also published a collection of rather stiff children's poems, *The Children's Garland* in 1862 (he had six children of his own); but Emily died of consumption in this year.

As a young man Patmore had been angular and rugged, and had suffered from often extreme mood swings. He was frequently haughty, imperious, combative, sardonic and essentially self-centred; but he also possessed a rapid intelligence and a certain charm. But in later life these character traits hardened into reactionary inflexibility. He (as we might expect from *The Angel in the House*) had little time for women's rights; but he also thought 1867 (which saw the Great Reform Act, greatly extending British democracy) 'the year of the great crime', and he called the Third Reform Act (which introduced universal male suffrage) 'the final destruction of the liberties of England'. This calcification was reflected in the rather curmudgeonly way he converted to Roman

Catholicism in 1864. He was drawn to what he saw as the timeless certainties of Catholic tradition, and some of the religiously inspired poems in *The Unknown Eros* (1877) and *Root, Rood and Flower* (1895) express a powerful sense of the religious mystery. But he also bitterly disliked the Catholic clergy in Britain, and found himself often at odds with his fellow Catholics. He worked for many years on his own reading of Catholic doctrine, to be called *Sponsa Dei*, but he destroyed the manuscript rather than publish, perhaps because it was too idiosyncratic. His second wife, Marianne (whom he married in 1864, the year of his conversion) was also Catholic. He retired from the British Library, and lived chiefly in Hastings. 1878's *Amelia, Tamerton Church-tower etc.* contained a characteristically dogmatic preface on English metrical law. In 1880 his second wife died (Patmore built a church in Hastings to commemorate her), and he married the former governess of his children. But later life was marred for Patmore by the death of his daughter Emily in 1882 and his son Henry in 1883.

Despite the prickliness of Patmore's character, the poetry of *The Angel in the House* is light, pleasant and even fairly entertaining. If never exactly witty, it does at least manage a certain penetrating verisimilitude in the anatomy of the ups and downs of courtship. But it, and its sequel, are nonetheless deeply reactionary poems. Often taken as paradigmatic expressions of Victorian domesticity they are actually both too extreme and old-fashioned to be so. Some contemporary critics would like to make out a place for Patmore as a great neglected figure of nineteenth-century poetics, but he is not; Patmore is more skilled as an epigrammaticist than a poet (either lyrical or narrative).

Pauline, A Fragment of a Confession (1833), By Robert Browning. 1031 lines, blank verse. Browning's first publication, and one he subsequently tried to suppress, although it was eventually reprinted in 1868.

The narrator is an unnamed young poet, who has many things in common with Browning himself. During the course of his rather fluid speech, we learn of his solitary and bookish childhood, and his powerful, imaginative self-consciousness ('I am made up of an intensest life'). Above all, we learn of the three most significant influences on his life. One is Shelley (referred to in the poem as 'Sun Treader') both in terms of his poetry and his political optimism ('Men were to be as gods, and earth as heaven'). The second is God, seen from the perspective of the narrator's wrestlings with atheism. The third is Pauline herself, the beautiful object of his love. By the end of the poem, the narrator has worked through a variety of spiritual dilemmas to emerge triumphantly ('I believe in God, and truth,/And love'). Browning sent a copy of the poem to John Stuart Mill, whose negative criticisms ('the writer seems to me to be possessed with a more intense and morbid self-consciousness than I ever knew in any sane man') encouraged him to forge a new, less 'confessional' style.

Pelican Island, The: A Poem in Nine Cantos (1827), by James Montgomery. 2939 lines, blank verse. Arguably Montgomery's masterpiece, the poem is based on a passage in Cpt. Flinder's *Voyage to Terra Australia* in which the ecostructure of a Pacific island is described in detail. Montgomery uses this basis to develop a fascinating picture of the interconnectedness of life, which (despite the unabashed Christian message of the whole) strikingly anticipates by thirty years evolutionary theory.

Canto First. The narrator begins: 'Methought I lived through ages, and beheld/Their generations pass so swiftly by me/That years were moments in their flight'. The scene is first set when 'sky, sun, and sea were all the universe'. Day passes back into night, and back into day. The first example of life appears (a Nautilus), and then a flying fish, and finally at sunset an oceanic revelry ('spouting Whales projected wat'ry columns,/That turn'd to arches at their height, and seem'd/The skeletons of crystal palaces/Built on the blue expanse'). *Canto Second*. 'Life's intermitting pulse' continues, above the waves and on the seabed. A coral reef slowly appears: 'atom by atom thus the burden grew'. *Canto Third*. Slowly the reef becomes an island, and vegetation grows upon it. It becomes inhabited with a wide variety of wildlife, and in particular 'birds, small and great, of endless shapes and colours'. A hurricane devastates the island. *Canto Fourth*. The poet looks 'with consternation' on the wreck of the island, but he has underestimated the power of 'glorious Nature'. The island is repopulated. A pair of Pelicans arrive, a sort of Pelican Adam and Eve, who breed a whole population of birds ('Thus wings were multiplied from year to year;/And here the patriarch-twain, in good old age,/Resign'd their breath beneath the ancient rest'). *Canto Fifth*. More coral islands appear, subsidiary to the main island. All manner of animals have turned the island into 'a land of births ... a land of deaths'. *Canto Sixth*. Time moves on. 'The islands moved like circles on the water,/Expanding till they touch'd each other, closed/The interjacent straits, and thus became/A spacious continent'. Animal life becomes more variegated, and the poet finally spies 'Man going forth amidst inferior creatures'. Sadly, at this stage, mankind's 'prime glory was insane debauch': war, pillage, cannibalism and so forth. *Canto Seventh*. Mankind expands, but the poet experiences 'heart-sickness to behold them thus/Perishing without knowledge'. A woman gives birth to a child, but murders the girl rather than have her grow up in so cruel a world, weeping 'O that my mother had done so to me!' *Canto Eighth.* The poet compares the misery of human experience with the generations of Pelicans. *Canto Ninth.* An elderly chieftain ('the glory of his tribe,/The terror of his enemies') is out with his grandchild when he experiences a divine revelation – '"My son!/My son! there is a GOD! there is a GOD!"' The poet concludes with advice to his reader to 'take this parable/Home to thy bosom'.

Peter Bell (1819), by William Wordsworth. 1320 lines, ballad metres. Written in 1798, but not published (in slightly revised form) until much later, Wordsworth's simple tale of a simple man's reformation excited some admiration, but a great deal more ridicule, including legion parodies (such as Reynold's *Peter Bell the Second* and Shelley's *Peter Bell the Third*).

Prologue. The narrator sets the scene by intimating the soaring power of his imagination ('I have a little boat/In shape just like the crescent moon./Fast through the clouds my boat can sail') before being called back to reality and a party in his garden, with several homely guests ('The Squire is there, and ... His pretty little daughter Bess', 'Parson Swan', 'Stephen Otter'). *Part First.* The narrator begins to tell his friends 'the Tale of Peter Bell' with the striking lines.

> All by the moonlight river side
> It gave three miserable groans
> 'Tis come then to a pretty pass',
> Said Peter to the groaning Ass,
> 'But I will bang your bones'.

His audience object, and insist that he tells the story from the beginning; which he does. Peter Bell is an itinerant Potter, a bad man, amoral, with 'a dozen wedded wives'. Coming across the ass, standing unattended by the pool, he thanks his luck; but all his beating and snarling cannot encourage the beast to move; instead it looks sadly at Peter and 'upon the pivot of his skull/Turns round his long left ear'. Suddenly Peter notices a man lying on the river bed. He faints. *Part Second.* Recovering from a swoon, Peter reasons that the dead man in the river was the Ass's master. Using a sapling, he retrieves the body from the water; whereupon the Ass is content to give him a ride. They set off. *Part Third.* Peter is terrified by a variety of apparently supernatural but actually natural phenomena (for instance, the noises he hears in the earth at his feet are actually Miners blasting a tunnel underground). Eventually the Ass returns to his master's house and widow. The strange events have effected a change in Peter; and he becomes 'a good and honest man'. The Ass 'by his labour' helps to maintain the widow's family.

Pleasures of Hope, The (1799), by Thomas Campbell. 1088 lines, heroic couplets. Modelled on Akenside's *Pleasures of Imagination* (1744) and, more immediately, on Rogers' *The Pleasures of Memory* (1792), this discursive pseudo-philosophical poem was Campbell's first publication.

Part 1. According to classical myth, when the guardian deities of mankind abandoned this world, Hope alone remained to comfort us ('Auspicious Hope! in thy sweet garden grow/Wreaths for each toil, a charm for every woe'). Hope sustains the seaman at his wintry watch, the soldier marching into battle, and so on. From various individual instances of Hope at work, the perspective shifts to hope for the political improvement of Society. Campbell is optimistic that 'bright Improvement' will 'rule the spacious world from clime to clime', but his present view of the world is less cheerful. The partition of Poland, the capture of Warsaw and all the horrors that attended it, are indignantly described ('Shall War's polluted banner ne'er be furled?'), as are the evils attendant on colonialism in Africa and India. *Part 2.* Love is apostrophized and praised, and the connection made between romantic attachment and Hope for the future. Love and imagination are hymned as inseparable, and the poem ends with pious reflections in the hope for life after death. Campbell attacks the sceptical philosopher ('hopeless, dark Idolator of Chance') who denies this state of affairs, and concludes with a peroration to 'Eternal Hope!'

POLLOK, Robert (1798–1827). Pollok was born in North Moorhouse, Eaglesham, Renfrewshire, the seventh of a Scots farmer's eight children. He tried to follow one of his brothers into cabinet making, and made four chairs in 1815; but the trade did not suit him. Ambitious to become a preacher, he went to Glasgow University in 1817, where he graduated with an MA in 1822. From 1822–27 he studied theology at United Secession Hall and Glasgow University. He began work upon his one major poem *The Course of Time* in 1825, also writing occasional poetry and essays. On 2 May 1827 he received his qualification as a probationer under the United Associated Synod and preached once in Edinburgh and three times in Slatefield, just outside the city. But his health was poor, and doctors advised him to travel and convalesce in Italy. He travelled by sea from Edinburgh to London, but there it was decided that he was too ill to travel further. *The Course of Time* was published in Edinburgh, 1827, and Pollok and his wife moved down to Shirley, just outside Southampton. He died there 18 September 1827.

Prelude, The, or, Growth of a Poet's Mind (1799, 1805, 1850), by William Wordsworth. 8487 lines, blank verse. Wordsworth first wrote a two-book version of this, his poetic autobiography, in 1798–99; at this stage the work was untitled (or, perhaps, called 'Poem to Coleridge', the addressee of these blank-verse ruminations). By 1805 Wordsworth had expanded the work to thirteen books, partly by incorporating previously written material and partly by original composition (it is the 1805 *Prelude* that is detailed here), but neither the 1799 nor the 1805 version was published. Wordsworth returned to the manuscript many times over the following forty-five years, tinkering and revising without radically altering the whole. It finally appeared in print after the poet's death in 1850, its title supplied by Mary Wordsworth. *The Prelude* is so-called because it was originally designed as a prelude to a much-larger philosophico-poetical work, to be called *The Recluse*, which Wordsworth never completed. *The Excursion* is a related work, an excursion from the main body of *The Recluse*.

Book I. Introduction – Childhood and School-Time. The poet begins by rejoicing in the 'gentle breeze/That blows from the green fields and from the clouds' as he leaves crowded, oppressive London for the natural world. He recalls his near-idyllic childhood in the Lake District ('Fair seedtime had my soul'), and mentions incidents such as iceskating, and rowing out over Ullswater and being overwhelmed by the 'huge Cliff' that seemed to rise up as he rowed. But the purpose here is less nostalgia and more an imaginative attempt to recreate the process by which Wordworth's poetic soul developed. He describes his childhood as a crucial time for this development: a time when 'I held unconscious intercourse/With the eternal Beauty, drinking in/A pure organic pleasure'. *Book II. School-Time (continued).* Wordsworth's childhood play (rowing on Windemere, riding horses) was as important a part in his 'schooling' as the actual attendance at School. *Book III. Residence at Cambridge.* Wordsworth went up to St Johns, Cambridge, October 1787, and here he recalls his Cambridge days amid the various colourful and peculiar types for which Cambridge is so famous: 'I was the Dreamer, they the Dream; I roamed/Delighted, through the motley spectacle;/Gowns grave or gaudy, Doctors, Students, Streets'. *Book IV. Summer Vacation.* With the holidays Wordsworth returns to the Lake District, 'a wild, unworldly-minded Youth, given up/To Nature and to Books'. Balanced with the previous book, the overall theme is an exploration of the conflict between false and true education. *Book V.*

Books. 'Hitherto,/In progress through this Verse', says the narrator, 'my mind hath looked/Upon the speaking face of earth and heaven'. But books were also important in the development of the poet's mind, and some are mentioned here: Cervantes, Arabian Nights – books that allowed for the fostering of the imagination, rather than the sort of narrowing texts prescribed by educational theories of the time (which the narrator attacks). *Book VI. Cambridge and the Alps.* In possibly the most famous section of the *Prelude*, Wordsworth details his trip through France and over the Alps to Italy in company with his friend Robert Jones. The sublimity of the Alps marks another important stage in the development of his poet's soul ('my heart leaped up'), and in a beautifully paced passage he describes the realization that he has actually crossed the Alps without being aware of it: adding a panegyric to 'Imagination!' that locates his earth-shattering epiphany not in the beautiful surroundings, but inside the poet himself. *Book VII. Residence in London.* Back in England, the narrator lives for a while among the hustle-bustle of London, and describes a visit to Bartholomew Fair. He does not much like the company of his urban fellows ('Crowd ... Barbarian and infernal! tis a dream/Monstrous in colour, motion, shape, sight, sound ... grimacing, writhing, screaming'). *Book VIII. Retrospect. – Love of Nature Leading to Love of Mankind.* The course of the poem has been, up to this time, a mostly chronological account of Wordsworth's life. In this book, the narrator meditates upon the positive virtues of a love of the natural world, returning as he does so to the Lakes ('Beauteous the domain/Where to the sense of beauty first my heart/Was opened'), contrasting the pleasant small-scale Helvellyn Fair with the anarchy of Bartholomew Fair in the previous book. The moral of the piece is that a true love of Nature is the gateway to 'union or communion' with 'human Creatures' and ultimately with God. *Book IX. Residence in France.* The narrative returns to the narrator's residence in London, and thence to the time spent living in France (1791–92). Recalling his own revolutionary enthusiasm ('my heart was all/Given to the People, and my love was theirs'), he obliquely refers to his love affair with Annette Vallon by including an earlier-written fictionalized account, 'Vaudracour and Julia' ('Oh! happy time of youthful Lovers!'). *Book X. Residence in France and French Revolution.* In a sense, this book charts Wordsworth's disillusionment with the French Revolution, following the rise of Robespierre and the Terror. To begin with the narrator keeps his faith ('rouzed up, I stuck/More firmly to the old tenets'), but on returning to England he eventually gives up the mental fight to justify revolution ('sick, wearied out with contrarieties') and by 'Nature's self, by human love/Assisted' (the human love coming from his sister, Dorothy), he is restored 'to my true self' ('though impaired and changed').

Book XI. Imagination. How Impaired and Restored. This mostly discursive book details the conflict between head and heart, and the primacy of the latter. He dwells on those moments of intense personal epiphany that he calls 'Spots of Time':

> There are in our existence spots of time,
> Which with distinct preeminence retain
> A renovating virtue, whence depressed
> By false opinion and contentious thought,
> Or aught of heavier or more deadly weight
> In trivial occupations and the round
> Of ordinary intercourse, our minds
> Are nourished and invisibly repaired.

He illustrates this with recollections of being strangely affected by seeing a woman by a pool in Penrith Beacon, and another occasion when a similar moment of intensity came while he was waiting for some horses. *Book XII. Same Subject (Continued).* This book actually picks up the story from Book X, and relates his emotional recovery from the crisis described there; a recovery enabled, surprise surprise, by Nature; 'Nature through all conditions hath a power/To consecrate'. *Book XIII. Conclusion.* The narrator concludes by recalling his ascent of Snowdon. With a friend, he sets off before dawn to climb the mountain in order to see the sun rise. Climbing in the dark, he describes a startling sudden illumination by the moon; this prompts 'a meditation' on the shaping power of the Imagination, and on Love (and those that Wordsworth has loved). The work concludes by again addressing Coleridge: 'O most loving soul,/Placed on this earth to love and understand'.

The expanded 14–book 1850 *Prelude*, in addition to various minor changes, effectively adds a book, mostly by dividing 1805's Book X ('Residence in France and French Revolution') into two: Book X, 'Residence in France – Continued', and Book XI, 'France – Concluded'.

Prince Hohensteil-Schwangau, Saviour of Society (1871), by Robert Browning. 2155 lines, blank verse. In this lengthy dramatic monologue, Browning explored his attitude towards Napoleon III, who, under an assumed name, is the speaker here.

The monologue is addressed to a Leicester Square prostitute. The Prince, fallen on hard times and exiled in England, explains his political history and ideology to her over coffee and cigars. His enemies (he says) have accused him of mere expediency; but he insists that he has always struggled to maintain, or 'save' society as he has found it – rather than making anything revolutionary or new. In the latter part he enters into a dialogue with an imaginary future-historian (whom he calls 'Sagacity'), explaining various of his political decisions and attitudes. At the end of the poem, a chiming clock awakens the Prince from his dream – he has been sleeping in his Imperial Palace all along, and dreaming of a (possible) future conversation with the prostitute.

Prince's Progress, The (1866), by Christina Rossetti. 540 lines, six-lined stanzas aaabab. Rossetti wrote this work at her brother Dante's suggestion to expand upon a mournful lyric called 'The Prince Who Arrived Too Late'; which lyric now constitutes the last 60 lines of the poem.

A princess is waiting for her Prince to come and marry her. The Prince, meanwhile, is 'taking his ease on cushion and mat' in his 'world-end palace'. Roused by a 'hundred sad voices' telling him to seize the day, he resolves to stop procrastinating and sets out on the journey to his bride-to-be. Along the way he accepts a drink of milk from a milkmaid, and stays with her for 'one idle day'. With dawn he sets off again, travelling across a ghastly desert landscape ('Some old volcanic upset must/Have rent the crust and blackened the crust;/Wrenched and ribbed it'). In this wilderness he encounters an alchemist who is creating an elixir of life, and stays to help him ('thinking "My love and I will live./If I tarry, why life is good,/And she may forgive"'). The alchemist eventually dies, and the Prince continues with a small phial of this elixir. He is nearly drowned in a river and nursed back to health by some kindly citizens, among whom he loiters. Finally he climbs the mountain and descends the other side to the palace of his bride, but discovers he has come too late: 'Too late! too late!/You loitered on the road too long ... The enchanted princess in her tower/Slept, died, behind the grate.'

Princess, The: A Medley (1847), by Alfred Tennyson. 3309 lines, blank verse with interspersed lyrics. Some of the best-known lyrics (including 'The splendour falls on castle walls') were not added to the work until the third edition, 1850.

Prologue. Sir Walter Vivian, English gentleman, has given over the grounds of his stately home to a summer fete. Among the guests are university friends of Vivian's son, one of whom is the narrator. Also present is the beautiful Lilia ('a rosebud set with little wilful thorns/And sweet as English air could make her'). The group of seven university friends agree to improvise a tale in seven parts, each taking one and carrying the story on. *One.* A prince, the narrator, has been betrothed since birth to the beautiful Princess Ida from the neighbouring kingdom (modelled on Lilia). On coming of age, the princess announces her conversion to a sort of feminism, declares she 'will not wed' and goes off to found a university, for women only, situated close to the border between the two kingdoms. With his two friends, Cyril and Florian, the prince disguises himself as a woman and the three gain entrance to the university as students. There are two main lecturers, Lady Pysche ('prettiest, best natured', and also Florian's sister) and the austere Lady Blanche. The interlopers enroll under the tutelage of the former. *Two.* Florian is recognised by Lady Pysche, who tearfully tells them that she must keep her vow to reveal any intruding men to the princess, and that the university operates under a law that decrees 'LET NO MAN ENTER IN ON PAIN OF DEATH'. Cyril, who has fallen in love with Psyche, declares that fear of death is no deterrent for him. Psyche agrees to keep their secret, and the men stroll about the university. *Three.* The men join a field-trip into the surrounding countryside to gather geological samples ('hammering and clinking, chattering stony names/Of shale and hornblend, rag and trap'). *Four.* Drunken horseplay by Cyril reveals to all that the Prince and his companions are men. Fleeing the scene the Princess falls into a river, and is rescued by the Prince. Despite his having saved her life, Ida is adamant that the Prince must die. The Prince's father sends an army ('You have our son: touch not a hair of his head:/Render him up unscathed'), and Ida reluctantly lets the Prince and his companions go. *Five.* The Princess's brother also appears on the scene at the head of a troop, and battle seems unavoidable. To avoid large-scale bloodshed, they decide on a chivalric tournament, where fifty men from each side can battle it out. They fight, and the prince is severely wounded: 'the blade glanced ... and dream and truth/Flow'd from me; darkness closed me; and I fell'. *Six.* The Princess makes a melodramatic speech ('behold our sanctuary/Is violate, our laws broken') from the roof of the university. The university is turned into a hospital to nurse all those injured in the tournament, and Ida herself nurses the wounded Prince. *Seven.* While nursing the Prince, Ida's harshness seems to dissipate, as she falls in love with him. 'Her falser self slipt from her like a robe/And left her woman'. Everything ends happily, with the Prince finally wedding his Princess, and his two companions also finding wives. *Conclusion.* The tale-tellers argue over the significance of their tale, and the narrator and Lilia go off together to contemplate social wrongs and the future, 'Maybe wildest dreams/Are but the needful prelude of the truth ... This fine old world of ours is but a child/Yet in the go-cart. Patience!'

Prisoner of Chillon, The (1816), by Lord Byron. 392 lines, various rhymed metres.

The narrator is a figure loosely based on a historical personage: Francois Bonivard, a sixteenth-century Genevan priest whose democratic affiliations resulted in incarceration at the hands of Duke Charles III from 1530 till 1536. In the poem, the narrator suggests that it 'was for my father's faith/I suffered chains and courted death'. His family has been hit hard by tyranny: his father 'perished at the stake/For tenets he would not forsake' and his seven children were imprisoned in Chillon castle. All are now dead save the narrator, who has suffered mightily in body, but suffered more profoundly in mind. After periods of madness ('I had no thought, no feeling – none –/Among the stones I stood a stone') he is brought back to full life by the song of a bird. He climbs to look out of his window at the beautiful scenes of Swiss nature outside the prison. But, ironically, the poem ends with the suggestion that the narrator has been immured so long that 'my very chains and I grew friends', and that 'even I/regained my freedom with a sigh'.

Psyche, or the Legend of Love (1805), by Mary Tighe. 3347 lines, Spenserian stanzas. All but ignored on its first publication, this work attracted rather more attention with an 1811 reprint following its author's consumptive death in 1810. Jonathan Wordsworth has called this neglected masterpiece 'one of the most accomplished long poems of the Romantic period'. It influenced Keats and Shelley, and is currently undergoing something of a renaissance of critical interest.

Canto 1. Venus, goddess of love, is envious of the beautiful mortal woman Psyche, who is so good-looking as to be distracting humanity from their proper worship. She sends Cupid to deal with her; 'deep let her heart thy sharpest arrow sting,/Its tempered barb in that black poison dyed./Let her … feel all the fury of thy fiercest flame/For some base wretch to foul disgrace allied'. But Cupid himself wants Psyche, and he applies one of his arrows in an erotically suggestive scene ('The dart which in his hand now trembling stood/As o'er the couch he bent with ravished eye'). Waking after what she takes to be a dream, Psyche is the subject of an oracle that insists she must be exposed on a tall rock so that 'a winged monster of no earthly race' can bear her away. Cupid builds an enchanted palace for his new bride, but remains hidden from her. He tells her that she must never look upon his face, although: 'solace thy mind with hopes of future joy:/In a dear infant thou shalt see my face,/Blessed mother soon of an immortal boy'. *Canto 2.* Returned to her family, Psyche awakens the jealousy of her sisters, who convince her that her new husband actually wants to hide his face because his looks are 'loathsome'. On her return to her palace Psyche disobeys Cupid by sneaking a look at him, and she is banished from the palace of love. 'Now prostrate on the bare unfriendly ground/She waits her doom in silent agony' until the voice of Cupid tells her that 'some happier hour/Thy banished steps may lead back to thy lover's bower'. Psyche sets off on her quest. *Canto 3*. Psyche meets a knight on a 'milk-white steed', who will be her champion; the knight keeps a Lion (allegorical representation of Passion) in check at his feet. She and her knight travel until weary, but Psyche takes refuge in the 'bower of loose Delight' (where 'white-bosomed nymphs' with 'loosened zones' attend the guests). She escapes from there and encounters allegorical personifications of Innocence, Vanity and Flattery, who distract her and trap her in the 'car of Ambition' (she tries to jump out but is restrained by 'a thousand silken trammels'). She is rescued from this perilous position by her knight. *Canto 4*. Continuing on her journey Psyche meets and has adventures with further allegorical figures, first Credulity and then Slander (or 'the blatant beast') with which ferocious creature her knight fights. Credulity leads Psyche away to the Castle of Suspicion ('the sad and dreary bower/Where sad Disfida held her gloomy state'). Disfida convinces Psyche that her knight has abandoned her. The canto ends with the knight rescuing her from this predicament. *Canto 5*. Psyche and her knight approach the 'well-defended gates' of the Palace of Chastity. She is invited in, but her knight ('the lion and her gallant lord') 'affright' the guardians on the gate and they shut him out. After Psyche's pleading, and the intermission of Hymen, the knight is allowed in. Psyche is so enamoured of what she finds inside the palace (she has a 'ravished ear') that she resolves to devote herself to Chastity. The knight is not happy at this ('farewell, mistaken Psyche! ... Since thy false heart a spouse divine disclaims/I leave thee to the pomp which here thy pride inflames'); but rather than allowing her to stay in the palace Queen Castabella sends her out to 'bear my fame/Even to the bowers where Love himself commands'. Psyche continues her journey over the sea; but a storm forces the ship against the coast of Spleen. She is tended by Patience. *Canto 6*. Psyche continues her journey, spends some time on the Island of Indifference but is rescued by her knight. Finally she makes her way back to the home of Cupid, and the poem ends happily.

Purgatory of Suicides, The: a Prison-Rhyme (1846), by Thomas Cooper ('the Chartist'). 8658 lines in Spenserian stanzas. Written in Stafford Gaol, where Cooper was confined for his Chartist activities, the poem is dedicated to Thomas Carlyle ('Right noble age-fellow, whose speech and thought/Proclaim thee other than the supple throng').

Book the First. After addressing the poor and oppressed masses ('Slaves toil no more! Why delve, and moil, and pine,/To glut the tyrant-forgers of your chain?') the narrator tells us 'I had a vision, on my prison-bed':

Methought I voyaged in the bark of Death, –
Himself the helmsman, – on a skyless sea,
Where none of all his passengers drew breath,
Yet each, instinct with strange vitality,
Glared from his ghastly eye-balls upon me,
And then upon that pilot, who upheld
One chill and fleshless hand so witheringly
That, while around the boat the hoarse waves swelled
It seemed as if their rage that solemn signal quelled.

The boat is full of the shades of suicides. It reaches the shore ('a gloomy land where startling visions lay') and the occupants disembark, travelling eventually to a huge cave. There the narrator sees various princely and royal suicides from history (Sardanapalus, Chow-Sin Emperor of China, Oedipus, Otho, Dido, Cleopatra and Boadicea among them). *Book the Second*. The narrator praises Milton ('Great minstrel ... I joy that my young heart a covenant made/To take thee for its guide'), before returning to his dream of the underworld. Empedocles and Calanus (an Indian who had immolated himself in front of Alexander the Great) discuss the parlous state of the living world, and hint at future utopia. *Book the Third*. Castlereagh ('Hah! Utter not thy name – that synonym/Of villainy!') is treated. He is remorseful for his earthly doings ('Ten thousand hells hath merited – my sin/Against ineffable Goodness! – How I rave/Amid my madness'). *Book the Fourth*. The narrator discusses the pitiful state of England with a robin redbreast nesting on the prison rampart. Returning to the dream-world, he meets the shades of Sappho and Lucretius who debate the respective merits of reason and passion. *Book the Fifth*. We meet the French revolutionary Buzot, and the Jacobin Le Bas. The shade of Samson ('huge, gray ... so stone-like, and so blind, yet stern of mien') rises up to condemn atheism. *Book the Sixth*. The narrator encounters famous suicides from the Greek, Roman and Hebrew traditions (Isocrates, Demosthenes, Themistocles, Zeno, Anthony, Marius, Photius, Saul, Zimri, Archite and others) and they all discuss Good and Evil, concluding optimistically ('Good shall result from Evil: woe/And want shall cease'). *Book the Seventh*. We meet Sophonius, Petronius and Apicus ('I saw by their antique/Eagle-beaked faces [they] were of Rome'), Vatel and Villeneuve from France, and two English lords, Lumley and Mordaunt. *Book the Eighth*. The narrator describes a body of 'sorrow's suicides ... in desponding phalanx ... wailing that they could not escape their being's load'. *Book the Ninth*. A wife comes to Stafford Gaol to see her husband for the last time before he is hanged. The narrator inveighs against capital punishment, and his sympathy with the woman ('Poor sufferer! ... O Woman! fairest, frailest, sweetest flower/Of Nature's garden, what rude storms thee bend!') leads him, in the dream-realm, to describe the souls of women forced to commit suicide to preserve their chastity ('Many a virgin whom old bards extol/For spotless chastity'). *Book the Tenth*. The final book builds to a Chartist peroration: 'I dreamt again, – but 'twas a gladsome dream ... a festival of Brotherhood and Mind/By suicidal spirits held ... mystically designed/To adumbrate future bliss for Earth and humankind'. The poem concludes:

> The dream o'erwrought me to a throe
> Of bliss; and I awoke to find my home
> A dungeon, – thence, to ponder when would come
> The day that Goodness shall the earth renew,
> And Truth's young light disperse old Error's gloom, –
> When Love shall Hate, and Meekness Pride subdue, –
> And when the Many cease their Slavery to the Few!

: *Q* :

Queen Mab; A Philosophical Poem (1813), by Percy Bysshe Shelley. 2304 lines, blank verse and various lyric metres. Shelley's youthful attack on much of establishment ideology is less remarkable as poetry (despite occasionally fine passages); more interesting are seventeen lengthy prose notes, amounting to a collection of passionately argued essays against (as Shelley was later to put it) 'Jesus Christ, & God the Father, & the King, & the Bishops, & Marriage, & the Devil knows what'. The work was especially popular among the quasi-underground community of English radicalism; a cheap version of the text went into fourteen editions by 1840.

I. The Fairy Queen Mab enters in her flying Chariot, and wakes the soul of the beautiful Ianthe. Ianthe's soul leaves her sleeping body and joins Mab in her chariot: 'the magic car moved on./The night was fair, and countless stars/Studded heaven's dark blue vault'. Eventually the pair leave the solar system altogether: 'The magic car noved on./Earth's distant orb appeared/The smallest light that twinkles in the heaven'. *II*. Mab and the Spirit enter the Hall of Spells, where Mab promises 'the past shall rise;/Thou shalt behold the present; I will teach/The secrets of the future'. She points out various historical disasters ('Where Athens, Rome, and Sparta stood,/There is a moral desert now'.) *III*. Mab summons up the vision of a King, who testifies to his own misery as well as the misery inflicted by tyrannical political systems: 'Nature rejects the monarch ... kings/And subjects [are] mutual foes'. *IV*. The Queen comments on the beauty of the night until 'dark red smoke' blots out 'the silver moon' – the fires of war. She dwells on the horrors of human conflict. *V*. Mab launches into an attack on 'the twin sister of religion, selfishness' observing that 'hence commerce springs'. Capitalism, in effect, is attacked as 'poison-breathing', a situation where everything 'even love is sold'. *VI*. Mab attacks 'religion! ... thou taintest all thou lookest upon!' *VII*. Discussion on religious questions continues. Mab summons the spirit of Ahasuerus, the Wandering Jew, to answer the question: 'Is there a God?' His answer ('aye, an almighty God,/Vengeful as almighty') represents humanity's spiritual imprisonment in the concept of a wrathful father-figure God. *VIII*. Mab now promises to reveal 'the secrets of the future'. She describes a glorious utopia. *IX*. More Utopian promises ('O happy Earth! reality of Heaven!'). Ianthe's spirit descends, and she wakes.

: R :

Red Cotton Night-Cap Country, or Turf and Towers (1873), by Robert Browning. 4247 lines, blank verse.

Part 1. The title is a variant on a phrase used by Carlyle ('White Cotton Night-Cap Country') to characterize the sleepy environs of rural France in terms of the peasant's distinctive head-wear. Browning changes the colour to indicate such bloody goings-on as the French Revolution and the Reign of Terror, and uses the occasion (after a lengthy introductory section) to tell a particularly grisly tale based on a contemporary true story. *Part 2*. Leonce Miranda, son and heir to a wealthy Spanish jeweller, lives in Paris under the watchful eye of his overbearing French mother. He falls in love with the already-married Clara Mulhausen; unable to legalize the relationship, Miranda gives his jewellery business over to an associate and goes to live with his lover in the countryside, a stately home at Clairvaux. For five years they are happy together. *Part 3*. Miranda is summoned back to Paris by his mother. She (a strict moralist) admonishes him, both for his adulterous liaison and his extravagant expenditure. Miranda, who had always been something of a mummy's-boy, first tries to commit suicide by throwing himself into the Seine. Clara nurses him back to health after this, but on returning to Paris Miranda discovers that his mother is dead. Certain cousins, hoping to preserve their inheritance from going into the hands of Clara, have arranged the shocking discovery of her body, laid out in state; they convince him that it was his behaviour that killed her. Unprepared for the shock Miranda is stunned. He agrees to foreswear Clara. The cousins discover him one day reading her old love letters by the fire. Miranda suddenly thrusts the box into the fire, holding it in the flames with both hands

> and held them there.
> 'Burn, burn and purify my past!' said he,
> Calmly, as if he felt no pain at all.

But this attempt to rid himself of his love for Clara is unsuccessful, and he eventually returns to Clairvaux. *Part 4*. Miranda is caught between the opposing forces of the corporal (his love for Clara, symbolized by the 'turf' of the poem's subtitle) and the spiritual (his love of God, the 'towers'). In Clairvaux his acts of piety are extreme, lavish; and then, after two years, he climbs to the top of the tower at Clairvaux and moments later is dead on the turf below. Browning imagines what must have gone through his mind: the hope, or even the certainty, of a miracle, an intercession from God. He sees himself flying through the sky, miraculously travelling to the Church of the Virgin Ravissante, where his hands would grow back. Millions would be brought to the Christian faith by this act, and Miranda would be able to take Clara as his lawful wife. In other words, what seems to be a suicide attempt is actually far more complex. The poem ends with news of the court proceedings that followed to decide whether the cousins or Clara should inherit Miranda's wealth. The matter is finally settled in favour of Clara.

Revolt of Islam, The (1818), by Percy Bysshe Shelley. 4817 lines, Spenserian stanzas. Shelley's great political epic was originally composed under the title *Laon and Cythna: or The Revolution in the Golden City, A Vision of the Nineteenth Century*. In a prose preface, Shelley explains that the poem was prompted by the 'panic which, like an epidemic transport, seized upon all classes of men during the excesses consequent upon the French Revolution'.

Canto I. In contrast to the rest of the poem, this first canto is an allegory: a spectator watches a stormy sky, and in particular 'an Eagle and a Serpent wreathed in fight' (the Eagle is 'Evil', the Serpent 'Good'). The Eagle seems to win: he shakes 'the strength of his unconquerable wings' and the serpent 'lifeless, stark and rent' falls to the sea. But the serpent is wounded, not killed, and a beautiful woman instructs the spectator not to lose hope. *Canto II.* Laon, our hero, comes from Greece ('Argolis beside the echoing sea') where Turkish tyranny had determined him to devote his life to revolution and freedom. A young girl called Cythna, brought up in Laon's home (in the original version of the poem, Cythna was Laon's sister), declares that she will join him: 'Can man be free if woman is a slave?' *Canto III.* Cythna is abducted by pirates, who leave Laon bound naked in a cage on top of a tower. He has strange, hallucinatory and masochistic dreams until rescued by a hermit. *Canto IV.* By the time Laon has recovered his health and sanity in the hermit's hut, seven years have passed. We learn that there has been a rebellion (lead by 'a maiden fair') in the Golden City of Constantinople, but 'the tyrant's guards' are fighting back 'fearless and fierce and hard as beasts of blood'. *Canto V.* Laon travels to the City to find that the tyrant's guards have slaughtered ten thousand people ('stabbed in their sleep'); he is afraid that the people will respond with similar brutality, and accordingly attempts to lead what we might today think of as a Gandhi-style revolt of peaceful non-retaliation. Stabbed in the arm by a soldier, Laon does not strike back, but speaks eloquently ('We are still brethren!'). The armies on both sides are won over, and fraternize with one another. They proceed to the Sultan's palace, where Laon demonstrates more compassion in not allowing the populace to kill the tyrant. A huge festival is held on the plain before the city to celebrate the revolt; here Laon is reunited with Cythna. *Canto VI*. The celebrations are barely over when the armies of fellow kings and emperors attack. The people fight gallantly ('myriads flocked in love and brotherhood to die') but it is hopeless. Cythna rescues Laon from the midst of battle, and the two slip away to a green 'recess' where they make love ('blend two restless frames in one reposing soul'). *Canto VII*. Cythna relates her adventures from the time she was abducted by pirates: her passage to Constantinople, her rape by the tyrant, a time of imprisonment and near-madness in a sea-cave and the birth of her daughter (who is stolen away and taken to the emperor). She was, she says, eventually freed from the cave by an earthquake, and picked up by a passing ship. *Canto VIII*. Cythna recalls preaching peace, freedom, atheism and other Shelleyan enthusiasms to the sailors, who are converted. *Canto IX*. Cythna recalls her arrival by ship at the Golden City, and the 'millions' of citizens gathering round her as a revolutionary leader. *Canto X*. The narrative of the poem returns to the present. While Laon and Cythna hide, the war rages on an apparently worldwide scale: 'the continent/Trembled, as with a zone of ruin bound,/ Beneath their feet, the sea shook with the Navies' sound ... myriads had come – millions were on the way'. For 'seven days' the army kills indiscriminantly, and 'there was peace anew'. But this peace is more terrible than the war: waste, famine and disease sweep the land. The rulers bicker among themselves as to reason for this disaster, and a 'Christian Priest' turns the occasion into a bigoted fundamentalist sermon. At his prompting, reprisals are taken against all non-believers. *Canto XI*. Cythna, still hiding with Laon, falls into a depression. Laon leaves her, hoping to find a cure for her melancholy even at the expense of his own life. Disguised as a priest he infiltrates the council of kings, where he exhorts them to abandon their evil ways: 'Ye Princes of the Earth, ye sit aghast/Amid the ruin which yourselves have made'. He (as priest) promises to deliver Laon to them if they grant amnesty to Cythna, that she might go to the 'land beyond the Oceans of the West' where 'Freedom and Truth/Are worshipped'. The tyrant agrees to this, and Laon foolishly reveals his identity. *Canto XII*. Laon is being taken to the execution pyre. Cythna appears suddenly on a black horse. The tyrant seems prepared to keep his word and let her go free, but the 'Christian Priest' insists that, as an atheist, she must be burnt. They are torched: 'the mighty veil/which doth divide the living and the dead/Was almost rent, the world grew dim and pale'. They both die, and awake to find themselves in a paradisical realm beyond death, where they realize that their sacrifice was not in vain: the revolution will eventually come about.

Ring and the Book, The (1868–69). Robert Browning's masterwork was published in four monthly parts from November 1868 to February 1870. Written in blank verse, its twelve books and 21,116 lines make it a massive work by any standard, although (as Carlyle pointed out) it was 'all spun out of a story but a few lines long' that 'only wanted forgetting'. Each of the poem's books is a lengthy dramatic monologue, and in the course of the work ten speakers give their various and partial perspectives of the narrative.

Book 1, The Ring and the Book. The narrator (identified with Browning himself) describes in turn the ring and the book of his title. The ring is an actual ring given to Browning by a friend, and is introduced as a metaphor for the process of literary creation, specifically the forging of a literary artefact out of an alloy composed of the artist's imagination and 'pure crude fact'. The book is similarly a real book, 'Small-quarto size, part print part manuscript:/A book in shape but, really, pure crude fact' that Browning had come across in June 1860 at a street market in Florence. This book was a collection of documents from an actual seventeenth-century Italian murder trial; its title is translated by Browning as follows:

> A Roman murder-case:
> Position of the entire criminal cause
> Of Guido Francheschini, nobleman,
> With certain Four the cutthroats in his pay,
> Tried, all five, and found guilty and put to death
> By heading or by hanging as befitted ranks,
> At Rome on February Twenty Two,
> Since our salvation Sixteen Ninety Eight:
> Wherein it is disputed if, and when,
> Husbands may kill adulterous wives, yet 'scape
> The customary forfeit.

The remainder of Book 1 is concerned with outlining the (factual) details of the murder, and anticipating the various speakers who will come forward. The circumstances are as follows: Count Guido, an impoverished Arezzo nobleman and minor churchman, marries Pompilia, the young daughter of an elderly Roman couple, in the mistaken belief that she is wealthy. At the beginning of the marriage, the parents live with Guido and Pompilia in Arezzo, but the marriage is unhappy, and the parents (Pietro and Violante) soon returned to Rome. Once there they sue Guido for the return of Pompilia's dowry, revealing that she was an illegitimate child (Violante having bought her from a prostitute and passed her off as her own). Eventually, an utterly miserable Pompilia flees her husband's house in the company of a young priest, Caponsacchi, and is pursued by Guido. Arrested on the outskirts of Rome, the priest is sent on internal exile for three years, and the (pregnant) Pompilia taken to a nunnery while the lawsuits are decided. At the time of her confinement, however, Pompilia is released into the care of her putative parents; and two weeks after the birth of a son, Guido and his accomplices burst into their house, murder the old couple and stab Pompilia repeatedly, wounding her fatally. Arrested for this crime, Guido claims justifiable homicide on the grounds of what he insists was his wife's adultery with the priest, Caponsacchi. Despite his plea, conviction follows, and Guido then pleads exemption on behalf of his (lowly) status in the Church. The Pope eventually rules, however, that Guido was guilty, and he is executed. The first book ends with an invocation to the spirit of Browning's dead wife, 'O lyric Love, half-angel and half-bird'. *Book 2, Half-Rome.* The speaker of 'Half-Rome' is a representative, and ordinary, Roman man. He expresses his sympathy for the husband – Guido was an honest man who had grown old waiting for a promised preferment in the Church: he had been easy prey for the wicked old couple. The result of Violante's scheming was that 'Guido's broad back was saddled to bear all – /Pietro, Violante, and Pompilia too'. His wicked parents-in-law had no sooner rid themselves of their daughter than they tried to snatch back the dowry, and Pompilia began an affair with the local priest. When Guido tried to obtain justice he was rebuffed in the courts, and when he heard of the birth of a boy – a boy who would be falsely presented as an heir – his patience gave way before his rage. *Book 3, The Other Half-Rome.* This speaker is chiefly moved by pity for the stabbed Pompilia ('A flower-like body, to frighten at a bruise/You'd think, yet now stabbed through and through again') and the dead parents. He argues that Guido was a brute of a husband, and Pompilia quite right to try and escape. Guido had no business appealing to the law in the first place, and then 'flying out of court' crying '"Honour's hurt the sword must cure!"' when the process did not go his way. *Book 4, Tertium Quid* ('third quantity'). This speaker, addressing a 'Highness' and an 'Excellency', is careful not to offend the prejudices of either. He sees no reason to assume that wrong is entirely on either side, and sums up the case in a fairly balanced way. *Book 5, Count Guido Franceschini.* Guido addresses the Court, having confessed to his crime under torture. He tries to elicit sympathy for his injuries ('aie, aie, aie,/Not your fault, sweet Sir! … the shoulder blade,/ The left one, that seems wrong i' the socket'), and his speech is characterized by a mixture of sycophancy and self-pity. He makes great play with certain alleged love letters between Pompilia and Caponsacchi, and with the fact that he whispered the name 'Caponsacchi' at the door on the night of the murder. If his wife had not been the priest's lover, she would not have opened the door at the sound of his name. *Book 6, Giuseppe Caponsacchi*. The priest now tells his side of the story. He confesses his love for Pompilia, but insists that love was pure and chaste. He helped her escape her monstrous husband out of compassion, and for no carnal reason. *Book 7, Pompilia*. Speaking on her deathbed, Pompilia asserts her innocence. She was never Caponsacchi's lover, the love letters supposedly from her to the priest are forgeries, for she cannot even read and write. She dies declaring that God shows 'His light/For us i' the dark to rise by. And I rise'. *Book 8, Dominus Hyacinthus de Archangelis* and *Book 9, Juris Doctor Johannes-Baptista Bottinius* constitute the speeches of the Court's legal advocates, the former speaking on Guido's behalf, the latter on Pompilia's. But both colossal examples of legal quibbling and pedantry are represented as equally beside the point. *Book 10, The Pope*. The trial has condemned Guido, and he has appealed to the Pope. From dawn until dark, the Pope has been studying the facts of the case, and his attempt to reach an authoritative judgement causes him to interrogate his deepest assumptions about God, man and religion. But, ultimately, Guido's action cannot be defended, and the Pope refuses to intercede. *Book 11, Guido*. Guido's second monologue sees him in his prison cell, and in the course of it his conciliatory mask slips to reveal a more ferocious, unrepentant figure. He announces that he has always hated the 'timid chalky ghost' who was his wife. Finally he hears the steps of the executioners on the stairs outside his cell and he breaks down, begging for his life.

> Life is all!
> I was just stark mad, – let the madman live
> Pressed by as many chains as you please pile!
> Don't open! Hold me from them! I am yours,
> I am the Granduke's – no, I am the Pope's!
> Abate, – Cardinal, – Christ, – Maria, – God, ...
> Pompilia, will you let them murder me?

Book 12, The Book and the Ring. The narrator concludes his artistic 'ring' with several letters from contemporaries describing the subsequent events, Guido's execution, the Pope's restoration of Pompilia's 'perfect fame' and various details of the political situation in the Rome of 1692. The book concludes with another dedication to the 'Lyric Love'.

The contemporary reception of the poem was universally positive, critics acknowledging the huge but tightly controlled scope of the work, its rich and detailed portrait of the multifariousness of life, and the complex vitality with which Browning interrogated issues of truth, love, law, and language. *The Ring and the Book* represents the pinnacle of Browning's achievement.

Roderick, the Last of the Goths; a Tragic Poem (1814), by Robert Southey. 7331 lines, 25 sections, blank verse. This epic, Southey's last, is based on the historical events surrounding the conquest of Spain by the Moors. Writing it, Southey was able to draw upon his own personal and extensive knowledge of the Iberian peninsular.

1–6. Roderick is the last king of the line of Spanish Wisi-Goths; partly as a result of a blood-feud, he rapes the daughter of a rival Lord, Count Julian. To take revenge on this act, Julian invites the Moors into Spain,

> And like a cloud of locusts, whom the South
> Wafts from the plain of wasted Africa,
> The Musselmen upon Iberia's shore
> Descend. A countless multitude they came.

Roderick fights bravely with his army, but is defeated; he goes into hiding as a monk, assuming the name of Father Maccabee, and vows to carry on the struggle against the Moors. Now penitent for his former crimes, Roderick decides to give up the throne. *7–17.* Roderick creeps into the Moorish camp at night to rescue one of the Gothic–Spanish prisoners, the nobleman Pelayo, and persuades him to lead the Spanish counter-insurgency. They raise an army. *18–25.* The Spaniards and the Moors meet at Covadonga: Roderick terrifies the enemy by riding into battle without armour ('"what man is this,"/Appalled they say, "Who to the front of war/Bareheaded offers thus his naked life?"'). The Moors are defeated, Roderick disappears and Pelayo is crowned King of Spain. 'Generations pass'd/And centuries held their course' before the resting place of Roderick was finally discovered: a humble tomb in a hermitage in a remote part of Spain.

Rokeby (1813), by Walter Scott. 5029 lines, octosyllabics with interspersed songs. *Rokeby* is Scott's fifth long poem, and his only to have an English setting (Rokeby is in Yorkshire). The scene is set in 1644, during the English civil war.

Canto First. It is a summer night, but Oswald Wycliffe cannot sleep. Eventually a messenger comes to his castle with news of the recent battle between Roundheads (Oswald's party) and Cavaliers at Marston Moor. But this is no ordinary messenger: it is the grizzled old veteran

Bertram Risingham, who plotted with Oswald to use to cover of the battle as an opportunity to kill Philip of Mortham, Bertram's captain. Oswald, as heir, stands to inherit Mortham's wealth, and has promised to pay off Bertram with booty from the Indes that Mortham has secreted inside Rokeby Castle. Oswald is eager to know whether Bertram has performed his evil action, and Bertram toys with him before revealing that as 'fierce Rupert thundered on our flank ... Twas then I fired my petronel/And Mortham, steed and rider, fell'. Bertram insists that Oswald go with him to the castle to enable him to claim his treasure, but the cowardly Oswald, uneasy in the presence of the ruffian, sends his fey, poetic young son, Wilfrid, in his place. *Canto Second.* On the way to the vault Bertram is convinced he sees the ghost of the man he killed, Philip of Mortham. In his confusion he reveals the plot to Wilfrid, who may be unwordly but does not lack courage: grabbing hold of Bertram crying 'should every fiend to whom thou art sold/Rise in thy aid, I keep my hold', he raises the alarm. Bertram easily throws him off, but is prevented from killing the boy by the intervention of (what seems to be) the ghost of Mortham. As help comes from Rokeby castle, including Rokeby's young page Redmond O'Neill, Bertram escapes into the woods. The lord of Rokeby, as a Royalist, is now (following Cromwell's vistory) the prisoner of Oswald, who decides that he will use this position of power to force Rokeby's beautiful daughter, Matilda, to marry his son Wilfrid. *Canto Third.* Bertram evades capture and falls in with a band of desperadoes, drawn from both camps in the Civil War. The outlaws reveal that they know a secret entrance into Rokeby castle. *Canto Fourth.* Matilda loves gentle poetic Wilfrid like a brother, but her heart belongs to gallant Redmond. Matilda and Redmond are in a green dell, when Bertram creeps up to shoot the young Royalist, 'but twice Matilda came between/The carabine and Redmond's breast'. He curses his fortune and withdraws. *Canto Fifth.* Wicked Oswald threatens to execute Rokeby unless his daughter agrees to marry his son, Wilfrid. But Wilfrid is too honourable to allow such blackmail. One of the outlaws, a young boy skilled as a harp-player, comes to Rokeby and plays various Yorkshire ballads; but this is just a ruse to distract the occupants while the other outlaws come through the secret entrance. Bertram bursts in, and 'behind their chief, the robber crew/Forth from the darkened portal drew'. A fight ensues, in which Redmond distinguishes himself, although Rokeby Castle catches fire and burns to the ground. *Canto Sixth.* It transpires that Mortham is not dead ('the coward shot/The steed, but harmed the rider nought'), and also that Redmond O'Neill, far from being a poor Irish boy, is actually Mortham's long-lost son and heir. Meanwhile, Oswald is carrying out his dastardly plan to execute Rokeby to force his daughter to marry Wilfrid. At the last minute

Bertram rides in, apparently overwhelmed with remorse for his evil ways. He shoots Oswald: 'from saddle bow his pistol drew ... Rung the report – the bullet sped –/And to his long account at last/Without a groan dark Oswald passed'. Oswald's soldiers kill Bertram, but he is granted an honourable burial: 'a soldier's cloak for winding sheet'. The way is clear for Matilda and Redmond to marry.

Romance. Many long poems in the nineteenth century described themselves as 'romances' (for instance Keats's *Endymion: A Poetic Romance*, or Byron's archaically designated *Childe Harold's Pilgrimage: A Romaunt*). Indeed, the Romantic period of English poetry is ostensibly named for the prevalence of writings that can be termed 'romance', although most critics of the period see crucial features of the age (the primacy of the imagination, the focus on the inner life rather than external actions, the cult of genius, bildungsroman, aesthetic criteria specifically and self-consciously opposed to 'classicism') as rather inimical to the romance mode as traditionally conceived. But romance flourished during the early years of the century, and formed a large feature of the poetic landscape throughout the Victorian age.

Romance is traditionally distinguished from *epic. Where epic was poetry of high seriousness relating the deeds of war and travel in a heroic age, romance (particularly in its widely occurring medieval format) was poetry of courtly and chivalric adventures, often to do with love, particularly the high-flown love of a Knight for a Courtly Lady (*amour cortois* or courtly love). Some of the most famous medieval romances are based on the 'Matter of Britain', or the Arthurian Legends (the twelfth-century *Gawain and the Green Knight* for instance, or the works of Chretien de Troyes).

A nineteenth-century poet, then, by calling his or her work a 'romance' is positioning it within this archaic tradition. But, more specifically, they were identifying a 'sentimental' strain in the work. 'Sentiment' was not a word that for the Victorians carried the negative connotations it now does; and sentimental literature (especially the novel of sentiment, or sensibility) was specifically geared to evoke pity and empathy, in order to educate the reader's heart in empathetic skills and thus make him or her a better human being. Tugging at the reader's heart strings, then, was no mere exercise in authorial power, but rather a profoundly ethically based exercise in humanizing. Since love stories were one straightforward way through which to reach the heart of the reader, many romances concerned themselves with the vicissitudes of love (and so it was that the word took on its twentieth-century connotations of being, exclusively, about love).

In fact, if we look at nineteenth-century long poetry from this perspective, almost all of it is 'romance' in a broad sense: which is to say, even the most deliberately tooled epics balanced the severity of their inheritance with a nineteenth-century fascination with 'pity' and the emotional life. The distinction between epic and romance becomes rather difficult to uphold in the face of this, and instead we see an aesthetic based on length itself which combines epic high ambition with romance focus on pity and love.

ROSSETTI, Christina (1830–94). Brother to D.G., Christina was educated at home, and spent most of her life in the domestic sphere, attending her sick mother and doing voluntary work associated with the church. She was a devout Anglican throughout her life, and rejected several marriage proposals ostensibly on the grounds of religious incompatibility (as, for example, the Pre-Raphaelite painter James Collinson, who converted to Roman Catholicism and so ended his chance of marrying Christina). Indeed her life is at first glance characterized by its lack of incident, and the Victorian virtues of meekness, submission and self-restraint that she so completely embodied in her self tend to emerge in much of her poetry as frustration, impotence and depression. Critics sometimes divide her poetic output into two categories of verse; on the one hand, lyric poetry, often devotional and of great beauty (she wrote the words to the hymn 'In the Bleak Midwinter'), sometimes more personal and expressive of individual sadness and desolation; on the other hand, children's verse, of which *Goblin Market and the shorter verses in the collection called *SingSong* (1871) are perhaps the most famous. Actually this twofold division ignores a wide spread of her poetry, including much powerful love poetry and a fine variety of sonnets.

She wrote poetry from an early age, and used her brother's connections with the Pre-Raphaelite Brotherhood to publish her works in the PRB journal, *The Germ*, in 1850. Other poems were printed in *Macmillan's Magazine* and *Once A Week*. Her first volume of poetry, *Goblin Market and other poems*, was printed by Macmillan in 1862; other volumes followed slowly, including *The Prince's Progress and other poems* (1866), and *A Pageant and other poems* (1881). Her health was not good during her adult years, and her eventual death from cancer was the culmination of much suffering. Death is a prominent theme in her poetry, but if her lyrics can sometimes be morbid her longer poetry rarely is, and her facility with the cadences of spoken English, the inventiveness and fecundity of her poetic imagination (always controlled by a rigorous aesthetic that balances play with austerity), are perhaps her most distinguishing features.

: S :

SCOTT, Sir Walter (1771–1832). It was Scott who fashioned the long poem into a commercially successful (in his case, astonishingly successful) commodity, and so laid the road that so many nineteenth-century imitators, from *Byron on, were to follow. If *Southey (and, in his little-known way, *Blake) attempted to refashion *epic as a mode for serious, psychologically acute and high-minded poetic enterprise, Scott created the alternate mode, the popular *romance. His long poems are indeed like his novels, not least in their narrative imperative as well as their enormous readership; and their success made long poetry one of the dominant modes of literary discourse for seventy years.

Scott was born into a moderately well-to-do Edinburgh family, educated in Edinburgh School and at the University, and trained for a career in law. He was called to the bar in 1792, and practised in a small way, although his career advancement owed more to his assiduous cultivation of Tory patronage (which resulted, for instance, in his near-sinecure post of Sheriff of Selkirkshire in 1799: £300 a year for doing very little). His duties allowed him a great deal of time to follow his interests as a gentleman amateur folklorist. He travelled the Border country, and collected a number of oral ballads and tales. During the 1790s, when the craze for German literature and tales hit the country, he translated a German ballad ('Der wilde Jager') as 'The Chase of William and Helen'. Other short pieces, imitative of German balladry, followed; but his first serious publication was the three-volume edition of Scottish ballads, The Minstrelsy of the Border (1802–03). The archaic, martial tone of the various ballads collected caught the public mood (in the middle of the Napoleonic wars), and the edition did well, selling nearly 10,000 copies by 1812, a very impressive number for a work of literary scholarship. Inspired by this success, Scott published his own composition, a long poem with clear connections with the Minstrelsy, *The Lay of the Last Minstrel (1805). Scott himself acknowledged the influence of *Southey's *Thalaba (1801) on this undertaking, although critics see a closer affinity with the work of Coleridge (his 'Christabel' was in the process of being written at this time). The poem was a tremendous success: critics and ordinary readers alike enthused. 15,000 copies were sold in a short time; everybody from the Prime Minister down was talking about the work. Scott decided that publishing was where his fortune lay. He (secretly) became a partner in a publishing venture organized by a friend, the hapless John Ballantyne, and wrote another work for this press. This poem, *Marmion* (1808), did even better business than the *Lay*, despite being written very quickly (the last canto was completed in four days, with pages being sent to the printer as soon as the ink dried) – a fact which shows in its sometimes creaky versification. Scott diversified his writing (for instance, editing an eighteen-volume edition of Dryden's works in 1806–07, or helping found the *Quarterly Review* in 1809), but it was the long poems that made the biggest impact. *The Lady of the Lake* (1810), his next big success, is perhaps his most characteristic piece; *The Vision of Don Roderick* followed in 1811 and *Rokeby* in 1813.

By this stage Scott was earning prodigiously (each of his poems brought him many thousands; plus, in 1812, he started receiving the income for another sinecure in the Court of Session: £800 a year for life). But his outgoings were also large. In 1811 he purchased, and modernized, the estate of Abbotsford on the Tweed. His reputation as a poet was so high (the Prince Regent was a fan) that Scott was offered the position of poet laureateship in 1813, although he declined and suggested his friend *Southey instead. But despite this success, Scott was increasingly uneasy with his role as poet. In large part this was because of the bursting onto the poetic scene of *Byron (in particular, the great success of *Childe Harold* on its first appearance in 1812). In the words of his biographer (and son-in-law) Lockhart, Scott 'discerned in Byron a rising star who was to carry the force of words into a deeper region of the soul than his own poetry could stir'. The financial considerations of a more successful rival (and better poet) were also a factor. *The Lord of the Isles* (1815) did not come flowing from his pen with his usual facility (he talked of the pain of having to 'grind verses'), and although the finished product looks like any other Scott long poem, it did less well than some of its predecessors. Scott decided to give up writing poetry (his only other effort, 1817's short *Harold the Dauntless*, fell completely flat); instead he turned his talents to prose, and published the first of the phenomenally successful Waverley novels (*Waverley*) in 1814. The remainder of Scott's life is rather beyond the scope of this study but the continued runaway success of the Waverley novels, and his own status as literature's first superstar, played their part in convincing later writers to follow in his footsteps. His exhausting rate of work never faltered; in fact, after the bankruptcy of his partner Ballantyne, and his own liability for debts amounting to £114,000, he upped his output. He cleared this debt, but at the cost of ruining his own health and bringing on a complete breakdown and early death through his overwork.

Denigration of Scott's poetic achievement began with Scott himself. Never comfortable with the role of poet, he described his poems as 'soap bubbles', and claimed 'my poetry has always passed from the desk to the printer in the most hurried manner possible, so that it is no wonder, I am sometimes puzzled to explain my own meaning'. James Ballantyne, Scott's publisher and partner, once asked Scott's daughter Sophia whether she had enjoyed *The Lady of the Lake*, only to receive the reply: 'Oh, I have not read it; papa says there's nothing so bad for young people as reading bad poetry'. Some of Scott's contemporaries agreed with this: Coleridge was aware of Scott's frequent plagiarisms, and compared Scott to a dog, lifting his leg six times to piss a canto. But, by the same token, there have been people extravagant in their praise. Reviewerish comparisons with Shakespeare were commonplace, and (in the 1920s) Hardy claimed to prefer *Marmion* to the *Iliad*. It is difficult to endorse so extreme an opinion; but it is nonetheless true that the complete eclipse of Scott as a poet (something that has not happened with his novels) is severely unjustified. The faults of his work, technical (particularly his feeble grasp of the principles of rhyme) and thematic (most critics see something rather adolescent in Scott's Tory enthusiasm for war and heroism), are so obvious as to be uninteresting. But his strengths are considerable. Above all, he gives poetry an impetus, a sense of movement and narrative drive, that had been almost lacking among the poise of the eighteenth century, and which contemporary poets like Southey lacked the skill (or inclination) to do. Of course, it is this very pace, this onrushing hurry about Scott's verse that opens him to criticisms of doggerel, but it is difficult to deny the narrative power of Scott's work.

Asked by a friend why he did not write in the more stately decasyllabics of most of his contemporaries, Scott conceded that his shorter line left too little room for the grander stylistic tricks associated with epic. But, he argued, his distinctive octosyllabics (derived from the onward push of ballad metres) created a sense of speed. Scott's poems play on this. They abound with scenes of chase and travel, weave often complex plot-lines together, and build to a big climax in the sixth canto (most usually a battle). This pattern perhaps comes over, in this brief summary of it, as crude, but it works – indeed, it seems to this critic that there is more narrative urgency about Scott's poems than there is in his celebrated but often overly-digressive novels. Scott, then, establishes an effective poetics of travelling, almost a movie (or travelogue) aesthetic; embroidered with the tourist features of detailed (and accurate) scenery-description and propelled by what are often creaky romance premises, but urgent and onward-moving all the same. So fluent is Scott's verse that his often pithy aphoristic touches can pass the unattending reader by. But it is striking how many of Scott's versified phrases have become commonplace, from *Marmion*'s 'O what a tangled web we weave/When

first we practise to deceive', to *The Lay of the Last Minstrel*'s 'breathes
there a man, with soul so dead,/Who never to himself hath said,/This is
my own, my native land!'

SHELLEY, Percy Bysshe (1792–1822). Shelley's genius is lyric, although
in his own day what reputation he had (and he was regarded as beyond
the pale by many) rested upon his philosophico-political long poem
Queen Mab, which became one the standard books of political radicals such as the Chartists.

Born in Horsham, Sussex, in 1792, Shelley grew up as the son of
wealthy MP Timothey Shelley, and grandson of the baronet and landowner Bysshe Shelley. He went to Eton in 1804, where his unconventional
modes of thinking already made him the butt of narrower minds (he
was bullied, and called 'Mad Shelley' or 'Atheist Shelley'). His first
publication, the adolescent Gothic novel *Zastrozzi*, was published in
1810, the same year Shelley entered University College Oxford. Here
Shelley's revolutionary sympathies were encouraged by reading the radical
writers of the day: Godwin and Paine in particular. In January 1811 he
met Harriet Westbrook, the daughter of a coffee-shop owner. In February he published a pamphlet attacking organized religion, *The Necessity
of Atheism*. After this, events in Shelley's life began speeding up. He was
expelled from Oxford for his pamphlet in March, and then eloped with
Harriet (she was sixteen). They were married in Edinburgh in August;
although Harriet was distressed by Shelley's suggestion that (as a dem-
onstration of how little regard they had for conventional living) she
sleep with his best friend, Hogg. In 1812 he travelled widely in Ireland,
Devon and Wales, publishing pamphlets, addressing meetings, posting
democratic broadsheets, and generally making a nuisance of himself for
the reactionary Government of the day. In 1813 this radical life bore
poetic fruit, as *Queen Mab* was published, complete with detailed and
inflammatory notes. Shortly after the publication of this volume, Shelley's daughter Ianthe (named after the protagonist of the poem) was
born.

In 1814 he abandoned Harriet (who gave birth to a son later in the
year) and eloped with Mary Wollstonecraft Godwin, the sixteen-year-old
daughter of Mary Wollstonecraft (the 'Mother of British Feminism') and
William Godwin (the radical writer and novelist). With Mary's stepsister
Claire Clairmont, they toured the Continent, returning to Britain in
September. The death of Shelley's grandfather meant that he inherited a
legacy of £1000 a year, a very large sum indeed, even if £200 of it was
paid to the solitary Harriet. Unable to get a divorce, Shelley could not
marry Mary, but he lived with her in a cottage on Windsor Great Park,

where he wrote *Alastor* (1816). Then he travelled for some months in Europe, where he struck up his famous friendship with *Byron; and where he wrote some of his most famous shorter pieces: 'Hymn to Intellectual Beauty' and 'Mont Blanc'. Harriet committed suicide later in that year (on 9 November although her body was not discovered until 10 December); Shelley straightaway married Mary (30 December) and began a Chancery case to obtain custody of his two children. He was to lose this case (his political radicalism and publications weighed against him), something that made him extremely bitter.

Throughout 1817 Shelley developed several friendships, and wrote a number of things, including *Laon and Cythna*, a lengthy political epic. It was published in December, but withdrawn almost immediately under threat of legal action. Shelley hastily revised the piece, and re-published it under the title *The Revolt of Islam* in January 1818. In March Shelley moved permanently to the Continent, travelling through Italy. In Venice, he composed 'Julian and Maddalo', a poetic version of his deep friendship with Byron; and between December 1818 and April 1819 he composed his masterpiece, *Prometheus Unbound*. 1819 was his annus mirabilis, the year in which he composed such famous works as 'The Mask of Anarchy' and 'Ode to the West Wind'. 1820 and 1821 saw this prodigious output of classic shorter pieces continuing ('Witch of Atlas', 'Sensitive Plant' and his elegy for Keats, 'Adonais'). He also composed his prose *Defence of Poetry*, one of the most influential pieces of criticism from the period. In 1822 he moved to a villa on the Italian Coastline at San Terenzo and bought a boat, which he called 'Ariel'. He met himself outside the villa one day (this spectral version of himself asked him 'for how long do you intend to remain content?') and shortly after his boat went down in a squall with him and a friend aboard. He drowned on 8 June 1822.

Perhaps the most powerful Romantic poet, certainly the Romantic with the most intense lyrical intensity, Shelley was never really able to command the architectonic coherence demanded by the long poem. His epics and his long verse-drama *Prometheus Bound* remain extraordinary resources of fine poetry, but Shelley's reputation was sustained not so much upon his work in these modes.

Siege of Corinth, The (1816), by Lord Byron. 1079 lines, octosyllabic couplets. Based on the historical siege of the Venetian-controlled Corinth by the Turks in 1715, this was the last of Byron's highly popular Eastern verse-tales.

The tale opens with the 'gleam of twice ten thousand spears' of 'the Moslem's leaguering lines' outside Venetian Corinth. The Turkish leader,

Alp (a Venetian who has converted to Islam) is in love with the beautiful Francesca, daughter of the city governor Minotti. Corinth's walls are breached, and 'with to-morrow's earliest dawn' the city will be overrun. Alp wanders along the beach in the moonlight, and makes his way to the ruin of an ancient Greek temple. There he meets a curiously spectral Francesca, who urges him to reconvert to Christianity; he refuses and she departs. The next day battle is joined, and the Turks overrun Corinth. Alp tells Minotti that he intends to marry Francesca; but the old man grimly informs him that she is already dead, having died the previous evening ('he saw Alp staggering bow/Before his words as with a blow'). Minotti makes his way to the arsenal with a torch, and blows Corinth sky-high, destroying defenders and attackers in one go:

> The shatter'd town – the walls thrown down –
> The waves a moment backward bent –
> The hills that shake, although unrent,
>   As if an earthquake pass'd –
> The thousand shapeless things all driven
> In cloud and flame athwart the heaven,
>   By that tremendous blast –

Sigurd the Volsung (1876) by William Morris (9729 lines, iambic-anapestic hexameters). Full title: *The Story of Sigurd the Volsung and the Fall of the Niblungs*. Morris himself regarded this retelling of the Volsunga saga as his greatest poetic work. Indeed, he thought that this body of Norse myth constituted 'the Great Story of the North' which 'should be to all our race what the Tale of Troy was to the Greeks'.

Book 1. Sigmund. King Volsung is marrying his daughter, Signy, to the Goth-king Siggeir. The wedding takes place in his great hall, the most striking feature of which is the huge tree growing through it, called the Branstock. In the middle of the ceremony Odin enters ('One ey'd and seeming ancient, yet bright his visage glowed') and plunges a great sword into the Branstock as a wedding gift. All the nobles try to pull the sword free, but only Sigmund, Volsung's son and Signy's brother, is able to do so. King Siggeir asks for the sword as a gift, but Sigmund refuses. Siggeir hides his bitterness. He invites the Volsungs to the land of the Goths after the marriage, but when they come they are ambushed by an army and King Volsung is slain. Sigmund and the surviving Volsung nobles are chained to a tree in the forest, and one by one eaten by wolves in the night. Only Sigmund survives (by biting the wolf to death as it tries to eat him: 'I, lord of the golden harness, the flame of the Glittering Heath,/Must snarl to the she-wolf's snarling, and snap with greedy teeth'). He lives for many years in the forest alone, amassing wealth by banditry. His sister Signy, now Queen of the Goths, discovers him. Together they incestuously conceive a son, Sinfiotli; and with his help Sigmund eventually takes revenge upon King Siggeir. Returning with great wealth to the Volsung's land, Sigmund marries Borghild; but she conceives a hatred for Sinfiotli and poisons him. Divorcing Borghild, Sigmund marries Hiordis. Shortly afterward Sigmund perishes in battle. Widowed Hiordis goes to stay with the Sea-king Elf, son of the Helper. *Book 2. Regin.* Sigmund's son Sigurd is born in the land of the Helper. As he grows to manhood he is trained by 'Regin the wise craftsmaster', a retainer at the court of king Elf ('So exceeding old was Regin, that no son of man could tell/In what year of the days passed over he came to that land to dwell'). Sigurd acquires the great horse Greyfell ('the tireless horse of Odin') and his own sword, 'The Wrath of Sigurd'. Regin then reveals that he is a survivor of the doomed race of Dwarfs, and tells him of the gold of Andvari amassed by his father the greedy Reidmar, and in particular of Andvari's ring, cursed by its maker, 'the Seed of Gold and of Grief' which brought about the downfall of Regin's own royal house. The hoard of gold is now guarded by a giant Dragon, the shape into which Regin's own brother Fafnir has metamorphosized as an expression of his greed and violence. Sigurd accepts the quest to recover the Gold from Regin. Sigurd and Regin ride to the Glittering Heath and have various adventures before Sigurd slays Fafnir the Serpent. Regin rips his brother's heart out of the dragon's corpse and orders Sigurd to cook it 'that I may eat it and live, and be thy master and more'. Sigurd obeys, but accidentally tastes the blood of the dragon ('he reacheth his hand to the roast to see if the cooking be o'er') thus achieving an ancient Dwarf-wisdom and feeling 'beset of evil in a world of many foes'. Sigurd then beheads Regin and steals the gold. On his return journey he encounters the beautiful Brynhild in a sort of trance. He wakes her and they fall in love. *Book 3. Brynhild.* Gudrun is the daughter of Giuki, the king of the Niblung people; she is jealous that Sigurd has betrothed himself to Brynhild, and with the aid of Grimhild the wise-wife (who brews her a magical potion) she tricks him into marrying her instead. Sigurd rides to battle with the Niblungs and does heroic deeds. He also persuades Brynhild to marry Gunnar, Gudrun's brother, who has inherited the throne of the Niblungs: 'there now is Brynild abiding as a Queen in the house of the Kings ... And no man knoweth her sorrow'. She sickens 'whereof none knoweth, and death o'er life prevails'. Sigurd, having tasted the dragon's blood, puts the ring of Andvari on his finger and knows the secrets of men's – and women's – hearts: he urges Brynhild 'O live, live, Brynhild beloved, and thee on the earth will I wed,/And put away Gudrun the Niblung', but she declares 'I will not wed thee, Sigurd, nor any man alive'. Sigurd is stabbed in his sleep ('It is Brynhild's deed' he murmurs as he dies, 'the woman that loves me well'). Gudrun's grief for her dead husband is profound. Brynhild commits suicide. *Book 4. Gudrun*. Gudrun weds an outland King called Atli, 'the lord of a mighty people, a man of marvellous fame', who invites the Niblung people to his land:

> Three days the Niblung warriors the ways of the mirk-wood ride
> Till they come to a land of cities and the peopled countryside, ...
> But nought will the Niblung tarry; swift through Atli's weal they wend,
> Their hearts are exceeding eager for their journey's latter end.
> Three days they ride that country, and many a city leave,
> But the fourth dawn mighty mountains by the inner sea upheave.
> They ride a little further and Atli's burg they see
> With the feet of the mountains mingled above the flowery lea,
> And yet a little further, and lo, its long white wall,
> And its high-built guarded gateways, and its towers o'erhung and tall.

They travel to Atli's kingdom, and into his hall ('Huge, dim is the hall of Atli, and faint and far aloof,/As stars in the misty even, yet hang the lamps in the roof') where Gudrun tells them that they are all doomed to die. A mighty battle takes place in the Hall and the Niblung kings are all slain; Gunnar is thrown into a snake pit where he makes a proud speech before dying. Atli speaks triumphantly to Gudrun ('There is glory now in the Eastland, and thy lord is king alone'), but Gudrun waits until Atli and all his warriors are dead drunk and sleeping, and sets fire to his hall, killing them all. She herself makes her way to the sea and addresses it ('O Sea, I stand before thee; and I who was Sigurd's wife!/By his brightness unforgotten I bid thee deliver my life/From ... the bitter wrong of my birth') before drowning herself.

SMITH, Alexander (1830–67). Born the son of a Kilmarnock lace-pattern maker, Smith went to school in Paisley (which education, his biographer tells us 'was rudimentary to a degree' leaving him 'a stranger to the classics, poorly versed in geography'). He began work as a pattern-designer, but showed little aptitude for his father's trade, and sought solace in reading and writing poetry. His first effusions were published in the *Eclectic Review* and *Critic* in 1851. Encouraged by friends in the Glasgow literary circle, he began work upon his first long poem **A Life Drama*. So promising was this work that London publishers vied among themselves to obtain it, Smith eventually being paid the extraordinary (for a first-time writer) sum of £100 for the copyright. The extraordinary, ingenious and often garish imagery of this work, and its episodic, fragmentary structure, marked it out as something highly individual. The poem, published in 1852, was a success, and in 1854 Smith was appointed secretary to Edinburgh University, a post he held to his death. He augmented his income with journalism, firstly as editor of the short-lived *Glasgow Miscellany*, later submitting articles to a variety of journals. He met Sydney *Dobell in 1854, and their jointly-composed sonnet-sequence *Sonnets on the War* (inspired by the Crimean debacle) emerged in 1855. 1855 was also the year in which A. J. *Aytoun's satirical *Firmilian* immortalized both Smith and Dobell, along with *Bailey, as *Spasmodics. Smith visited Skye many times (his prose travel book *A Summer in Skye*, 1865, remains a thoroughly entertaining portrait of the island) and in 1857 married Flora Macdonald, the eldest daughter of Macdonald of Ord in Skye. He was paid an advance of £250 for his next collection, *City Poems* (1857), but the often finely written and powerful poems in this collection failed to make an impact on the public. He spent the next four years writing his last large-scale poetic undertaking, the historical epic *Edwin of Deira* (1861). Despite (or perhaps because) of the fact that this was a much more restrained performance than *A Life Drama*, it fell flat; reviewers thought little of it, and accused Smith of plagiary, particularly from Tennyson. Discouraged by the fate of *Edwin*, Smith concentrated on writing prose until his death from typhoid fever complicated by diphtheria in 1867.

Despite justifiable charges of poetic immaturity and ill-discipline, much of *A Life Drama* remains a powerful and bracing poetic experience – not, however, in the manner which Smith probably intended it (which is to say, as a psychologically acute portrait of a sensitive soul growing beyond introspection and into mental health) – but rather as a collage of bizarre, striking and surreal images that builds to a powerfully dislocated portrait of aesthetic and social alienation. Apart from this the 'spasmodic' label has done its job, reducing Smith's output in our eyes to a caricature of post-Keatsian poetry. There has been next to no critical interest in his work during this century.

Sohrab and Rustum. An Episode (1853), by Matthew Arnold. 892 lines, blank verse. Arnold considered this one of his most successful attempts at epic grandeur, simplicity and directness.

Sohrab, the young Tartar warrior, is searching for his father Rustum, the leader of the Persian army. Rustum, however, believes his lost child to have been a daughter. When the Tartar and Persian armies meet on the battlefield, Sohrab and Rustum meet in single combat, unaware of their mutual relationship. Only when Rustum has mortally wounded Sohrab do matters become plain ('Truth is on the lips of dying men'). The poem ends with a beautiful invocation to the river Oxus, that flows through the battlefield: 'But the majestic river floated on,/Out of the mist and hum of that low land,/Into the frosty starlight'.

> Oxus, forgetting the bright speed he had
> In his high mountain cradle in Pamere,
> A foiled circuitous wanderer – till at last
> The longed-for dash of waves is heard, and wide
> His luminous home of waters opens, bright
> And tranquil, from whose floor the new-bathed stars
> Emerge, and shine upon the Aral sea.

Sordello (1840), by Robert Browning. 5982 lines, heroic couplets. *Sordello* has a good claim to the title 'most notorious poem of the nineteenth century'. Browning laboured upon this vast epic for the best part of a decade; but it was received with widespread bafflement, astonishment and derision, swiftly becoming a byword for artistic incomprehensibility and affectation. Jane Carlyle claimed that she had read through the whole thing without working out whether Sordello was a man, a book or a city. Tennyson similarly claimed to have read it, but said he only understood the first line ('Who will, may hear Sordello's story told') and the last ('Who would has heard Sordello's story told'), and that they were both lies. It took Browning's reputation nearly thirty years to recover from *Sordello*, although modern critics see it as massively significant, not merely in terms of Browning's development, but in its sustained and muscular attempts to wrestle with the problems of poetic meaning.

To understand *Sordello*, a reader needs to have a sense of the history of late twelfth- and early thirteenth-century Italy; and in particular the battle for power in Lombardy between the Pope-backed Guelfs (including the Marquis of Este) and the Austrian-Emperor-backed Ghibellins (including Ecelin Romano, and the soldier-kingmaker Taurello Salinguerra). The historical Sordello was a Mantuan poet, mentioned by Dante in the *Purgatorio* but otherwise rather obscure. Browning makes Sordello Salinguerra's son, brought up secretly and under a false identity

Book the First. The poem opens dramatically ('Lo, the past is hurled/In twain: up-thrust, out-staggering on the world ... appears Verona') at the time of the formation of the (Guelph) Lombard League. After outlining the two factions, the narration moves to distant Goito castle, where the refined beautiful boy Sordello is described. He has no duties, and lives the life of his imagination, summoning imagined companions and enjoying imagined adventures. Having once caught a glimpse of the young Palma (Eccelino's daughter, and therefore a Ghibelline) he is able to weave an elaborate fantasy life about her, in which she is Daphne and he Apollo. *Book the Second*. Now a man, Sordello wanders one day to the walls of Mantua, where Palma is holding a 'Court of Love'. With an extempore effusion, Sordello defeats Palma's minstrel and wins the prize, which is to become Palma's minstrel himself. In the months that follow, he struggles to produce perfect poetry, but falls short. *Book the Third*. Returning to Goito, Sordello attempts to bury himself in the contemplation of Nature; but he is conscious of a sense of life passing him by, 'youth once gone is gone,/Deeds let escape are never to be done'. Then he receives a message from Palma summoning him to Verona. At this point the poem embarks on a lengthy digression, in which Browning recalls things he has seen on his own nineteenth-century trip to Venice, and muses on some of the ethical issues associated with the Sordello story. The book closes with Browning paying tribute to his friend, the poet Walter Savage Landor, 'whose great verse blares unintermittent on'. *Book the Fourth*. We are introduced to Salinguerra, the soldier and man of action, in his palace in Ferrara, as he muses on the events of the past. Sordello comes with Palma to Ferrara, to see for the first time a town ravaged by war. He is greatly struck, sees the world as 'consigned to chaos and discgrace' and sees life in terms of 'petty enjoyments and huge miseries'. He determines to adopt 'the people's cause', but an interview with Salinguerra convinces him that both Guelf and Ghibelline are equally unjust and cruel as far as ordinary people are concerned. Eventually he decides that the truth must lie on the side of religion, which means supporting the Pope and therefore the Guelf cause. *Book the Fifth*. Despairing in the face of his apparent helplessness, Sordello hears a voice:

> Sordello, wake!
> God has conceded two sights to a man –
> One, of men's whole work, time's completed plan,
> The other, of the minute's work, man's first
> Step to the plan's completeness.

He realizes that he cannot achieve everything, but that his small contribution is valuable nonetheless. He returns to Salinguerra to try and influence him (and the Ghibellines) in the cause of the people. But instead of convincing him to adopt the Guelf cause, Sordello is propositioned by Salinguerra to join the Ghibellines, and marry Palma. Almost involuntarily, Salinguerra crowns Sordello as Eccelin's successor. After this event, Palma comes in and relates the true story of Sordello's birth. *Book the Sixth*. Sordello wrestles with the possibilities available to him, the realities of power. He argues the pros and cons with himself, but it becomes apparent in his increasing feverishness that he is dying. He seems to decide to sacrifice the egotistical possibilities of wordly power, but dies before he is able to realize the possibilities.

SOUTHEY, Robert (1774–1843). More than any other poet of the Romantic period, Southey's name was associated with long poems. Southey persevered writing epics despite degrees of public disinterest (Madame de Stael, famously, called such works 'Southey's unsaleables'), a fact Southey ruefully acknowledged. During work on *Madoc, he wrote to a friend that this epic contained 'some of my best workmanship', but added 'I shall get by it less money than fame, and less fame than envy'. After completing *The Curse of Kehama, he wrote to his son that 'very very few people will like Kehama' but opined that 'every generation will afford me some half-dozen admirers of it, and the everlasting column of Dante's fame does not stand upon a wider base'. The comparison with Dante seems ill-judged. Of the major Romantics his is really the only reputation that has stubbornly refused to be reflated by contemporary scholarship.

The son of a Bristol linen-draper, Southey experienced a lonely childhood, long portions of which were spent in the house of his maternal aunt. Poorly schooled, largely self-educated, he attended Westminster school until expelled for editing a student's magazine The Flagellant (not pornographic, despite its name: Southey was actually expelled for writing an article attacking corporal punishment). He went up to Balliol College, Oxford, and met Coleridge, with whom he planned a utopian community in North America ('Pantisocracy', Coleridge's name for this movement, means 'government by the all'). Nothing came of this project, but Southey and Coleridge remained close friends, sharing revolutionary ideals and collaborating on several literary undertakings, such as the Jacobinical *Joan of Arc and a play the pair wrote in twenty-four hours, The Fall of Robespierre. Southey also wrote the republican drama Wat Tyler.

In 1795 Southey married Edith Fricker; in 1796 he travelled through Portugal and Spain. Returning to England he settled down to a (not very well renumerated) career as a writer, producing a prodigious stream of travel books, biographies (most famously a Life of Nelson in 1813), histories (a three-volume History of Brazil appeared 1810–19), editions (notably of Malory's Morte D'Arthur, 1817), essays, one novel (the Tristram Shandy-like The Doctor, 1834–35) and myriad reviews for the Quarterly and Annual Review. He raised a large family, and became an almost wholly sedentary man, more comfortable in his library than in the world at large. His political views decayed (or matured, depending on your perspective) into Conservatism in the manner of Wordsworth or Coleridge. This perceived apostasy lead the younger generation of Romantic poets to regard him with some disdain. His appointment (in 1813) as poet laureate only confirmed to writers such as Francis Jeffrey, Hazlitt and (most famously) Byron his Establishment status. Enemies republished his youthful, revolutionary *Wat Tyler* in 1817 to much ridicule of its now Tory author; and Byron never missed any opportunity to ridicule him, a campaign culminating in the brilliant parody of Southey's laureate ode on the death of George III, *A Vision of Judgement.

Southey wrote an immense amount of poetry, in all modes, and his long poems represent the most sustained attempt to refashion the epic idiom that the Romantic period witnessed. As a schoolboy he had planned to write a series of epics, each one based on a different mythological and religious scheme; in adulthood he began to put this plan into action. *Thalaba the Destroyer* (1801) utilizes Arabian sources and mythological apparatus. *Madoc* (1805) invokes the Aztec civilisation of South America, and *The Curse of Kehama* (1810) is based on Hindu religion and tradition. In each case Southey undertook extensive research before writing the work, so much so that this poetry is sometimes difficult to follow without the copious explanatory annotation he himself provided. Nonetheless, this is poetry that often rises to a genuinely epic grandeur. Even his enemy Byron conceded that, while 'there is, perhaps, too much [of Southey's poetry] for the present generation', nonetheless 'he has *passages* equal to anything'. The cumulative effect of *Thalaba*, for instance, is surprisingly bracing in its narrative sweep. His last attempt at epic, based on the Moorish invasion of Spain, was *Roderick; the Last of the Goths* (1814). The remaining two decades of his life were given over mostly to prose. His wife died in 1837 and he remarried two years later, but his health, never good, was giving out. The last few years of his life witnessed mental deterioration, and he died in 1843.

For all his faults, Southey does not deserve the almost total neglect under which he languishes today. As a writer of epics he surpassed all his contemporaries except perhaps *Blake, and as a genuine internationalist and poetic explorer he was preeminent in his time.

Spanish Gypsy, The (1868), by George Eliot (Marian Evans). 7177 lines, blank verse with interspersed lyrics. Despite its chiefly dramatic form, this is a work that functions as a *verse-novel, in the manner of Eliot's dry historical *Romola*.

Book 1. The scene is set in fifteenth-century Spain. Duke de Silva is charged with the 'high trust' to 'keep the Christian frontier'. The war against the Moslem forces has been waging for a while, and de Silva has arrested the local Gypsies ('strong and cunning knaves' Silva calls them). The scene opens with a group in a Tavern in the Spanish city of Bedmar discussing the current situation, and in particular the inactivity of the soldiery ('We make no sally:' observes Lopez, a soldier, 'we sit still here and wait whate'er the Moor/Shall please to do') on account of the Duke's forthcoming marriage to the duskily beautiful Fedalma. There is some controversy in this, on account of Fedalma's looks (a Prior advises Silva against marrying her because 'she bears the marks/Of races unbaptised, that never bowed/Before the holy signs', but Silva insists 'Fedalma is no Jewess'). Fedalma watches the Gypsy prisoners lead across the square and feels a strange interest in them. One night she receives a message tied to a little bird: *'Dear Child, Fedalma/Be brave, give no alarm – your Father comes'*. Zarca, King of the Gypsies, then climbs through her window (he has, we learn, escaped imprisonment with the help of a file 'hid in his shaggy hair'). He tells her how she was snatched as a child by 'marauding Spaniards', and how he recognizes her by the necklace she still wears. He tells her that her destiny is 'to be the angel of a homeless tribe'; Fedalma seems ready to go along with him ('Father, your child is ready!'), but is torn by her love for Silva ('the chief half of my soul/Where lies my love'). Father and daughter bicker, but she eventually flees, after leaving a note for her husband-to-be. *Book II*. Silva returns to find the Gypsies escaped and Fedalma gone. He vows to recover her. Zarca knows of a secret entrance into the city, and writes to the Moslem King El Zagal with the promise of entry to the city if in return El Zagal grant the Gypsies an African kingdom. *Book III*. Fedalma is not happy ('Oh, I am sick at heart'). Silva comes to her in the night in the Gypsy camp; as they embrace Zarca comes upon them and draws his sword. Forced to choose between lover and father, Fedalma chooses the latter ('slowly she moved to choose sublimer pain;/Yearning, yet shrinking'). Da Silva, in desperation, renounces his nobility and vows to join the Gypsies, in the hope of being able to marry Fedalma. *Book IV*. The Gypsies and Moors capture the town of Bedmar with much slaughter. Silva rages at Zarca ('You never warned me/That you had linked yourself with Moorish men/To take this town'). Zarca attempts to burn the priest Isidor, and Silva refuses to allow it ('Stand aside, my lord!' Zarca commands, 'you vowed obedience/To me, your chief'), so Silva renounces his Gypsy affiliation. As Father Isidor burns, and the crowd is distracted with his agony, Silva dashes at Zarca and stabs him. Fedalma is brought to her dying father, who urges her to 'save our people' as its Queen; he also instructs the Gypsies holding Silva to let him go, 'I charge you let him go unharmed and free/Now through your midst ... '. He dies. *Book V*. Fedalma and Silva meet one last time on the seashore, as the Gypsies are boarding Moorish boats to carry them to their new kingdom in Africa. Silva announces that he will visit the Pope ('I go to be absolved, to have my life/Washed into fitness for an offering/To injured Spain'). Fedalma goes off to lead her people, and yet she insists even at their parting that 'we are wed;/ For we shall carry each the pressure deep/Of the other's soul'.

Spasmodic. A term of satirical abuse coined by *Aytoun to characterize a particular sort of psychological, intense and morbid style of poetry. The classic Spasmodics are Alexander *Smith, Philip James *Bailey and Sydney *Dobell, although some early *Browning is sometimes spoken of as sharing some of these characteristics. As we might expect from the provenance of the word ('spasmodic' was originally a medical term, meaning 'pertaining to cramp or convulsion, or hauling of the sinews'), these characteristics are mostly stylistic abruptness and infelicity, bathos and inflated diction, repetition and non-sequiturs. In terms of subject, a typical Spasmodic poem will concern the inner life or psychological profile of an intense, self-absorbed young man, often a poet or thinker, agonizing over various issues. Chambers, in his 1860 *Cyclopedia of English Literature*, described these poets in the following terms: 'they heap up images and sentiments, the ornaments of poetry, without aiming at order, consistency, and the natural development of passion or feeling'. The great error of Spasmodic poetry, according to Chambers, is 'want of simplicity and nature'. Many Spasmodic techniques, however, are fairly in tune with more recent poetic theories, and much Spasmodic poetry appears very beautiful to present-day readers. The following, for instance, is from *Smith's *A Life Drama*:

> Unrest! Unrest! The passion-panting sea
> Watches the unveiled beauty of the stars
> Like a great hungry soul. The unquiet clouds
> Break and dissolve, then gather in a mass,
> And float like mighty icebergs through the blue.
> Summers, like blushes, sweep the face of earth;
> Heaven yearns in stars. Down comes the frantic rain;
> We hear the wail of the remorseful winds
> In their strange penance. And this wretched orb
> Knows not the taste of rest; a maniac world,
> Homeless and sobbing through the deep she goes.

Story of Doom, A (1867), by Jean Ingelow. 2520 lines, blank verse. Paul Turner describes this nine-book epic on the last days before the Flood as 'all too aptly named.'.

Book 1. Noah tells his wife, Niloiya, that he is troubled by the message he has received from God to build the Ark. The Ark is already under construction, but Niloiya announces that she would rather die than live 'rolling among the furrows of the unquiet,/Unconsecrate, unfriendly, dreadful sea'. She says that a ghost of her mother has visited her to warn that Noah is a fool, and that there will be no flood. To answer her uneasiness, Noah relates the command from God, his initial wariness, and his eventual surrender to God's will. Niloiya seems satisfied. *Book 2*. Noah works on the Ark. He, in the company of a female slave, visits the house of the aged Methuselah (a house once occupied by Adam himself, and constructed of 'forest-trunks, brought whole and set together'). Methuselah prophesies (causing those 'that were about him' to run away or stop their ears) the doom about to engulf mankind. Noah wanders off 'into the waste to meet the Voice of God'. *Book 3*. Two demons on Methuselah's roof overhear his prophesy of the flood, coming thereby to hidden knowledge about the future. They hurry off to tell Satan ('the old dragon lay/Coiled in the cavern where he dwelt') who resolves to go about the world, to incite the giants to rebellion against God, and to 'drive out/The women, the abhorred of my soul.' *Book 4*. Noah encounters his sons, and is best pleased with Japhet, to whom he says 'that the drenched world,/When risen clean washed from water, shall receive/From thee her lordliest governors'. *Book 5*. Niloiya goes off to fetch her son Japhet a wife. Unable to find one, she offers him a slave-woman. After some reluctance, Japhet embraces the prospect. *Book 6*. One night, Japhet ponders the difficulties ahead of them. Satan, meanwhile, prompts the giants to revolution by dwelling on the injustices of God (to good effect: 'they cried out in rage and wrath'). *Book 7*. Noah and Japhet arrive in the middle of Satan's speechifying to announce to the giants that 'God is wroth'. While Satan appears to sleep, curled up on a central dias, the giants debate and then reject Noah's warnings. *Book 8*. Noah returns to the Ark; Japhet marries. *Book 9*. Noah prays to God. Noah and his family board the ark and wait for the Deluge.

SWINBURNE, Algernon Charles (1837–1909). Swinburne's aristocratic background (he was the son of an Admiral and went to Eton) helped shape his particular view of the world. He himself considered the parallels between his own existence and *Shelley's so strong as to be remarkable. In an important sense, Swinburne worked to refigure the poetry of Shelley for a *fin-de-siècle* aesthetic. He copied his idol's atheism, his republicanism, and strove in his own way to be as outrageous as Shelley had been; in particular, the habit the young Shelley picked up of drinking to extreme. At Oxford Swinburne became friendly with Dante Rossetti and Edward Burne Jones, and after being sent down from university he lived for a while in Rossetti's London house.

Swinburne first came to fame with the publication of *Atalanta in Calydon* in 1865, modelled on the forms of Greek tragedy, but written with a vigour and energy that was in stark contrast to previous dull, solid works written in that form (such as Arnold's boring *Merope*). A collection of short poems followed the following year (*Poems and Ballads*) and caused no small storm of indignation and horror. Swinburne's paganism, his fascination with sexual sadism, hermaphroditism and disgusting disease, all reflected in the subject and style of these pieces. In setting out to *epater les bourgoise* Swinburne looks forward to the aestheticism of the *fin de siècle*. Swinburne's dissipated lifestyle, his drinking, his visiting a brothel in St John's Wood (where he paid a prostitute to beat him), his diminutive body, bright red hair and manic excitability – all this contributed to a certain mythos of the new school of poetry. Swinburne wrote fluently, publishing two politically radical works (*Song for Italy* in 1868 and *Songs Before Sunrise* in 1871) and expressing his paganism again in *Erechtheus* (1876). He put out a second collection of short poems (*Poems and Ballads: Second Series*) in 1878. The heated, even febrile tone of much of this poetry is not particularly compatible with writing long poetry.

What happened next marks the major change in Swinburne's life. By 1879 it was clear that he was drinking himself to death, and would not have lasted much longer. But a friend, Theodore Watts (later Watts-Dunton) took him away to his Putney home, 'The Pines'. There he managed to wean Swinburne off the drink, and to provide a settled, regular environment. Not only did this mean Swinburne was able to live (and write) through to the end of the century and even beyond, it gave him the calm to start producing lengthy poetry. Swinburne at this stage in his life admired Victor Hugo above all other living poets, and thought particularly highly of Hugo's enormous poem *Les Legendes des Siècles*. 1882 saw the publication of his first epic, the amazing **Tristram of Lyonesse*, and after various shorter pieces and editorial projects Swinburne returned to Arthurian myth with **The Tale of Balen* (1896). He also wrote a large number of plays (none of which were performed) and a significant body of prose criticism.

Tale of Balen (1896), by Algernon Charles Swinburne. Seven sections, 2367 lines, ballad stanzas (Swinburne uses the same stanzas as Tennyson's 'The Lady of Shalott'). Swinburne's last Arthurian work, and his last long poem.

1. Sir Balen, a passionate 'northern child of earth and sea', whose 'life of blood and breath/Sang out within him', rides from Tyneside to Camelot. There he is insulted by a 'churl of royal seed', with whom he fights. Killing the man, he is sent to prison for 'six dark months'. *2.* A distressed maiden comes to the court with a mighty sword chained to her side. Only a knight of exceptional purity ('a passing perfect knight/ Not great alone in force and fight') can free her from this burden, and various figures, from Arthur down, try in vain to release her. Eventually Balen tries, and is successful; but he refuses to give back the sword (whose name, we later learn, is Malison): 'Nay, for mine/It is till force shall make it thine'. The maiden utters a prophetic warning:

> For with it thou shalt surely slay
> Of all that look upon the day
> The man best loved of thee, and lay
>   Thine own life down for his.

3. The Lady of the Lake comes to Camelot, and demands the head of Balen. Balen, accusing the Lady of the Lake of causing his mother's death, chops off her head with the sword. He then rides off to Wales to kill Ryons, Arthur's enemy, and so restore his favour with the King, and hot-blooded Sir Launceor rides after him to avenge the wrong he had done in slaying the Lady of the Lake. Merlin reveals that the sword Malison was wrought with evil charms by the maiden who had brought it to Camelot, to use to kill her own brother. *4.* Balen and Launceor fight ('Balen's spear through Launceor's shield/Clove as a ploughshare cleaves the field/And pierced the hauberk triple-steeled/That horse and horseman stricken reeled') and Launceor is slain. Launceor's lover appears, and kills herself with his sword. Balen then meets his brother Balan, and they decide to ride together against the Welsh king. A dwarf rides up, and warns Balen that Launceor's many kin will now seek him out for revenge, although Balen is unmoved by this news. King Mark of Cornwall arrives, and promises to build the lovers a fine tomb. *5.* Aided by Merlin, Balen and Balan surprise the Welsh king Ryons with a small band of guards. The brothers bring Ryons as a prisoner to Camelot.

The 'wild brother' of this 'wild foe' attacks, attempting to free him, and battle is joined. King Lot 'and all his host of sea-born men' comes to the aid of the wild king, hoping to overthrow Arthur, but Merlin casts a spell to distract him (he sees a vision of his 'lustrous wife' floating over the battle), Lot is slain by Sir Pellinore, and the battle is won. 6. Some time later, a dolorous knight passes Arthur, and the king sends Balen to fetch him back and explain the reason for his sorrow; but on the return the knight is killed by an apparently invisible foe. Balen sets out to track this foe in the company of the dead knight's bereaved maiden; they fall in with a second knight, who vows to join them: but he too is slain by 'the invisible evil', 'fleet as the lightning's laugh and flame.' Balen and the maiden are hospitably received by a third knight, who tells them that the man they seek is called Garlon, that he is King Pellam's brother, and 'he walks and slays as plague's blind breath ... Hid round by charms from all men's sight.' At a tournament put on by King Pellam, Balen encounters Garlon and kills him. Pellam attempts to revenge his brother's death, but is also killed. 7. Balen meets the sorrowful Sir Garnysshe of the Mount, who has been crossed in love. He comes across his beloved with another man, slays them both, and then kills himself. 'Balen, seeing him dead,/Rode hence, lest folk would say he had slain/Those three.' Travelling on, he learns of a knight who guards an island against all comers, and resolves to take him on: since his own shield is battered and bashed, he borrows a shield from another knight. But the knight he rides against is his own brother Balan, and the change of shield prevents him being recognized. The two brothers fight:

> Balan smote Balen first, and clove
> His lifted shield that rose and strove
> In vain against the stroke that drove
> Down: as the web that morning wove
> Of glimmering pearl from spray to spray
> Dies when the strong sun strikes it, so
> Shrank the steel, tempered thrice to show
> Strength, and the mad might of the blow
> Shore Balen's helm away.

Balen retaliates, and both brothers are killed.

Temple of Nature, The (1803), by Erasmus Darwin. 1928 lines, heroic couplets. Darwin's last poem is a detailed exposition of the evolutionary theories that Darwin spent his life developing (and that were to influence his more famous grandson, Charles).

Canto 1. The Production of Life. After an invocation to various personifications (to Darwin's Muse, to Love, to Nature and so on) the poem begins with the first stirrings of life on Earth. 'Nurs'd by warm sun-beams in primeval caves,/Organic life began beneath the waves ... without parent by spontaneous birth/Rise the first specks of animated earth'. From these microscopic beginnings, Darwin sketches in the entire evolutionary process:

> ORGANIC LIFE beneath the shoreless waves
> Was born and nurs'd in Ocean's pearly caves;
> First forms minute, unseen by spheric glass,
> Move on the mud, or pierce the watery mass;
> These, as successive generations bloom,
> New powers acquire, and larger limbs assume;
> Whence countless groups of vegetation spring,
> And breathing realms of fin, and feet and wing.

Canto II. Reproduction of Life. After dealing with asexual reproduction ('So the lone Truffle, lodged beneath the earth,/Shoots from paternal roots the tuberous birth'), this canto details the varieties of sex: 'hail the DEITIES OF SEXUAL LOVE!/All forms of Life shall this fond Pair delight,/And sex to sex the willing world unite'. The canto ends with the Goddess and the Muse sharing a taste of the Forbidden Fruit from the Tree of Knowledge. *Canto III. Progress of the Mind.* The Goddess and the Muse converse, discussing humanity's achievements.

TENNYSON, ALFRED, from 1884 First Baron Tennyson (1809–92). Tennyson was born at Somersby, Lincolnshire, the third son of the rector, George Tennyson. An introverted and gloomy youth, influenced by the melancholia (and eventual breakdown) of his alcoholic father, Tennyson went up to Trinity College, Cambridge, excessively shy (he once ran away from a lecture hall because it was too full of people). His time at Cambridge saw him coming out of his shell, in large part due to the friendships he made there – most notably the intense connection he made with Arthur Hallam. Hallam swiftly became more than a friend to the poet, and became engaged to Tennyson's sister Emily.

Tennyson won the University's chancellor's medal for English verse with 'Timbuctoo' in 1829. His verses had already appeared in a volume entitled *Poems by Two Brothers* (1827), which actually contained three brothers' work (Alfred, Charles and Frederick Tennyson). More successful in his own eyes was his 1830 collection, *Poems, Mostly Lyrical*, which contained some of his most enduring verses, including 'Mariana'. The collection was, however, savagely reviewed by some influential critics. Tennyson was greatly discouraged (as his later autobiographical poem 'Merlin and the Gleam' makes plain). His 1832 collection, *Poems*, included masterpieces such as 'The Lotos Eaters', 'The Kraken' and

'The Lady of Shalott'. It is difficult, however, to avoid seeing all this as nothing more than a prelude to the event of the following year which was to constitute the central shaping incident of Tennyson's life. When visiting Italy in 1833, Arthur Hallam, aged twenty-two, suddenly dropped dead of an aneurism. Tennyson was overwhelmed with grief.

The poetry Tennyson wrote in the aftermath of this bereavement was almost exclusively concerned with articulating his devastating sense of desolation and loss. Many of the lyrics that were later incorporated into *In Memoriam date from this period, as well as 'Break, break, break', 'Tithonus', 'The Morte D'Arthur' and many others. Tennyson did not publish another collection of poetry until 1842, and it was not until 1847, with the publication of *The Princess, that Tennyson really began to achieve wide public prominence. During the 1830s, Tennyson had become engaged to Emily Sellwood, but the engagement had faltered, possibly because of fears that Tennyson might have inherited his father's tendency towards madness.

The breakthrough year for Tennyson was 1850. He finally published, as *In Memoriam A.H.H., the lengthy collection of elegiac lyrics occasioned by the loss of Arthur Hallam. This work struck an immediate chord with the Victorian reading public, and was almost universally praised. Queen Victoria, who would later turn to the work for consolation on the death of Albert, greatly admired it. Wordsworth having died earlier in the year, it was decided to make Tennyson Poet Laureate. 1850 was also the year that Tennyson finally married Emily Sellwood.

From here on, Tennyson's position as the chief poet of his age was unassailable. *Maud (1855) and the first four *Idylls of the King (1859) sold in prodigious numbers, and Tennyson enjoyed a wide circle of friends and admirers. A son, Hallam Tennyson, was born in 1852, and another, Lionel, in 1854. Tennyson wrote copiously, and to an increasingly admiring audience. *Enoch Arden came out in 1864, and Tennyson put great effort into the completion of his vast Arthurian epic. The Holy Grail and Other Poems (1869) and Gareth and Lynette, etc. (1872) added to the collection of Arthurian idylls, and a collection of them was published as Idylls of the King in 1872. He was offered a baronetcy in 1865, and in 1873, 1874 and 1880, but refused it each time, only eventually agreeing to the honour in 1884.

By 1875, when Tennyson was sixty-six, he decided to begin a career as a playwright. Queen Mary was published in 1875 and produced for the stage the following year. Other plays included Harold (1877), The Falcon (1879), Beckett (1884) and The Foresters (1892). His final illness and death occurred in 1892, and he was buried in Westminster Abbey.

Tennyson's reputation has sunk and risen, but is currently high. Criticism has never really refuted Auden's opinion that 'his genius was lyrical', and that he lacked the necessary narrative and architectonic powers to produce long and epic poetry. Yet his sensibility was, of all Victorian poets, the one most precisely attuned to the spirit (or spirits) of his age. His engagements with issues of doubt and faith, action and lassitude, duty and desire are rendered not only with technical virtuosity, but with a profound and often neglected dialecticism.

Thalaba the Destroyer (1801), by Robert Southey. 6097 lines, varied unrhymed metres. The poem was attacked by the critics and sold relatively poorly, but it remains an intermittently powerful work, the first of Southey's mature productions.

The First Book. Zeinab is wandering the Arabian desert with her son Thalaba, bewailing the recent murder of her husband. They come across a stately palace, inhabited by the solitary Aswad. He tells the tale of how divine retribution came upon his tribe, the builders of the splendid palace (Irem), because of their worshipping of Idols. Only Aswad is spared, although he is magically prevented from ever leaving the palace; 'so many weary ages have gone by!/And still I linger here'. The Death Angel descends and releases Aswad and Zeinab from their sufferings, telling Thalaba 'thou art chosen forth/To do the will of Heaven;/To avenge thy father's death,/The murder of thy race'. *The Second Book.* The scene shifts to the 'Domdaniel Caverns/ Under the Roots of the Ocean', the habitation of the evil magicians responsible for the destruction of the race of Hodeirah (Thalaba's people). Despite going to every length, including interrogating the reanimated corpse of Hodeirah, these 'Masters of the Spell' cannot locate Thalaba (protected by the spirit of Mahommed) to finish the job. The Magician Abdaldar sets out on foot across Arabia to seek him. Coming across him in a desert camp he raises his arm to strike him down, but is himself destroyed by the Simoom, 'the Blast of the Desert'. *The Third Book.* Thalaba takes the magic ring from dead Abdaldar's finger and wears it. A demon, summoned up by the ring, reveals the evil plot of the Magicians. Thalaba grows to manhood, and falls in love with his adoptive sister Oneiza. One day he reads a message in the magic ring telling him to depart. *The Fourth Book.* Thalaba travels to Baghdad, avoiding assassination attempts by the Magician Lobaba. *The Fifth Book.* Arriving in Baghdad, Thalaba is directed to the 'Cave of Horrors' in search of a magic talisman. Inside, his guide Mohareb turns out to be another disguised Magician, whose attempt to kill Thalaba fails. A disembodied voice announces 'the Talisman is Faith'. *The Sixth Book.* Thalaba travels to an Edenic garden inside a mountain, where those 'marked by their horoscope' for mighty deeds, are allowed 'a foretaste of the full beatitude' of paradise; it turns out to be another diabolic plot to trap Thalaba. Returning to the desert, he overhears a cry of help from 'his own Oneiza, his Arabian Maid'. *The Seventh Book*. Saved from assault, Oneiza accompanies Thalaba back into the garden, where he destroys 'the Paradise of Sin' by slaying the presiding Magician. Thalaba is rewarded by the local Sultan, and he and Oneiza plan to marry. *The Eighth Book*. Azrael, the angel of Death, has taken Oneiza from her marriage bed; Thalaba for a time runs wild with grief. Eventually he resolves to continue his quest. He travels north and is captured by a Sorceress, whereupon he is carried by a magic flying car to Mohareb's Island. *The Ninth Book*. Thalaba is cast into a dungeon, but attempts to destroy him fail. His prison is dismantled by the whirlwind of 'the Genii of the Air'. *The Tenth Book*. Thalaba struggles across the snowy wilderness. He takes shelter at the house of the beautiful Laila, whose supernatural father keeps her isolated from mankind. The Guardian is revealed to be Okba, the murderer of Thalaba's father; but fate decrees that Thalaba cannot kill him yet, and he scorns to take his revenge upon Okba's daughter. When Okba tries to stab Thalaba, his daughter rushes between them and receives the fatal stroke. *The Eleventh Book*. Laila's spirit, in the shape of a green bird of paradise, guides Thalaba to the presence of the Bird of Ages, the Simorg. This creature in turn directs Thalaba to the Cavern under the Seabed. He travels down a river in a little boat, 'without an oar, without a sail' navigated by a mysterious Damsel, and eventually alights. *The Twelfth Book*. Thalaba discards his magic ring, passes through adamantine gates and descends into the realm of the Magicians. They try to disbar him, but 'vain are all spells! the Destroyer/Treads the Domdaniel floor ... to crush the single foe', scattering magicians around him as he approaches the Idol of Eblis (Satan). He meets Okba, his father's murderer but, for Laila's sake, cannot kill him. The Prophet's voice is heard: 'thou hast done well, my Servant!' Okba is pitied and forgiven, Thalaba destroys the Idol of Eblis and is received into Paradise to meet again with his wife, Oneiza.

Theodric: A Domestic Tale (1824), by Thomas Campbell. 1181 lines, heroic couplets.

The narrator and a friend are visiting Switzerland. In a country graveyard they notice 'a maiden's grave', a woman (the inscription reveals) young and beautiful and courted by many, but one who had died of an unrequited love. The narrator's companion tells the tale: Julia (for it is she) had dwelt with her father 'where yonder Castle shines/O'er clustering trees and terrace-mantling vines'. Her younger brother, Udolph, had gone to fight in the Austrian army, where his eager letters home had so effectively sung the praise of his commanding officer, Theodric, that Julia had fallen in love with him without even seeing him. After Theodric had saved young Udolph's life, he was invited back to this Swiss Castle; but before going there he travelled to England (he always had been, we are told, 'a glad enthusiast' for things English). There he had fallen in love with Constance, an Englishwoman of rank, and they had become betrothed. On arriving in Switzerland he became aware of Julia's feelings, and felt duty bound to disabuse her, which he did gently. He later married Constance and settled in England. Julia, left in Switzerland sickened with lost love and was brought near to death. She sent Udolph to ask Theodric if she might see him one more time; Theodric goes, but as he attends Julia's deathbed news reaches him that his own wife, Constance, is close to death. He rushes back to England, but is too late. The poem closes with a letter his wife had left for him, and the soothing effect this had on his mind.

TIGHE, Mary (1772–1810). Born Mary Blachford in Dublin. Her father died in 1773, and she was raised by her independently-minded but religiously devout mother. She married her cousin, Henry Tighe (pronounced 'Tyee') in 1793, an Irish MP. It seems clear that their marriage was not a success; there were no children, and Tighe did not really love her husband (she had, according to the rumour of the time, been in love with somebody else, but did not have the heart to turn down Henry's proposal). The couple moved to London, and while her husband studied for the Bar she learnt Latin, wrote poetry and prose. In 1801 the couple returned to Ireland, and Mary composed her single great poem, *Psyche, in 1803. This work circulated in manuscript for over a year (one of its readers was the poet Thomas *Moore), and it was published in a small private edition in 1805. But by now Tighe's health was poor; she had her first symptoms of consumption in 1804. She spent her final years in Ireland, and continued to write short poetry. She died 24 March 1810.

After her death Psyche was published in 1811, collected with other poems and edited by her brother-in-law William Tighe. This 1811 edition of Tighe's allegorical poem was a great success (it had gone into its fourth edition by the end of the year), and it proved particularly influential upon the young John *Keats. But after the poem's vogue had passed it was chiefly as a quarry for phrases and images in Keats's poetry that it was known at all. Nowadays Tighe's reputation is rising again, and many critics see in Psyche one of the neglected masterpieces of English poetry. Duncan Wu, for instance, calls it 'one of the great love poems in the language'.

Tristram and Iseult (1852), by Matthew Arnold. 789 lines, various metres, the poem first appeared in *Empedocles on Etna and Other Poems*. Arnold's only attempt at Arthurian literature, this poem was the first modern treatment of the Tristram myth in English.

1. *Tristram*. Tristram loves Iseult of Ireland; but she is married to King Mark of Cornwall, and he is married to Iseult of Brittany (also called Iseult of the White Hand). The poem opens on Tristram, wounded and sick, being nursed by his wife in Brittany. He has sent message to Iseult of Ireland, asking her to come to him, but she has not yet arrived. 2. *Iseult of Ireland*. Iseult arrives, and tries to rally him ('Tristram! Tristram! let thy heart not fail!'), but it is too late ('Hush, 'tis vain, I feel my end approaching!'). He dies, and so does she, presumably of a broken heart. The narrative perspective shifts abruptly to a figure on the tapestry on the wall. A huntsman on this 'ghostly tapestry' is given sudden sentience.

> What place is this and who are they?
> Who is that kneeling Lady fair?
> And on his pillows that pale Knight
> Who seems of marble on a tomb?
> How comes it here, this chamber bright,
> Through whose mullioned windows clear
> The castle-court all wet with rain,
> The drawbridge and the moat appear,
> And then the beach, and, marked with spray,
> The sunken reefs, and far away
> The unquiet bright Atlantic plain?

3. *Iseult of Brittany*. A year later, Iseult tells her children the story of how the wizard Merlin was entranced and destroyed by the beautiful but evil Vivian.

Tristram of Lyonesse (1882), by Algernon Charles Swinburne. 4468 lines, heroic couplets. Swinburne himself regarded this arresting hybrid lyric-epic as his greatest work, although critical opinion has only recently begun taking it seriously. The eroticism of the poem created a climate of some small notoriety. Swinburne wrote to Rossetti that he hoped 'to make the copulative passages of the poem more warm and provocative of sinful appetite than anything my chaste Muse has yet attempted'.

Prelude: Tristram and Iseult. The poet invokes 'Love, that is the first and last of all things made,/The light that has the living world for shade'. 1. *The Sailing of the Swallow*. Tristram, the premier warrior at the court of King Mark of Cornwall, escorts Iseult of Ireland over the sea to Cornwall to marry the king. Iseult's maid, Brangwain, has a love potion for Iseult and Mark to drink on her wedding night, such that 'having drunk, they twain should have one heart'. But Iseult and Tristram accidentally drink from the golden cup.

> And with light lips yet full of their swift smile,
> And hands that wist not though they dug a grave,
> Undid the hasps of gold, and drank, and gave,
> And he drank after, a deep glad kingly draught:
> And all their life changed in them, for they quaffed
> Death;

2. *The Queen's Pleasance.* The boat arrives at Cornwall, but Tristram and Iseult are already lovers. Iseult and Mark are married, 'and all the loud time of the marriage feast/One thought within three hearts was as a fire/Where craft and faith took counsel with desire'. Brangwain substitutes herself for Iseult on the wedding night, that Mark should not realize his wife has been unfaithful to him. A stranger comes to Mark's court in the likeness of a minstrel ('A knight unchristened yet of unknown name,/Swart Palamede'); when Mark grants him a boon, he asks for Iseult. Mark is unhappy, but having given his word cannot back down ('And he bowed/His head, and wept'). Palamede spends the night with Iseult, but 'shame at heart stung nigh to death desire' and he only watches her as she sleeps. The following day Tristram and Palamede fight, and Palamede is left for dead as Tristram and Iseult ride off to a hidden bower. Together, they spend many nights. 3. *Tristram in Brittany.* Three years have passed, and Tristram stands by the sea in Brittany musing on all that has passed. He has travelled far and had many adventures, returning at last to the court of the Breton high king, whose daughter, Iseult of the White Hand, loves him. They marry. 4. *The Maiden Marriage.* Tristram, whose heart is with Iseult of Ireland, does not consummate his marriage. 5. *Iseult at Tintagel.* On Tristram's wedding night, Iseult of Ireland is meditating in her chamber in Tintagel. Her monologue is interspersed with the antiphonal responses of the sea and wind ('And as man's anguish clamouring cried the wind,/And as God's anger answering rang the sea'). 6. *Joyous Gard.* Tristram travels to Cornwall with his brother-in-law Ganhardine. He meets secretly with Iseult, and Ganhardine falls in love with her serving-maid Brangwain. Tristram and Iseult elope, and fly first to Camelot, and thence to Lancelot's north-eastern fortress, Joyous Gard. There they spend a happy summer together. 7. *The Wife's Vigil.* Meanwhile, 'all that year in Brittany forlorn ... dwelt the white-handed Iseult, maid and wife'. 8. *The Last Pilgrimage.* Tristram is commanded by Arthur to help support Triamour, King Of Wales, against the attacks of Urgan, 'an iron bulk of giant mould'. Iseult returns to Mark in Tintagel. Tristram slays the giant and returns to Brittany, where Ganhardine tells him a strange

knight has kidnapped his wife, Brangwain. The two ride after the stranger and rescue her, but in the battle Tristram is 'wounded nigh to slow dark death'. 9. *The Sailing of the Swan*. Tristram, dying, asks Ganhardine to take his ship (called the Swan) over the sea to Tintagel and fetch Iseult to him. But Iseult of the White Hand, overhearing his request, burns with 'a virgin lust for vengeance'. She kills her husband just before the arrival of the Swan; and when Iseult from Ireland comes across the dead Tristram she dies of grief. King Mark builds a chapel to bury the two lovers in. The poem ends apocalyptically with a vision of the chapel consumed by the sea.

> For many a fathom gleams and moves and moans
> The tide that sweeps above their coffined bones
> In the wrecked chancel by the shivered shrine:
> Nor where they sleep shall moon or sunlight shine
> Nor man look down for ever: none shall say,
> Here once, or here, Tristram and Iseult lay:
> But peace they have that none may gain who live,
> And rest about them that no love can give,
> And over them, while death and life shall be,
> The light and sound and darkness of the sea.

Troubadour, The (1825), by L.E.L. [Letitia Landon]. 1543 lines, octosyllabic couplets with various interspersed lyrics and other metres.

Canto 1. Raymond is a soldier and a poet in fourteenth-century Toulouse, and is singing songs to the beautiful Eva (a half-faery woman) in his tower. The summons comes from Lady Clothilde for Raymond to lead her troops into battle, something he is eager to do (it will mean a knighthood). That night, Eva gives him an 'amber-scented chain' with a cross on it. *Canto 2*. Raymond distinguishes himself in battle, and becomes enamoured of the raven-haired Lady Adeline; but after singing her one of his troubadour songs, he gallops away as 'deep shame mingled with remorse'. He decides to go on the Crusades, returns to the tower to bid farewell to Eva, and departs. *Canto 3*. In Spain, Raymond saves the life of Eva's father, but is himself captured and incarcerated by the Moors. Rescued from the dungeon by Leila, a beautiful Moorish maiden, he is nursed back to health. Leila falls in love with Raymond, but he leaves her to return to Eva and she dies. The poem ends with Raymond and Eva joyously reunited.

: V :

Vala, or the Four Zoas (unpublished; written 1795–1804), by William Blake. 4227 lines, Blakean long line. Blake's first attempt at long epic (as opposed to the brief epics such as *The Marriage of Heaven and Hell*), this poem remained unpublished until long after Blake's death. He worked on it over a long period, revising and rewriting and overlaying the existent text and narrative with not always compatible alterations. It remains an inchoate version of the mythology expressed more cogently in *Milton and *Jerusalem. Consequently it is a difficult poem to summarize, partly because of this sometimes muddled narrative line, and partly because of the complexity of the immanent symbolic schema, Blake's personal mythology, of which *Vala* is a rambling exposition. For a brief expression of this schema, see the note to Blake's life.

The text was originally called *The Four Zoas*, a 'zoa' (from the Greek for 'a living thing') being an eternal living principle, a fragment of a complete, whole Eternal Man. The fall of this harmonious, free being and his shattering into four elements is the starting point of the poem; these four elements each embodies a different aspect of the whole being. Urizen embodies conscious, rational thought and is the limiting or superego principle; Luvah is passion and sexuality, and approximates to the id; Urthona (also known as Los) is the imagination, prone to wrath, and (as the zoa most like Blake's own character) is a sort of ego; Tharmas is compassion and pity. Each of these characters (they approximate to the gods of classical epic) has a female partner, a mate, called an emanation. Urizen's is Ahania, Luvah's is Vala (she is a devious femme fatale, and her mischief provokes much of the poem's narrative, hence the work's alternate title), Urthona's is Enitharmon, Tharmis's is Enion. The broad sweep of the narrative concerns the fall of the Eternal Man into the realm of time and his separation into these four zoas and their emanations; the epic ends with the reassimilation of the Eternal Man.

Night the First. Tharmas (compassion) has taken pity on another female (Blake does not seem to have made up his mind as to whether this woman is Enitharmon or 'Jerusalem'); his emanation Enion is jealous. The two quarrel, and Enion binds Tharmas in a sort of cocoon ('from her bosom weaving soft in sinewy threads') from which his spectre arises. The two mate, and their offspring is a debased version of Urthona (called Los) and Enitharmon. By this means, Urthona/Los and

Enitharmon are trapped in the temporal world woven by Enion ('the circle of destiny'), for which has been drawn 'seven thousand years' out of the timelessness of eternity (although in every emprisoning year, Blake tells us, there are 'windows into Eden'). Los and Enitharmon, thrust into this fallen world, fight among themselves and reject their mother Enion, who wanders 'on the verge of non-being'. A council of gods ('those in great Eternity met in the Council of God/As one Man') debate this pitiable state of affairs. *Night the Second*. Los, raging against Enitharmon, smites her upon the earth, an action which apparently opens an obviously sexual cleft:

> Los saw the wound of his blow; he saw, he pitied, he wept.
> Los now repented that he had smitten Enitharmon; he felt love
> Arise in all his veins; he threw his arms around her loins
> To heal the wound of his smiting.

The result of this coupling will emerge eventually (in the fifth night) as Orc. Meanwhile, tyrannical Urizen (Rational Will) has invaded and subdued this new world with a vast army: 'ten thousand thousand were his hosts of spirits on the wind'. The Zoas are at war with one another, and the Eternal Man (made up of these elements) sinks closer to annihilation; this Man, in his weariness, deliberately (and wrongly) hands over power to Urizen, who consolidates his hold on the temporal world. But he is not happy, and enviously regards Los and Enitharmon, who are bickering in the idyllic landscapes of the new world. The Night ends with a lament from Enion, wandering woeful on the edge of non-being, that powerfully expresses the oppresiveness of suffering in this world. *Night the Third*. Urizen 'upon his high and starry throne' is unhappy; his emanation Ahania attempts to comfort him, but he reveals his vision that a boy (the yet-to-be-born child of Los and Enitharmon, Orc) will usurp his powers. Ahania tells him her own vision, an elaborate allegory about the Eternal Man neglecting his Rational Will (Urizen) and following only his sexual passion (Luvah), before realizing his error and overcompensating by throwing Luvah out altogether and resurrecting Urizen. Urizen is enraged by this vision, and throws Ahania 'from his bosom obdurate. She fell like lightning'. A terrible, chaotic flood ensues ('the swelling sea/Burst from its bounds'). Tharmas (compassion) emerges from the destruction, but he too hates his emanation, Enion, who has accordingly faded away to nothing more than a voice; her plaintive lament concludes the night. *Night the Fourth*. Urizen's world, and Urizen himself, were broken in Night Three; all the zoas except Luvah are now dwelling in the 'abyss'. Tharmas (compassion) carries away Los's emanation, Enitharmon, and thereby shatters Los (he becomes a spectre, 'a shadow blue, obscure, & dismal'). But Tharmas has delu-

sions of grandeur, and thinks himself God (each of the zoas believes this
in turn): 'Now,' he declares, 'all comes into the power of Tharmas.
Urizen is fallen'. Tharmas now reconstructs Urizen, putting him into the
body of a man. *Night the Fifth*. The narrative returns to Los (imagination) and his emanation Enitharmon, whose coupling now gives birth to
Orc, a sort of Blakean messiah figure, a fiery Christ. Los, jealous of his
son, binds him to an iron mountain-top with the chains of jealousy. It
transpires that Orc is the fallen state of Luvah (just as Los is the fallen
form of Urthona). The night ends with a lament by the reborn Urizen,
who is 'shut up in the deep dens of Urthona'. *Night the Sixth*. Urizen
explores his dens; he meets his three (unnamed) daughters, but when
they do not answer him he curses them ('for their colours of loveliness/I
will give blackness; for jewels, hoary frost; for ornament, deformity').
This curse has terrible consequences in his already ruined world ('he
had time enough to repent of his rashly threatened curse'). Urizen looks
with despair upon the world he has traversed.

> When he had passed these southern terrors, he approached the east,
> Void, pathless, beaten with iron, sleet & eternal hail & rain.
> No form was there, no living thing, & yet his way lay through
> This dismal world.

Urizen attempts to build a golden palace in this chaos, but his building
backfires as a tyrannical 'vast chain' binding and imprisoning his reality. He wanders on disconsolate, until he encounters Tharmas, Orc and
the spectre of Urthona. *Night the Seventh*. Urizen confronts Orc in the
cave where he is fettered ('a caverned universe of flaming fire'); a
'deadly root' grows through the cavern floor, and grows swiftly into an
Urizenic Tree of Mystery. Orc changes himself into a giant serpent,
which Urizen forces to twine about the tree. The perspective of the
poem changes to reveal Enitharmon's spectre entering the shadowy
world of Urizen in which Los and Urthona are imprisoned; here Urthona
and Enitharmon mate to produce a 'wonder horrible', the shadow of
Vala. Orc, in his malign serpent-form, breaks free from the tree and a
terrible war begins. Vala allies herself with Urizen. The Night ends with
the reconciliation of Los and Enitharmon, who agree to unite to combat
Urizen. *Night the Eighth*. The Council of God meets again 'as one Man,
even Jesus, upon Gilead & Harmon'; now Luvah (sexual passion, the
unfallen form of Orc) becomes identified with the Lamb of God. Urizen
is prosecuting his war, but he cannot resist the sexual wiles of Vala –
'Urizen/Sitting within his temple furious, felt the numbing stupor'. Despite this stupor, Urizen embodies himself forth as the Synagogue of
Satan, at the centre of which is the harlot Rahab (who in turn is another
version of Vala). This cruel gathering crucifies the Lamb of God upon

the Tree of Mystery. Urizen is finally overthrown by the triumphant Vala ('he felt his pores/Drink in the deadly dull delusion'); he is transformed into a petrified dragon form. 'Rahab triumphs over all'. *Night the Ninth*. This apocalyptic night owes much to the Biblical *Revelation of St John*. Los and Enitharmon build Jerusalem 'weeping over the sepulchre & over the crucified body'. The Eternal Man, who has throughout the poem been sick and asleep on a rock, begins to stir, aware of the 'war within his members'. The Man calls to Urizen (to whom he had handed his power on the second Night); this call rouses the Zoa from his stony-dragon form, and he emerges in human shape 'glorious bright, exulting in his joy'. Urizen confesses his error, is promised reconciliation with his emanation Ahania. The world ends: 'riven link from link, the bursting universe explodes'. A mob of souls converges in a huge riot: slaves revenging themselves upon the warriors who enslaved them, the oppressed upon the oppressor, unjustly convicted criminals upon wicked judges and so on. 'After the flames appears the cloud of the Son of Man'. The terror passes, and the Eternal Man rises to meet the vision. There follows a lengthy harvest of all the souls the temporal world has housed. Urizen ploughs souls like seeds into the earth in an eternal spring; Orc, the inferior form of Luvah, is burnt away in the eternal summer, and Luvah is reunited with Vala; Tharmas and Enion are similarly reconnected. The harvest is gathered in the eternal autumn, and bread and wine made from the wheat and grapes as autumn gives way to winter. 'And Man walks forth from the midst of the fires, the evil is all consumed'.

Victories of Love, The (1863), by Coventry Patmore. 3842 lines, octosyllabic couplets. For the general circumstances of the composition of this work, see *Angel in the House* to which it is a sort of sequel. This is the story of Frederick Graham, once a suitor for the hand of Honoria (who, in *Angel in the House*, married Felix).

Book 1. The narrative is made up of letters mostly from Frederick to his mother, and her replies, with some others from actors in the drama. Frederick is rather prone to fall in love, and does so with the beautiful Honoria (from *Angel in the House*), although in a rather highfalutin way ('*I* love Miss Churchill? Ah, no, no./I view, enchanted, from afar,/ And love her as I love a star'). When Honoria becomes engaged to Felix, Frederick reacts manfully ('Dearest Honoria ... Heaven bless you!') but is heartbroken. He goes to sea (he is a naval officer), but two years later, upon returning to England, he is still smitten. He marries Jane (with her features 'somewhat plainly set' and her 'homely manners'), but he does so from affection and companionship rather than love. Jane is understandably 'miserable' ('he never said he loved me!'); but she nurses him back to health after he falls dangerously ill. *Book 2.* During the second book Frederick, inspired by his wife's unflagging devotion, kindness and love, learns slowly to love her in return. As Jane falls ill herself, and sickens towards death, Frederick truly realizes what he is about to lose ('Oh Father,' he prays, 'take her not away'). Jane dies happy, her 'last doubts gone' about Frederick's love.

Verse novel. A distinctively Victorian phenomenon, the verse-novel parallels the rise to prominence of the prose-novel as the chief mode of writing in the period. The chief point that distinguishes a 'verse novel' from an *epic or a *romance is its novelistic focus on the contemporary. If we wished to be more specific, we could separate the celebrations of bourgeois values (family, romantic love, the smoothing over of ideological aporias) with a more oblique embodiment of those values in historical or otherwise distancing frames of epic and romance.

The pre-eminent verse novel of the nineteenth century remains *Barrett-Browning's *Aurora Leigh* (1857). As early as 8 October 1844 (in a letter to her friend John Kenyon) she was talking about her 'fancy for writing some day a longer poem':

> a poem comprehending the aspect and the manners of modern life, and flinching at nothing of the conventional .... Now I do think that a true poetical novel – modern, and on the level of the manners of the day – might be as good a poem as any other, and much more popular besides. Do you not think so?

Later in the same year she declared: 'I want to write a poem of a new class, in a new measure – a Don Juan without the mockery and impurity'. The reference to *Byron's masterpiece suggests that the establishment of a tradition of verse-novel writing was drawing much of its inspiration from a work radically opposed to bourgeois values. We might expect the versification of the novel format to be a tactic for raising the tone, in effect for gentrifying a middle-class mode of writing. But many nineteenth-century verse-novels follow the Byronic model more thoroughly than is altogether compatible with purging that same mode of the 'mockery and impurity' that Victorians found so unpalatable. Clough's *Amours de Voyage* (1858) certainly engages with exactly the same bourgeois family/love-story concerns as the novel itself; but its downbeat ending and subversive humour undermines these pieties. We find something similar in works such as *Lytton's *Lucile* (1860) or the extreme violence of *Browning's *Inn Album* (1875).

210 VISION OF DON RODERICK, THE

Vision of Don Roderick, The (1811), by Walter Scott. 837 lines, Spenserian stanzas. Profits from this, Scott's fourth long poem, were donated to a fund to help victims of the Peninsular war.

Don Roderick, the last Gothic King of Spain (in the eighth century) spends the night in a Cathedral vault in Toledo, despite the fact that prophecy had declared that any king who dared descend into the vault would be doomed to defeat. Inside this 'fated room', the Don has three visions: the first foretelling the Moorish invasion of Spain, and Don Roderick's own death on the battlefield, the second looking forward to the period of the Inquisition, and the third detailing the glorious Iberian actions of Wellington's forces in the Napoleonic wars. Scott, in this last vision, gives particularly prominence to the Highland regiments: 'But ne'er in battlefield throbb'd heart so brave/As that which beats beneath a Scottish plaid'.

Vision of Judgement, A (1821), by Robert Southey. 640 lines, unrhymed hexameters. Southey's poem is doomed to live forever in the shadow of Byron's superb parody (see below).

1. The Trance. An evening bell tolls the passing of George III; the narrator is cogitating sadly on this death when he hears 'a startling Voice from the twilight' that says 'Come and behold!'. He falls into a trance. *2. The Vault.* He finds himself in the vault of a mausoleum, but the King's coffin is empty; he hears beautiful music and the vault melts away from around him. *3. The Awakening.* 'Then I beheld the King. From a cloud which cover'd the pavement/His reverend form arose: heavenward his face was directed'. Perceval, the former Prime Minister, attends the monarch, telling him that everything in the kingdom is in an excellent state of affairs ('Right in his Father's steps hath the Regent trod' and so forth). *4. The Gate of Heaven.* The surrounding space dilates, and the scene shifts to the 'Gate of Bliss'. An angel announces 'Ho! ... King George of England cometh to Judgement'. Crowds of good and bad angels assemble. *5. The Accusers.* The king stands alone before a 'Presence/Veil'd with excess of light'. A demon comes forward to accuse George, and he summons the shades of two radicals (John Wilkes and Junius) to produce specifics; but in the face of the divine light they are unable to speak and the demon angrily sends them away again. *6. The Absolvers.* From the souls of the blessed, George Washington comes forward to announce that 'albeit in life opposed to each other' George had an 'upright heart' and always acted 'true to his sacred trust'. *7. The Beatification.* 'Well done, thou good and faithful servant' says a 'Voice from the Brightness'; the King drinks from the Well of Life outside Heaven's Gate, and rises 'to bliss everlasting appointed'. *8. The Sovereigns.* Inside heaven, we are told, George is anticipated by various righteous monarchs, including Charles I, Elizabeth, Richard Lionheart and others. *9. The Elder Worthies.* Various worthies are also waiting: Chaucer, Shakespeare, Milton, Newton and so forth. *10. The Worthies of the Georgian Age.* This list continues to include Wolfe, Reynolds, Hogarth, Wesley, Burke and Cowper. *11. The Young Spirits.* Various soldiers and sailors from the Napoleonic wars, Davy and Chatterton are added. *12. The Meeting.* George meets his recently departed Queen, and the narrator says 'when I beheld them meet, the desire of my soul overcame me'. He attempts to follow, but his earthly status prevents him and he awakes in the twilight.

Vision of Judgement, The (1822), by Lord Byron. 842 lines, ottava rima. The preface to Southey's *Vision of Judgement* had deplored 'the lewdness and impiety with which English poetry has, in our day, first been polluted', and castigated what he called 'the Satanic School' of verse. Although not mentioned by name, Byron was clearly under attack; and he responded with this energetic and powerful parody of Southey's laureate sycophancies.

Saint Peter is waiting at the gate of Heaven when a cherub arrives with the news that 'George the Third is dead' ('"And who *is* George the Third?" replied the apostle:/"*What George? what Third?*"'). The shade of the king then arrives, amongst a host of good and bad angels, Satan and the Archangel Michael included. Satan has come to make a claim for the Old King's Soul:

> He ever warred with freedom and the free:
>   Nations as men, home subjects, foreign foes,
> So that they uttered the word 'Liberty!'
>   Found George the Third their first opponent. Whose
> History was ever stained as his will be
>   With national and individual woes?

Satan calls witnesses to this cause, but so large a group comes forward that Wilkes and Junius are set to speak for them all, which they both do. Then a devil arrives carrying Southey under his wing ('Confound the renegado!' says the devil, 'I have sprained/My left wing, he's so heavy'). Southey explains that 'he meant no harm in scribbling', but had to be a turncoat in order to make a literary living. He offers to write the biographies of both Michael and the Devil, and then begins to read his *Vision of Judgement*. It is so awful that the angels flee and 'the Devils rans howling, deafened, down to Hell'. Saint Peter knocks the poet down with his keys, and in all the confusion King George slips, unnoticed, into Heaven.

Wanderer of Switzerland, The: A Poem in Six Parts (1806), by James Montgomery. 844 lines, ballad quatrains. Occasioned by the Napoleonic suppression of the ancient Swiss democracy in 1798, and demonstrating Montgomery's political radicalism to good effect.

Part I. The Wanderer of the title has left Switzerland with his family; over the border he meets up with the Shepherd, and explains the doleful situation ('In a day and hour accurst,/O'er the wretched land of TELL,/ Thus the Gallic ruin burst'). *Part II.* The Shepherd offers the traveller supper, and is treated to more stories of French aggression. *Part III.* The Wanderer continues his narrative, describing the terrible battle of Underwalden. *Part IV.* The story deals with the death of the Swiss hero, Albert. *Part V.* The Wanderer travels after the battle. *Part VI.* He tells the Shepherd of his intention to emigrate to America.

West Indies, The: A Poem in Four Parts, Written in Honour of the Abolition of the African Slave Trade, by the British Legislature, in 1807 (1808), by James Montgomery. 1025 lines, heroic couplets. Originally written to accompany a series of engravings (by Bowyer) and published as a memorial of the abolition of slavery.

Part I. Columbus's discovery of the West Indies is related, and the destruction of the 'Charib' people deplored. *Part II.* We are told about Africa, and there are some well-meaning but rather patronizing descriptions of Africans ('rude Caffraria, where the giraffes browse ... the Negro, nature's outcast child ... Is he not *man*, though knowledge never shed/ Her quickening beams on his neglected head?'). *Part III.* After insisting that all races are equally home-loving, the poet goes on to describe harrowing tales of the brutality and savagery of the slave trade. *Part IV.* The poem closes with a brief account of the abolition debate in England, and some pious observations on the need to evangelize the whole of Africa.

Whistlecraft (1817), by John Hookham Frere. 1524 lines, ottava rima. The full title of this work gives some sense of its pleasantly digressive comedy: *Prospectus and Specimen of an Intended National Work by William and Robert Whistlecraft, of Slow Market, in Suffolk, Harness and collarmakers, Intended to Comprise the Most Interesting Particu-*

lars Relating to King Arthur and the Round Table. A likeable although none-too-stretching work, it is chiefly remembered today as one of the inspirations for Byron's *Don Juan.*

Canto 1. After a prelude in which the author confesses that he had always wanted to write a book, the narrative begins: 'The Great King Arthur made a sumptuous Feast'. We are given extensive lists of food-stuffs, drinks, and guests, including the great Knights of the Round Table, Lancelot (of English Knights 'the best,/Except, perhaps, Lord Wellington in Spain'), Tristram and Gawain 'brave as his own sword'. *Canto 2.* The narrator decides he has written enough to begin another canto ('I've finished three hundred lines and more,/And therefore I begin Canto the Second'). The feast is interrupted by news that Britain's 'Aboriginal Giants' have abducted some ladies and taken them off to their fort. The knights ride out to the rescue. Gawain tries to parley 'but in vain – /A true bred Giant never trusts a Knight', and the giants rain down stones upon their attackers. The fort is blockaded and then raided by the Knights, who achieve much slaughter: Tristan beheads one (the Giant's torso remains standing for twenty seconds, 'but ulti-mately fell from loss of blood') and Gawain slays 'a brace of Giants out of hand,/Sliced downwards from the shoulder to the waist'. The Giants are all killed (except one bedridden Giant, on whose behalf the rescued ladies intercede: after all, the Giants only devoured two of the fatter, older ladies). *Canto 3.* The narrator's attention shifts to some nearby monks, who have long maintained friendly relations with the Giants in their Fort. But 'Giants abominate the sound of bells', and are incensed at the 'tintinabular uproar' coming from the convent. They attack. *Canto 4.* The Giants lay waste to the land outside the convent wall, but the monks inside are happy enough with 'plenteous' supplies of 'Bacon and pickled-herring, pork and peas', not to mention 'bottled-ale'. For a while the Giants 'bang with clubs and maces at the gate', but then they mysteriously retreat. The monks cannot understand why this should be:

> But though they could not, you, perhaps, may guess;
> They went, in short, upon their last adventure,
> After the ladies – neither more nor less.

White Doe of Rylstone, The (1815), by William Wordsworth. 1910 lines, rhymed tetrameter couplets.

Canto First. Bolton Priory, in Yorkshire, is in ruins; but the chapel still stands, and a crowd of country people fill it to hear a sermon. Then 'comes gliding in with lovely gleam ... a solitary Doe' that wanders round the ruin and eventually settles down 'beside the ridge of a grassy grave'. It seems that this white Doe comes from Rylstone to perform this office every Sunday. The locals have various 'superstitious fancies' to explain this behaviour – it is the soul of the woman who originally founded the Priory, it is a 'gracious Fairy' and so on. *Canto Second*. We are taken back to the rebellion of the North under Percy and Neville against Queen Elizabeth. Old Richard Norton and eight of his sons join the rising, despite attempts by his eldest son Francis to dissuade them. Francis stays behind with his sister Emily as the others ride away, gloomily prophesying 'we/Are doomed to perish utterly'. He resolves to go 'unarmed and naked' after his father and brothers. *Canto Third*. 'Now was the North in arms: – they shine/In warlike trim from Tweed to Tyne'. Old Norton joins the force, with Francis following incognito. Faced with Sussex's army opposing them, the army of the North retreats to Durham. Francis approaches his Father but cannot persuade him to abandon the cause. *Canto Fourth*. Night-time at Bolton Priory. Emily sits with the white Doe in the moonlight. She sends an old man off to find out what is going on in the battle. *Canto Fifth*. Via the old man, Emily learns of the slaughter at the battle of Neville's Cross. All the family killed save Francis, who has carried away the family Standard. *Canto Sixth*. Francis, with the banner, is pursued and cut down by Sussex's men. His body is brought back to the Priory. *Canto Seventh*. Nowadays 'despoil and desolation/O'er Rylstone's fair domain have blown'. Emily, after 'wander[ing], long and far', befriended a white Doe (such that the Doe 'tracked with faithful pace/The Lady to her dwelling place ... her last and living friend'). After Emily's death, the Doe continues to visit her grave.

WORDSWORTH, William (1770–1850). In a sense, Wordsworth's contribution to the traditions of the nineteenth-century long poem rests on an epic he did not write. *The Recluse*, a proposed work of brontosaurean dimensions, occupied a great deal of the poet's emotional energy during the last fifty years of his life. In the event he wrote a small section of the first part (published as 'Home at Grasmere'), and the whole second part (the ten-thousand line *Excursion), but nothing of the third. He also produced a prelude to the whole, *The Prelude; but the complete article never emerged. Unlike Coleridge's fragmentary shards of proposed epics (where the very fragmentation is intimately linked to theme) this poses a problem; for *The Recluse* was always going to be a poem about wholeness, unity, the spiritual health and integrity that Imagination, God and Nature can engender when taken together. The failure to realize the larger vision is (it seems to this critic) evident throughout the two completed sections, where professions of harmony are consistently undercut by aporia, misanthropy, contradiction and a curious double-edgedness of texture and style (sometimes extraordinarily beautiful, often rambling and tedious).

Contradiction is also, arguably, the keynote to Wordsworth's life. Born in Cumbria, he was sent (after the death of his mother in 1778) to Hawkshead Grammar School in the Lake District. His father died in 1783, leaving the intensely sensitive adolescent an orphan; this goes some way towards explaining why the young Wordsworth became so very attached to people (his sister Dorothy, his friend Coleridge) and places (the Lakes in particular). It is this period of his life that receives the most detailed treatment in his autobiography, *The Prelude*. In 1787 Wordsworth attended St John's, Cambridge, an experience that was not an unalloyed success. In 1790 he and a friend undertook a walking tour through France and the Alps (recorded in *The Prelude*, Book Six); and in 1791 Wordsworth returned to France, passionately excited by the ideals of the French Revolution ('Bliss was it in that dawn to be alive/And to be young was very heaven'). He had an affair with Annette Vallon and fathered a daughter, but he abandoned both mother and daughter to return to England. Guilt and remorse apparently dogged him over his actions for several years to come (see 'Vaudracour and Julia', written 1804), but they did not dog him sufficiently closely as to do anything about it. With the outbreak of war between France and England, and the degeneration of Revolution into the Terror, Wordsworth began a lengthy process of disillusionment with his political idealism.

A legacy of £900 helped, in 1795, to alleviate Wordsworth's financial difficulties, and ensure that he devoted himself to his poetry. Living with his sister Dorothy (with whom he was unusually and possibly illegally close) in Alfoxden, Somerset, Wordsworth struck up a friendship with Coleridge. Together the two poets worked at the job of, effectively, redefining English poetry. The publication of the jointly-authored volume *Lyrical Ballads* in 1798 marked a watershed in Romanticism, and arguably in the course of English poetry as a whole. So revolutionary was the volume that, on its second edition (enlarged) in 1800 Wordsworth felt moved to write a Preface which explains to potential readers that they are about to encounter a new sort of poetry, and explains how they are to read it.

In 1799 Wordsworth and Dorothy settled in the Lake District, at Grasmere; and 1802 saw the addition of a wife to the household in the shape of Mary Hutchinson. Now in the middle of his celebrated 'Great Decade' (1797–1807), Wordsworth was writing many of his most famous short lyrics (the Lucy poems, the Immortality Ode, 'Resolution and Independence') which were eventually published in *Poems in Two*

Volumes (1807). Wordsworth's first child, John, was born in 1803; he was to have five children in all. The period was, for a time, idyllic: but a series of events began to mark a change in Wordsworth's life. His brother John drowned in 1805; two of his children died young; and the friendship with Coleridge, that had given Wordsworth so much artistically and emotionally, began to fall apart. An argument and estrangement in 1810 was made up, but only to be repeated a few years later. The ostensible reasons for the quarrel are relatively unimportant; in fact it marks the point of difference between two wholly unlike characters. The quarrel also functions as an index to the change in Wordsworth's own personality; he was moving so far from his youthful anti-establishment and revolutionary idealism as to turn into a reactionary Tory.

He had been working, on and off, on *The Recluse* since the late 1790s; but the publication of a part of it as his first long poem *The Excursion* in 1814 was something of a disappointment. Wordsworth priced the volume at the very high figure of three guineas, expecting it to sell quickly and so enable him to print a cheaper version. But the reception was mixed, and this in turn sent him back to revision of the *Prelude*. *The White Doe of Rylstone* appeared in 1815, *Miscellaneous Poems* in 1815, and *Peter Bell* and *The Wagoner* in 1819. Indeed, he continued writing poetry for the rest of his life, but the poetry he wrote was (depending on your perspective) bad but with the saving grace of some topographical interest, or otherwise just bad. He had been appointed Stamp Distributor for Westmorland in 1813, a post that, quite apart from bringing in £400 pounds a year, signalled his acquiescence with the establishment. His civil list pension of £300 in 1843 served the same function, and in 1843 he followed *Southey into the post of Poet Laureate. Indeed, he had more in common with Southey than just this post: like the older man, the patriotism and Conservatism of his dotage were so pronounced as to make an effective mockery of his youthful political affiliations (see *Browning's 'The Lost Leader': 'Just for a handful of silver he left us,/Just for a riband to stick in his coat'). He spent 1849 revising his *Collected Works* (which appeared in six volumes), and died in 1850. *The Prelude* was published posthumously.

Wordsworth's genius is most apparent in his shorter poetry; and many of the lyrics and odes from the Great Decade have had an overwhelming, and justifiable, impact on the subsequent development of poetry. But as a poet of long poems Wordsworth cannot overcome his internal contradictions because he does not recognize that they are contradictions, just as he himself saw no fundamental difference between his early and late political views. Only in isolated moments of quasi-mystical intensity, the 'Spots of Time' (very beautifully rendered in *The Prelude* in particular), does sheer imaginative force fuse the opposites. Otherwise, and despite the huge critical industry that has grown up around him, Wordsworth remains the least likeable of all major poets.

World Before the Flood, The: A Poem in Ten Cantos (1813), by James Montgomery. 3103 lines, heroic couplets. Pious and mostly still-born epic of the sub-Miltonic variety. Epics on antediluvian topics had something of a vogue in the nineteenth-century – see, for instance, Byron's drama *Cain*, or Jean Ingelow's *A Story of Doom*.

Canto First. Following the expulsion from the Garden of Eden, humankind has divided into two main groups. One, pious and associated with the Biblical patriarchs, still lives in sight of Paradise; the evil other is descended from Cain and commanded by the Giants that had issued from the union between the Sons of God and the daughters of Men (Genesis 6:4). The descendants of Cain are now making war on their peaceful relatives. On the night before the battle, young Javan slips out of the Giants' camp. He was raised by Enoch among the patriarchs, but had been prey to the restlessness of youth and had run away to wander the world. For a while he made his way as a minstrel, and was a favoured bard in the camp of the evil Tubal-Cain. Now his conscience is twitching. *Canto Second.* Javan meets his former lover, the beautiful Zillah, in a shady spot. *Canto Third.* Javan makes his way to Enoch's house, where he is welcomed. The patriarch shows him round, and explains why the family of Seth first came to this valley. *Canto Fourth.* Enoch relates the death of Adam ('He closed his eyelids with a tranquil smile,/And seem'd to rest in silent prayer awhile'). *Canto Fifth.* Juval attends the annual ceremony on the anniversary of Adam's death. *Canto Sixth.* Javan reasserts his love for Zillah, but she refuses to believe him (she asks, not unreasonably: 'could Javan love me through the world, yet leave/Her whom he loved, for hopeless years, to grieve?') *Canto Seventh.* At midnight 'eager warriors from the host of Cain' capture the Patriarchs and everybody in their community and carry them away. *Canto Eighth.* On a mountain-top the Giants are assembled around their king; they hear a minstrel sing his praises, and he outlines military strategy. *Canto Ninth.* The patriarchs are brought before the king, and told that they are to be sacrificed to summon up demons so that he can conquer Eden itself. Javan is unbowed, and Zillah (also present) declares her love for him. Enoch appears. *Canto Tenth.* After a lengthy prophecy ('the proud shall perish' and so forth) Enoch is translated directly into heaven; the Giants straightaway assault Paradise, where they are all killed 'by whirlwinds driven,/In mighty volumes, through the vault of heaven'. Javan marries Zillah, and 'there did his wanderings and afflictions cease;/His youth was penitence, his age was peace'.

Select bibliography of secondary critical material

Anderson, Warren, *Matthew Arnold and the Classical Tradition* (Ann Arbor, MI: University of Michigan Press, 1965).

Barrell, John, *Poetry, Language & Politics* (Manchester: Manchester University Press, 1988).

Beatty, Bernard, *Byron's Don Juan* (New Jersey: Barnes and Noble, 1985).

Burrow, Colin, *Epic Romance: Homer to Virgil* (Oxford: Clarendon, 1993).

Christ, Carol T., 'Myth, history, and the structure of the long poem', in *Victorian and Modern Poetics* (Chicago and London: University of Chicago Press, 1984).

Curran, Stuart, *Poetic Form and British Romanticism* (Oxford: Oxford University Press, 1986).

———, *Shelley's Annus Mirabilis: The Maturing of an Epic Vision* (San Marino, CA: Huntingdon Library Press, 1975).

———, '"The Mental Pinnacle": *Paradise Regained* and the Romantic four book epic', in Joseph Wittreich (ed.), *Calm of Mind* (Cleveland, OH: Case Western Reserve University Press, 1971).

Frye, Northrop, *Anatomy of Criticism: Four Essays* (Princeton, NJ: Princeton University Press, 1957).

Hartman, Geoffrey, *Wordsworth's Poetry 1787–1814* (New Haven, CT: Yale University Press, 1964).

Highet, Geoffrey, *The Classical Tradition: Greek and Romance Influence on Western Literature* (2nd edn, Oxford: Oxford University Press, 1951).

Jenkyns, Richard, *The Victorians and Ancient Greece* (Oxford: Blackwell, 1980).

Leighton, Angela, *Elizabeth Barrett Browning* (Brighton: Harvester Press, 1986).

McFarland, Thomas, *Romanticsm and the Forms of Ruin: Wordsworth, Coleridge and Modalities of Fragmentation* (Princeton, NJ: Princeton University Press, 1981).

McGann, Jerome, *Don Juan in Context* (London: John Murray, 1976).

Merchant, Paul, *The Epic* (London: Methuen, 'The Critical Idiom', 1971).

Shaffer, E. S., '*The Fall of Jerusalem*: Coleridge's unwritten epic', in

'Kubla Khan' and The Fall of Jerusalem: *The Mythological School in Biblical Criticism and Secular Literature* (Cambridge: Cambridge University Press, 1975).

Shaw, W. David, *The Lucid Veil: Poetic Truth in the Victorian Age* (London: Athlone, 1987).

Tillyard, E. M. W., *The English Epic and Its Background* (London: Chatto and Windus, 1954).

Turner, Frank, *The Greek Heritage in Victorian Britain* (New Haven, CT: Yale University Press, 1981).

Turner, Paul, *Victorian Poetry, Drama, and Miscellaneous Prose 1832–1890* (Oxford: Clarendon, 1989).

Vogler, Thomas A., *Preludes to Vision: The Epic Venture in Blake, Wordsworth, Keats and Hart Crane* (Berkeley, CA: University of California Press, 1971).

Wilkie, Brian, *Romantic Poets and Epic Tradition* (Madison and Milwaukee, WI: University of Madison Press, 1965).

Wordsworth, Jonathan, *William Wordsworth: the Borders of Vision* (Oxford: Clarendon Press, 1982).

Index